The Complete
Step-by-Step Guide
to Designing and Teaching
Online Courses

The Complete
Step-by-Step Guide
to Designing and Teaching
Online Courses

Joan Thormann

Isa Kaftal Zimmerman

Foreword by Grant Wiggins

Teachers College
Columbia University
New York and London

Published by Teachers College Press, 1234 Amsterdam Avenue, New York, NY 10027

Figures 2.5, 2.7, 2.8, 3.5, and 6.6 contain screenshots from Blackboard. Used with permission.

Figure 6.5 is adapted from a rubric on the Rubistar website (http://www.rubistar.4teachers.org). Used with permission from the Advanced Learning Technologies in Education Consortia (ALTEC).

Library of Congress Cataloging-in-Publication Data

Thormann, Joan, 1945-
  The complete step-by-step guide to designing and teaching online courses / Joan Thormann,
    Isa Kaftal Zimmerman ; foreword by Grant Wiggins.
      p. cm.
  Includes bibliographical references and index.
  ISBN 978-0-8077-5309-5 (pbk. : alk. paper)
    1. Web-based instruction. 2. Instructional systems—Design. I. Zimmerman, Isa Kaftal. II.
  Title.
  LB1044.87.T57 2012
  371.33'44678—dc23   2011050710

ISBN 978-0-8077-5309-5 (paper)

Printed on acid-free paper
Manufactured in the United States of America

19 18 17 16 15 14 13 12   8 7 6 5 4 3 2 1

Contents

Foreword

You can't "wing it" in an online course as an instructor. There are countless logistic, technical, and planning issues to consider as you work, step-by-step, to build an effective and engaging experience for users.

There is a more pressing social reason to consult this book as a guide: while online learning is growing by leaps and bounds, there has been little quality control to ensure that the experience is a good one for learners. I have seen dozens of online courses, from both individual teachers and big commercial vendors, and most of them are of poor pedagogical quality: a high-tech way to deliver low-level information.

So, on many counts, it comes as a great relief and delight to have this guide by Joan Thormann and Isa Kaftal Zimmerman to take you through your paces and avoid all the many pitfalls of online course development. It's a near-perfect blend of theory and practice: advice on the pedagogy and practical tips on how to make the user feel comfortable; an overview of the history of online learning and concrete templates and worksheets for building a robust and coherent course.

Indeed, many of these chapters provide invaluable tools for *any* teacher, in any teaching situation or school. Chapter 4, for example—where the templates and examples of assignment types can be found—offers an incredibly useful jump-start to the development of appropriate goal-related experiences. Whether it is working on essays, case studies, or research, the authors have supplied a priceless overview of how to ensure that learning is well thought out and implemented to ensure maximal effectiveness. Similarly, the feedback templates in Chapter 5 provide an elegant solution to a common problem for all educators: how to give many students custom feedback as efficiently as possible. Finally, their rich experience also shows in their clear and helpful counsel on how to deal with (inevitable) plagiarism as part of the excellent chapter on dilemmas. This is must reading for all teachers, online instructors or not, who are striving for intellectual integrity and honesty in their work as learners.

In short, this is a rare book in education: one that is not only highly useful but also intellectually coherent and based on robust, transferable principles of learning and teaching. All educators—in online environments and in brick-and-mortar schools—will find this an invaluable resource.

—Grant Wiggins

Acknowledgments

Thanks to the organizations and individuals who supported us in this project. Lesley University granted Joan a sabbatical, a Russell Fellowship, and a Faculty Development Grant, all of which allowed her the time to focus on writing this book. In addition, Lesley provided a skilled and helpful assistant, Maggi Smith-Dalton, through the Graduate Assistant Program.

We appreciated the time generously given to us by our colleagues and friends. They include Diana Bander, George Blakeslee, Susan Cusack, Chris Dede, João Fernandes, João Freitas, Kathleen Fulton, Iris Geik, Barbara Gibson, Sarah Haavind, Jim Keefe, Dan Lake, Romeo Marquis, Steve Mashburn, Linda Triplett, and Maureen Yoder. Over the years, we have learned a tremendous amount from our students, and for this we are extremely grateful.

A special thanks to Gail Greenberg, who cheered us on and gave us useful feedback. Thanks to Ingrid Hahn for allowing Joan to use her serene refuge high above Lago Maggiore. Thanks also to Mike Thormann for his warm and gracious hospitality in allowing Joan to use his Florida home.

Last and most important, thanks to our husbands. To Joan's wonderful husband, Judah Schwartz, who read, rearranged, and edited; he gave an occasional needed word and his constant support and encouragement. Thanks to Isa's remarkable husband, George Zimmerman, who provided support and patience.

CHAPTER 1

Introduction;
and How to Use This Book

We are living in a world of unprecedented change. The evolution of technology is more accurately described as the *revolution* of technology. Products are regularly updated or reinvented.

Although less has changed in education than in other sectors, there have been some significant developments. Alternative approaches and formats have emerged: charter schools, virtual schools, online and **blended learning***, longer school days and years, more time-on-task, after-school programs, and home schooling. These alternatives signal that competition from differing practices and formats will change traditional brick-and-mortar schooling. The *one-educator-to-25-students* paradigm will continue to shift. There is no going back to a world that does not use technology in teaching and learning. Online learning in particular is becoming an important aspect of all levels of education. As Kathleen Fulton of the National Commission on Teaching and America's Future (NCTAF) has stated,

> The reality is that a blended form of learning is already central to education today, with students supplementing face-to-face classes with online courses when they aren't offered at their home schools, or when they don't have a chance to do "regular" schooling (when homebound due to illness or injury, incarcerated, travelling or other special cases). And of course, for home schooling, it can be the difference between having a limited repertoire of teaching and the world of courses and teachers available to them. In higher education the online learning opportunities are endless—and very profitable for higher education providers—so likely only to expand (email communication, November 2010)

IMPACT OF ONLINE TEACHING AND LEARNING: TRANSFORMATIONS IN SCHOOLING

The International Association for K–12 Online Learning (iNACOL) reports that 45 of the 50 states and the District of Columbia provide some form of virtual education. Many virtual schools show annual growth rates between 20% and 45%. iNACOL

---

*As you read, look out for terms in bold. These words have corresponding entries in the glossary (Appendix A).

(2010) also found that "72% of school districts with distance education programs planned to expand online offerings in the coming year" (p. 1).

These data show the movement toward online learning in K–12. Students can now have access to courses and learning experiences that are not available locally or that are not offered because of underenrollment. Online courses provide access to expert knowledge and resources. Students are not constrained by time and place and can learn with other students from all over the world. Private companies, state agencies, and school districts are developing or seeking out courses for K–12 students.

According to Allen and Seaman (2010), "Online enrollments in U.S. higher education show no signs of slowing. . . . More than one out of four college and university students now take at least one course online" (p. 1). Some universities have established entire departments to help instructors understand how to teach online, and some, like the University of Southern California, have put whole degree programs online.

It is becoming almost universally accepted that instructors will teach online and students will learn online for some portion of a program or in some cases, an entire program. Students may now enroll in high-quality learning experiences without needing to be on campus. Changes such as this will require instructors at all levels to transform their teaching styles.

Understanding the New Realities of Learning and Teaching Online

Prabhu (2010) states that the "sharp rise in students' media use challenges educators to make lessons more engaging." In one particularly telling example of the capabilities of Wi-Fi, Dillon (2010) reports:

> School officials mounted a mobile Internet router to bus No. 92's sheet-metal frame, enabling students to surf the Web. The students call it the Internet Bus, and what began as a high-tech experiment has had an old-fashioned—and unexpected—result. Wi-Fi access has transformed what was often a boisterous bus ride into a rolling study hall, and behavioral problems have virtually disappeared. (Wi-fi turns rowdy, para. 3).

Because of the absence of physical boundaries and access to resources that were not available before, students can learn anything, anytime, anywhere. Instructors who teach elementary students can create websites specifically for a unit, topic, or subject. They can thus protect their students from dangerous websites by directing them to a manageable number of resources. They can also create **webquests**, which are usually teacher-developed websites designed to guide students to use the web to study a particular topic. Instructors have been using the Internet for teaching purposes since the mid-1990s. All of this reflects the new reality of teaching.

Differences Between Online and Face-to-Face Courses

Interviews with colleagues confirm our experience of moving face-to-face courses online and creating new online courses. We have found two major categories of differences between online and face-to-face courses: the design of the course and its implementation. While these differences are addressed throughout this book, along with how to create successful online courses step-by-step, here we present some of the principal features that differentiate online from face-to-face teaching.

Designing for online. Designing the course assignments, number of assignments, time required, and planning for discourse differs in the two approaches. All need to be considered before an online course starts. We create activities and assignments that ask students to investigate one component of a topic, share their opinions, conduct research on student-selected topics, and examine their own settings. These assignments are shaped by each student's circumstances and interests.

Once students complete and post assignments, they can learn from each other. Traditional courses typically have students do the same assignment. In face-to-face courses students frequently have the experience of learning from each other only once or twice a semester because of time constraints. We construct assignments that reduce isolation by requiring students to ask questions and post comments about classmates' work on the Discussion Board. They also complete assignments in pairs or small groups.

Since online students do not spend time face-to-face, we factor that amount of time into the coursework students do each week by combining it with homework. In a typical higher education face-to-face semester-long course, students have a midterm, a final exam, and perhaps a few quizzes. At the K–12 level, students have quizzes and tests every few weeks and submit homework assignments regularly. Assignments and activities in online courses, at all levels, must be more frequent. The number and scope of assignments depend on the students' level. For younger students assignments need to be frequent and short. More mature students can handle larger assignments. However, we find that all students need to do, at minimum, one assignment a week to remain engaged.

We agree with Sarah Haavind, a faculty member at Lesley University, who, in an interview with Joan Thormann in September 2009, remarked that she was "able to be much more **constructivist** and inquiry-based" when teaching online. Instructors, she asserted, "can much more easily stay to the side and guide . . . rather than ask leading questions to get to the next point because 'we only had 15 more minutes' in a face-to-face class." Online students are able to take greater control of class work. We require substantive interaction among students. Because of this, they generally work diligently to understand the course topic. No one is allowed to sit at the back of the classroom and be unresponsive (-:.

To ensure that we have attended to all the necessary course elements prior to starting a course, we use a task checklist as seen in Figure 1.1.

In a face-to-face course, students object less to changes in the curriculum, since the instructor can easily explain the reasons. Online students object more to changes because their schedules are typically arranged from day one. The checklist also serves as a "tickler" for us. Online we do not have weekly meetings with students to remind us of organizational tasks we need to complete. Some of the tasks in the checklist occur

Figure 1.1. Task Checklist

DONE	1. Copy course from previous Blackboard course
DONE	2. Post new welcome announcement
DONE	3. Revise assignments and post
DONE	4. Revise syllabus and post
DONE	5. Revise assignment table and post
DONE	a. Alter assignments as necessary
DONE	b. Review number of points per assignment
DONE	6. Fix grade center to match current syllabus
DONE	7. Post quotes from previous student evaluations
DONE	8. Revise Discussion Board forum descriptions and due dates
DONE	9. Post message about Skype names in the Teachers' Room
DONE	10. Post schedule of Skype meeting times for appropriate weeks
DONE	11. Revise Course Guidelines and post
DONE	12. Update instructor resume and post
DONE	13. Develop checklist of assignment completions
DONE	14. Check streamed videos and URLs for currency

once a semester. Others need to be repeated. In this book we provide many examples of course elements: task lists, assignments, web pages, and activities.

Implementing online. Once the course is designed, the implementation of an online course needs to support the principles of online engagement. Some of the features that characterize online teaching include the need to check in with students frequently, writing communications with great care, engaging in much more written informal communication than in most face-to-face courses, and consciously supporting student social interactions to build community.

While *wait time* is important in any teaching situation, wait time online can be extended to hours and days rather than minutes. Having the luxury of prolonged wait time due to the **asynchronous** nature of the communication elicits the expertise of group members. When an instructor does not need to "jump in" to redirect a discussion during the last ten minutes of class, students find it much more conducive to contributing their ideas.

The limited time structure of face-to-face teaching and learning can constrain instruction. Haavind shared with us that sometimes if she waits for a day or two and "sits on her hands" a student will make a comment on the Discussion Board that adds significantly to the dialogue. This type of interaction is difficult to achieve in a face-to-face environment.

Discussions with two students who enrolled in online courses illustrate different approaches and also provide cautionary notes. Both students found their online course experience unsatisfactory. Andrea D. took a course in which she listened to a live lecture once a week and followed up with readings, tests, and a required paper. The course was a face-to-face class offered simultaneously online. During our interview, Andrea frowned and said, "Even if I was sitting in the lecture hall the course probably wouldn't be so great." She then explained that she had another online course in which "the teacher was terrific because she had the students do interesting assignments," had them working together in groups, and communicated with the class and individuals frequently (Personal communication, September 2009).

The second student, Rachel B., complained about the isolation she experienced in her online course. The instructor only responded to emails and coursework on Fridays. This student tried to engage her classmates in a discussion about coursework but was unable to get a reaction. The instructor did not encourage or create opportunities for classmates to interact and build a community of learners (Personal communication, November 2009).

Reaching Difficult-to-Teach Students

Because online learning has no physical boundaries, some students who are unable to attend face-to-face classes because of behavioral problems or who find the school environment difficult to manage can benefit from online learning. The instructor's ability to individualize the approach and the student's ability to manage time allow students to learn in ways more responsive to their strengths. The flexibility of the online setting can offer them more opportunities for success than when they are in a classroom for a predetermined period of time. However, the challenge is also the instructor's, to direct and work with these students, to find appropriate and viable resources, and to fashion the optimal structure that supports their individual needs.

Teaching and Learning Difficult Topics

The simultaneous access to multiple resources and modalities that the online environment offers is beneficial for teaching and learning difficult topics. Students can be guided to use multiple resources as part of their online experience in a way that students in a classroom cannot, unless each student has constant access to a computer and the time to explore. For example, in high school, geometry learning is greatly enhanced through online, manipulated visualization. Experiments with potentially dangerous chemical reactions can be conducted using an online simulation. In learning a foreign language, virtually unlimited repetition from a native speaker can be provided. Students' English compositions can be edited and reedited by instructors and peers in an online environment using such tools as a **wiki** or Google Docs. Some of these learning activities can be completed in face-to-face courses, but time limitations and accommodating the variety of skill levels in the classroom make it signifcantly more challenging to orchestrate in that environment.

Replacing Bricks and Mortar

Online teaching and learning may enable some K–12 schools and institutions of higher education to reduce their costs in a variety of ways. They may not have to build new physical facilities and therefore not pay for maintenance, heating/cooling, and transportation. If students are not at a central location, the institution does not have to invest in security, student activities, and other additional services.

Not everyone agrees that there are cost savings. Higher education institutions have discovered that maintaining an online instructional program has costs. Contracting for or hiring staff to manage a learning management system (LMS) like Blackboard or **Moodle** comes with fees. Course development, support for student and instructor LMS use, and professional development for use of new tools present additional costs. The decrease in face-to-face courses will undoubtedly take place over a long period, while the cost for the LMS and other supports are immediate, thus requiring financing for two infrastructures simultaneously.

The replacement of bricks and mortar is not solely a financial issue. For centuries, schooling has been associated with a physical location in a community where people of all ages come together to learn and socialize. Learning is, in part, a social activity, and online education must provide an arena for social interaction to occur. Online education challenges a deeply held belief by some of our colleagues that learning occurs best face-to-face. However, over a short period (a decade), we have seen our colleagues move from *"You cannot replace real classroom experiences with something on the computer"* to *"I'm teaching courses online and having a great time."*

Addressing Resistance to Change

In every institution, there are early adopters who explore online teaching and learning. Initially, we struggled with inadequate support such as primitive technology, minimal infrastructure, and the absence of personnel to assist our students and us. We developed our version of an LMS and taught ourselves how to teach online through trial and error. Most of our colleagues were not willing to do this but, as noted, resistance is diminishing.

Before this change occurred another development was serving to convince colleagues and administrators that online learning was as valid as face-to-face education and was, in fact, the *wave of the future*: The marketplace and the constant evolution of technology were overcoming the objections of those who initially ignored or criticized online teaching. Because the movement is now inevitable, many instructors, including our colleagues, are adopting online instruction. With widespread implementation, the deficiencies that we experienced initially have greatly decreased. Now the tools and methods for teaching online are substantial and constantly maturing.

HOW TO USE THIS BOOK

This book is designed so that, at the end, if all the suggested step-by-step activities are completed, the reader will have gained the skills needed to develop the foundation of an online course and will understand how to teach that course. In planning future online courses, the reader can return to these step-by-step activities to assist in the process. Most courses and students referred to in the book come from Joan Thormann's experience as a professor at Lesley University. We have respected the style of the authors/speakers in verbatim quotations. Because websites change frequently, some of the Web addresses we cite may cease to be viable long before the instructions detailed in this book. We have placed the links in context so a reader can explore other similar sites.

This book can be used by

- university faculty as a guide for teaching online or as a text to teach students how to teach online
- experienced instructors in K–12 and higher education who are taking a course about teaching online
- novice instructors in K–12 and higher education assigned the job of developing an online course or teaching it
- instructors who have already taught online who wish to validate and extend their knowledge as well as fill in gaps
- administrators wanting to know more about online teaching or supervising online teachers
- students who want to learn about online education and want to nudge their instructors to teach online

As can be seen from the table of contents, each chapter deals with a different aspect of teaching and learning online. Throughout the book, you will notice certain key terms are in boldface. We have included a glossary of definitions for those items in the appendix to save the reader time.

Student feedback has been an important aspect of developing our online courses. Throughout the text we have highlighted key quotes from students with a *Student Voice* icon.

The reader may progress through each chapter and do all the activities or focus on those that will augment the particular course(s) taught. Also, the reader may go directly to a chapter that is most urgently needed or where reconsideration is desired.

CHAPTER DESCRIPTIONS

Chapter 2, "Course Design and Development," covers the philosophy of education for teaching online and the pedagogy of online instruction. The latter addresses pre-planning, syllabus development, and technology decisions. Chapter 3, "Instructional Methods, Models, and Strategies," includes real-world authentic learning, learning communities, collaboration, and interactivity.

We think Chapter 4, "Assignment Templates and Examples," is invaluable for all those who do and will teach online, from novice to veteran. This chapter contains assignment, activity, and lesson templates and samples. They can be modified to meet individual instructors' goals and objectives in most content areas.

Interaction among students and with an instructor is particularly important as part of a student's learning experience. Online instructors need to be explicit in facilitating these interactions. Chapter 5, "Facilitation and Building Online Community," provides guidance and many concrete techniques such as icebreakers, peer mentoring, and use of Skype for achieving interaction that enhances student learning.

Chapter 6, "Evaluation and Assessment in Online Teaching," deals with a topic that is often controversial in online learning. We discuss a variety of approaches ranging from how to implement formative and summative **evaluation**, authentic assessment, and grading criteria to technology choices for assessment.

In today's online teaching and learning environment understanding and accommodating diversity is essential to the achievement of all students. Chapter 7, "Teaching Diverse Students Online," covers issues related to teaching students with special needs, **English language learners (ELL)**, **gifted and talented (G&T)** students, and at-risk students and explains how instructors can support these students online. Ideas for employing Universal Design for Learning (UDL) are described in detail.

Since online teaching is relatively new, there are still unresolved issues to grapple with. In Chapter 8, "Dealing with Dilemmas," we explore some challenges and suggest solutions. These challenges range from skills readiness, plagiarism, professional obligations, and student retention.

Chapter 9, "Looking to, and at, the Future; and Conclusions," touches upon how both technology and education are evolving and examines globalization and preparation for the future.

SUMMARY

In this chapter we have explained why online learning is no longer an experiment or a luxury. Online learning is a viable alternative for many students, K–12 schools, higher education institutions, and communities. The stage is set for the expansion of this format and the information, observations, templates, checklists, and suggestions in the chapters to follow are designed to help both beginners and experienced colleagues embark on this new educational journey.

CHAPTER 2

Course Design and Development

Before a course can be taught, a lot of planning must occur. In this chapter, we propose the necessary steps. The first is deciding on an online teaching philosophy. Next is developing learning goals, objectives, and outcomes. Then comes the selection of online instructional approaches, technology, and delivery methods. Through this process, we develop an evolving syllabus. With these components in place, the course is under way.

PHILOSOPHY OF EDUCATION FOR TEACHING ONLINE

In developing any course or presenting any topic, whether face-to-face or online, it is essential to think through a philosophy of teaching. It will dictate the way material is presented and how students interact with it. Instructors sometimes grumble at the prospect of this task. When we started teaching online, there were no guidelines to help us develop courses. We stumbled along for a while before we realized that we were using a constructivist teaching philosophy, just as we do in face-to-face teaching. The online courses we taught initially were neither as coherent nor as engaging as the ones we developed when we understood the role our philosophy played.

A philosophy, consistently and explicitly applied, and based on the instructor's knowledge, beliefs, and experiences, provides guidelines and boundaries for everyone. Within this philosophical approach, instructors need to consider the learning skills they want students to acquire and exercise.

A good starting point is to examine how a philosophy guides face-to-face instruction. The philosophy can then be adopted or modified for the online context. Since the online format does not afford immediate and constant visual and auditory feedback with students, the philosophical framework is even more important in informing assignments and activities.

It is useful for students to be aware of the philosophy so they can handle the differences between online and face-to-face learning. For example, online we deliberately create learning situations in which students have to participate "visibly." We use student moderators, cooperative learning techniques, and required interaction. We find that a transparent teaching philosophy, consistently applied, results in more confident students, since they can anticipate how they will be taught and what is required for success.

**Step-by-Step Course-Building Activity #1:
Educational Philosophy and How It Applies in Online Teaching**

The following activity will allow you to reflect on an educational philosophy and how it applies in online teaching.

1. Briefly, describe your personal educational philosophy.
2. You may wish to read the articles below or other articles relating to teaching philosophy and teaching online to extend your thinking.
3. Discuss/exchange your teaching philosophy with colleagues, instructors, or others.
4. Write a second statement, with a description of how to apply your philosophy in online learning.

Cowan, K. (2009). Learning across distance. *The Education Digest, 74*(9), 4–9.
Hughes, M., Ventura, S., & Dando, M. (2007). Assessing social presence in online discussion groups: A replication study. *Innovations in Education and Teaching International, 44*(1), 17–29.
King, A. (1993). From sage on the stage to guide on the side. *College Teaching, 41*(1), 30–36.
Miller, K. (2008). Teaching science methods online: Myths about inquiry-based online learning. *Science Educator, 17*(2), 80–87.
On the Horizon. (2008). Adaptive individualization: The next generation of online education. *On the Horizon, 16*(1), 44–47.
Wighting, M. J., Liu, J., & Rovai, A. P. (2008). Distinguishing sense of community and motivation characteristics between online and traditional college students. *Quarterly Review of Distance Education, 9*(3), 285–298.

Sharon Johnston of the Spokane Public Schools' Virtual Learning program writes about using an educational philosophy as the foundation for course design and development, asserting that "researching and implementing a model that aligns with the educational beliefs of the instructors and the goals of the institution are the best way to ensure informed, quality instruction" (as cited in Cavanaugh & Blomeyer, 2007, p. 22).

Some instructors may find the prospect of adapting their teaching philosophy to an online setting sufficiently difficult that they decide that the online environment is currently not a viable option. However, most instructors find these exercises interesting, challenging, and helpful.

PEDAGOGY OF ONLINE INSTRUCTION

Thoughtful preparation and care in crafting instructional presentation are fundamental to good teaching of anything, anywhere, anytime. They help keep the instructor focused on students and their progress. Well-organized materials enhance the probability of capturing students' interest, keeping them engaged, achieving learning objectives, and constructing their own meaning.

Preplanning

In the online format, assignments and learning activities are communicated primarily through text documents. Some are also shared in audio and video postings. Regardless of the medium, it is important to provide clear directions and have materials ready from the outset of the course. Online teaching is most successful when the entire course is developed in advance so the instructor can focus on course content and student interaction rather than **provisioning** the next activity. In our role as advisors, we hear from students that a few of their past instructors were disorganized and kept changing the assignments. In some cases students were in the dark about what they were supposed to do from week to week. Students expressed anxiety and frustration in these situations.

There are two approaches to distributing course assignments: (1) revealing assignments as the course progresses, and (2) providing assignments for the entire course at the outset.

We prefer providing all the assignments and materials in advance (approach #2) so that students have a total picture of the learning experience to come. In addition, if students choose to work on drafts ahead of time, they have the option to do so.

One reason for revealing assignments slowly (approach #1) is to prevent students from jumping ahead and losing the learning progression. To avoid this, we establish assignment due dates with a grade penalty for prior posting. We also do not provide all assignments in one document. Instead we divide the list and post assignments individually with separate links. This enables students to see all the assignments but deal with them one at a time.

This subject has been the basis of lively discussions among the instructors at our university. Our colleagues argue convincingly on both sides of the issue. One contends that her assignments are too complex to share with students from the beginning of the course. Others want to be in control. In the end, we all decided, it is a matter of personal teaching style.

Whichever approach one selects, we believe it is important to ensure that assignments are scaffolded and that students undertake them in a logical sequence. Others (Chou, 2003; Cole & Foster, 2008; Dede, 2004) imply or suggest that a sequential or developmental approach is not always necessary. Some students are able to impose their own structure or sequence on the activities/assignments, especially online. We do not advocate this, because it makes it difficult to have group discussions. Assignment distribution is just one of the areas in which the instructor needs to make decisions.

Learning Goals, Objectives, and Outcomes

Establishing goals, objectives, and outcomes is part of giving clear directions and communicating expectations in any learning environment. Instructors sometimes regard writing goals and objectives as an administrative exercise. However, these benchmarks are not just for administrators.

In our role at the university, we review student evaluations. Students occasionally report that there is no relationship between goals and objectives in the courses taught by some instructors. Students appreciate knowing what they are going to learn. They are also grateful when the course aligns with standards and state guidelines they need for certification or licensure.

Developing and establishing learning goals (also known as performance or achievement goals), objectives, and outcomes for an online course are basically the same as for face-to-face and blended courses.

It is important to distinguish among goals, objectives, and outcomes. Goals are "broad, generalized statements about what is to be learned" (p. 2, http://www.personal.psu.edu/bxb11/Objectives/). They are overall intentions and thus intangible, abstract, and hard-to-assess attainments. For example, the following is the learning goal for our class ECOMP 5007 *21st Century Teaching: Supporting All Learners on the Ability Spectrum*: "To increase awareness of the abilities and disabilities of all learners and to explore ways to meet their needs through technology."

Objectives are narrow and precise statements that can be validated (http://edweb.sdsu.edu/courses/EDTEC540/objectives/Difference.html). For example, in our ECOMP 5007 course, one of the objectives is "To to be able to integrate technology to support curriculum for inclusive classrooms."

Outcomes are statements of behavior desired at the end of the learning process. This is an example of an outcome statement from the same course: Students will describe characteristics of students with special needs and how technology can be used to benefit those students.

In defining the goals, objectives, and outcomes the instructor must attend to the following issues:

- What students know coming into the course.
- The observable and measurable actions students will be able to engage in during the course.
- The degree of content and skill mastery during and at end of the course.

The challenge here is that the objectives, and outcomes need to be measurable online. Examples of Web-based activities with measurable outcomes might include a posting such as a case study, a simulation, Web-based labs, a video, or an Elluminate conference (with or without preserved artifacts).

Figure 2.1 presents an example in which the criteria for writing goals, objectives, and outcomes are met.

Successful course development defines outcomes derived from meeting goals through the objectives. Activities and assignments align with goals and objectives that produce the outcome. Although some instructors think this is busywork, we have learned that this helps us provide accountability. The goals, objectives, and outcomes are course guides, serving as checkpoints to ensure that coursework is focused and assessment is valid.

Figure 2.1. Sample Goals, Objectives, and Outcomes

ECOMP 7104 *Technology in Education* Thesis Project

Course Description: The CAGS/Educational Specialist thesis project course is designed to assist students in developing and implementing a project that contributes to the field of educational technology. The project also helps to demonstrate that, at the end of the EdS (Educational Specialist) or CAGS (Certificate of Advanced Graduate Study) program, students have learned how to plan a major initiative, synthesize information, and present the work to an appropriate and critical audience.

Course Goal: To prepare students for post-master's-degree-level contributions to the profession through significant and extensive project work.

Objectives: To engage in critical review of previous research and projects.

- To extend personal and field knowledge in a selected area of study.
- To develop skills in knowledge production.
- To enhance the ability to work collegially.
- To plan, implement, and complete a major project.

Outcomes: The student will be able to

- Form a learning community with other educators.
- Critically review educational literature and projects.
- Develop an annotated bibliography.
- Develop a literature review.
- Develop a methodology section of a research study.
- Develop discussion, implications, and conclusions based on a research study.
- Stay on schedule while completing a major project.
- Give and receive substantive feedback.
- Develop leadership skills in class discussions.
- Complete multiple drafts of projects and make revisions.
- Submit a project that contributes to the field of technology in education.

Alignment with State, National, and Professional Standards

The adoption of academic standards (such as the Common Core State Standards) for students, teachers, and the profession in the K–12 setting represents a change in the educational scene. Most of the national professional associations, for example, the National Association of Teachers of Mathematics (NCTM) and the International Society for Technology in Education (ISTE) have well-developed learning standards describing what students and teachers should be able to do and know.

To find acceptance and use in schools these days, all curriculum must be mapped to the appropriate standards and related high-stakes testing. Most states mandate this testing for K–12 students. The tests are correlated to the standards, so it is essential to ensure curriculum alignment. Standards, however, are often set at a reasonable level and thus do not limit the goals for an online class.

We have tied our courses to ISTE standards since Lesley University's Technology in Education division offers courses throughout the United States and internationally. ISTE standards will undoubtedly be revised to include many common core, state, and content area organization standards, which now incorporate the use of technology. Figure 2.2 presents an example of how one of our courses is aligned to ISTE standards.

K–12 instructors will want to align with subject, grade-level, district, state, and Common Core standards. Higher education instructors need to use the most appropriate standards for their field.

Figure 2.2. Alignment with ISTE Standards

ECOMP 6008 *The World Wide Web as an Educational Resource*

Goal: In this course, students will learn skills for using the tools of telecommunications to communicate and collaborate with others so they can be responsible and articulate spokespersons on issues related to educational telecommunications, the changing nature of information, and the web.

Objectives: Students will

- Communicate and collaborate using various telecommunications tools such as list servers, **threaded discussions,** weblogs, chat, and instant messaging. (ISTE standards 1b, 1d)
- Complete online research to locate, select, evaluate, and acquire information using appropriate tools. (ISTE standards 2a, 2b, 3d)
- Adapt and integrate telecommunications experiences and create inquiry-oriented, standards-based student-centered activities. (ISTE standards 1a, 2a)
- Design, create, and publish a website for education. (ISTE standards 2a, 2b, 3a, 3b, 3c, 5a, 5d)
- Demonstrate an awareness of **Web accessibility** issues and requirements. (ISTE standards 2c, 4b)
- Identify appropriate online instructional resources and tools. (ISTE standards 2a, 2b, 3d)
- Articulate an awareness of current and emerging telecommunications technologies and their impact on education. (ISTE standards 1a, 1d, 4d, 5c)
- Become conversant with telecommunications issues, including ethics, security, privacy, copyright, acceptable use, and personal safety. (ISTE standards 4a, 4c)

ISTE National Education Technology Standards (NETS) standards can be found on the web at http://www.iste.org/standards.aspx

> ### Step-by-Step Course-Building Activity #2:
> ### Align Goals, Objectives, Activities, Assignments, Outcomes, and Standards
>
> The following activity takes you through the steps necessary to align goals, objectives, activities, assignments, outcomes, and standards.
>
> 1. Choose a course you plan to teach online.
> 2. Develop goals and objectives. Make sure that they are connected. The objectives should flow from the goals.
> 3. Start to think about activities and assignments that will align with your objectives.
> 4. Write measurable outcomes that align with the goals, objectives, activities, and assignments you have selected.
> 5. Determine the appropriate standards that your course will need to comply with. Match your course goals and objectives to those standards.
>
> Note: Some prefer to do "backward design" and start with standards.

Syllabus Development

Developing a syllabus for online is similar to developing a syllabus for a face-to-face course. The syllabus has several purposes. It serves as a guide for students, giving them an overview of the projected learning experience and vital course details such as goals, schedules, and contact information. It also is a *contract* between the instructor and student about requirements and expectations.

We urge instructors to make their syllabi clear and complete. We once had a student who threatened legal action after her work had unfortunately earned her a failing grade. She insisted that the instructor was at fault, claiming a lack of clear criteria for assignments and grading in the syllabus. The instructor, the division director, the dean, and an appointed ombudsperson reviewed the student's claims. The university was concerned about its reputation and many people spent a great deal of time on the problem.

Luckily in this case the university's standards were upheld, since the omissions in the syllabus were not the cause of the student's failure. We use this example to urge instructors to make their syllabi clear and complete.

Similarity to face-to-face. We use a face-to-face syllabus and make adjustments in assignments, activities, and schedule for online. Other elements such as course goals and the contract with the student are the same. We have observed that students typically ask more questions and there is more discussion about what we intend to do in online than in face-to-face courses. We surmise that, since these students cannot see us, they use these questions to create a connection with us and learn how we will react to them.

An example of a request for clarity and of making contact occurred when a student emailed the following question about Turnitin, an online plagiarism prevention and detection site, on the second day of the course: "When submitting a paper to Turnitin, what percentage of similarities should we be under?"

We responded by thanking her and answering her question. In addition we asked her to post her question in the Teachers' Room forum for discussion with the whole class. She did this and four classmates responded with their opinions and rationales.

Some schools require peer or administrative approval of curriculum and syllabi. We have found that it has taken a while for members of those committees to realize that a syllabus for an online course does not have to be substantially different from that for a face-to-face course. Understanding that developing a syllabus for any format results in almost the same syllabus was difficult for non-online instructors to grasp. A syllabus is a syllabus is a syllabus . . .

Essential components. For recommendations of what to include in a syllabus, see Figure 2.3. The requirements of the institution or organization sponsoring the course must be followed. Lesley University's requirements are included in our example. We delve more deeply into syllabus development in subsequent chapters.

Figure 2.3. Syllabus Components

Course Title and Number

- Faculty contact information
- Course dates
- Course description
- Course goals, objectives, and outcomes/expectations
- Course requirements
- Required reading
- List of assignment titles/brief description by module (if applicable) and by week or day.

A table with headings for module, week number, assignment name and number, due date, and group composition. (Alternately, include brief descriptions of major assignments, due dates, and how each will be weighted.)

- Grade range table
- Generic **rubrics**
- Discussion participation rubrics
- Specific course equipment that might be needed
- Evaluation criteria
- Policy statement on academic integrity
- Online attendance policy
- Policy statement on disabilities
- Bibliography

Step-by-Step Course-Building Activity #3: Building a Syllabus

The following is an activity to start you thinking about building a syllabus.

1. Find out what your institution's syllabus requirements are. List the items that you must include.
2. Using your institution's format or the one shown in Figure 2.3, fill in as much of the information as you can.
3. Write down your goals and objectives, which you may change as you proceed.
4. Continue to work on completing more components of the syllabus, save a copy of your draft, and add to the syllabus as you read this book.

Online Instructional Approaches

Of the many instructional approaches that are commonly practiced, we discuss three of the most prevalent online: programmed learning, teacher-centered learning, and constructivist/student-centered learning. We also detail two subcategories or strategies commonly associated with constructivist/student-centered learning: project-based learning and authentic learning.

Programmed learning. Programmed learning, or self-paced learning, has its roots in B. F. Skinner's (1963) theories of **behaviorism.** However, programmed learning has developed considerably since Skinner's time. Now a student can read, listen to, or view material online and move from level to level by taking mastery tests or quizzes.

Work is completed independently and the content and method of learning are predetermined. Programmed learning may be simply a series of readings followed by multiple-choice or fill-in-the-blank questions to test comprehension. On the other hand, programmed learning may entail sophisticated knowledge branching or **artificial intelligence (AI)** techniques.

The advantage of programmed learning is that students can work at their own pace, depending on their skills, interest, and available time. If the course is well designed, it can be a set of sequential steps or a more complex branching of steps. The student can repeat lessons multiple times to master the material. In some cases programmed learning is available to students in school computer labs or alternative school sites where a knowledgeable assistant can help them. This instruction may add to the expense of offering the program, but in these cases it is considered important to help students stay on track. Many schools are currently using programmed learning to help students who have not been successful in the face-to-face classroom, who need an extra "boost," or who want to accelerate their learning (Brenner, 2007; Chalker & Stelsel, 2009; Claybaugh, 2005; Doe, 2007).

Adult learners use online programmed instruction to follow an interest, to continue their education, or to earn a certificate. A student we know earned a Microsoft Certified Professional Developer (MCPD) certificate. He commented,

Student Voice *Achieving Microsoft certification via self-study can be done but requires discipline and the willingness and motivation to put in extra hours outside of work and regular life. You definitely cannot do it just by reading but have to actually program. The exams that have been easiest have almost always been the ones where I've had more real-world experience than the ones where I've relied more on readings and practice exams.*

From an academic point of view, course content and assessment can be standardized so that students learn the same material. The instructional methodology is consistent because there is no instructor involved. There is no subjectivity in grading or passing students to the next level because they are "well behaved and try hard." Finally, if educational and content experts develop the course, good instructional practices can be implemented.

Not all courses or content areas lend themselves well to programmed learning. It is typically geared toward skills-based knowledge and rote learning, for example, learning facts in a social studies course or rules when learning a language. Teaching problem-solving skills is difficult to accomplish in this context, since a right or wrong answer is usually required. Even when using more advanced knowledge-branching techniques, the possibility of appropriate responses to the myriad of potential student inputs is limited.

Because self-paced learning can also be isolating for the student, the successful use of this kind of instruction requires students to be self-motivated, to have some self-teaching or learning skills, and to be able to work independently. Generally, there is not an instructor or classmate available who can respond to questions or discuss issues that interest or stymie the student. The developer sets the curriculum, so the student is completely dependent on that perspective of the subject matter and the way the material is presented.

In many cases this form of online learning has earned a negative reputation in part because the programs lack good teaching principles. However, some companies and universities are making inroads into the field by using experts to develop programmed courses that include a more interesting delivery format and AI techniques that allow for addressing a greater variety of **learning styles**.

Teacher-centered learning. A second online teaching approach is the teacher-centered method. The key feature is that interaction is primarily between the instructor and individual student, precluding much student-to-student exchange. The instructor assigns readings, prescribes specific assignments and activities, leads discussions, gives feedback, and presents lectures that are recorded and viewed as streamed material or downloaded. The instructor is the focal point in the process. The student is a receiver of knowledge. Student-initiated participation is not promoted.

Some students and instructors are most comfortable with this traditional-teacher, *sage on the stage* mode. In this context the instructor is the authority. Students may be reassured that the instructor will tell them what to do and the instructor is able to stay in control of both the class and content. This also means that the instructor is essentially doing multiple tutorials or individual courses in parallel with each student rather than teaching a group of students.

There are some drawbacks to a teacher-centered approach in the online environment. By receiving feedback solely from the instructor, the student gains only the instructor's insights and perspective. The student is dependent on the instructor's opinion and presentation style and sometimes neither engages fully with the material nor strives to *own* the learning process and content. Students miss useful ideas and views from peers.

We sometimes have graduate students who are most comfortable with teacher-centered learning. They demonstrate this by asking us what *we* want them to do to earn a good grade. We explain that the course is not *our* course, but *theirs*, and that we hope they will be learning what they need and want within the boundaries of the course. We assume that students at all levels are interested in taking ownership of their own learning. The teacher-centered approach limits this ownership.

In some teacher-centered courses, discussions among students are required or encouraged. Doing so opens the content beyond the instructor–student dyad. However, with a teacher-centered approach, the instructor's comments, directions, and guidance shape and focus the discussion.

Although we started teaching online using instructor-originated and facilitated discussions, we discovered that we could not engage students fully in discourse. We felt that something was missing. Because of this, we developed a student moderator approach. A complete discussion and directions on how to use student moderators can be found in Chapter 5.

In a teacher-centered approach, some students are less likely to express their ideas, since they may be concerned about contradicting the instructor and the effect this might have on their grade. Students may also feel that if the instructor has already made a comment or stated an opinion, the student does not (or should not) have anything to say or add. In this situation, students often think the instructor knows everything. Isn't this true? (-:

Instructors can ask probing questions so students think more deeply about a topic. However, in the teacher-centered approach, the students' primary role is to respond to the instructor's questions or comments rather than to engage with the subject. This method can become a *game* of guessing what the instructor wants the student to say. The focus can move away from the content to the instructor.

The degree of student interaction and the instructor's ability to probe deeply distinguish teacher-centered from student-centered approaches. On a continuum of interaction, at the most structured end, the instructor dictates all interaction, while at the other end everyone participates equally without facilitation. In our view, to meet everyone's needs, an approach that includes a high degree of student interaction as well as instructor guidance is preferable.

Constructivist/student-centered learning. With the increase of online education, inquiry-based constructivist or student-centered approaches to teaching seem to dominate as modes of instruction. This switch from the instructor's being *sage on the stage* to his or her acting as *guide on the side* is widely reported in the literature for all teaching formats (Cowan, 2009; Hughes, Ventura, & Dando, 2007; King, 1993; K. Miller, 2008; Wighting, Liu, & Rovai, 2008). Teaching online is an opportunity to examine and expand implementation of constructivist ways of engaging students.

The constructivist approach to teaching face-to-face and online, in particular, has taken center stage in much of U.S. education. While emphasis on standards and testing has reined in constructivist teaching in K–12, it still has the respect of many educators. The educational theories of Dewey and Vygotsky, which underlie the constructivist approach, stress learning by doing and having students engage with each other and the instructor to create their own meaning. It is examined and supported by many online learning researchers (Alonso, Manrique, & Vines, 2009; Legg, Adelman, Mueller, & Levitt, 2009; K. Murphy, Mahoney, Chen, Mendoza-Diaz, & Yang, 2005; E. Murphy & Rodriguez-Manzanares, 2009).

While widespread in face-to-face teaching, constructivist theories are also well suited to online instruction. Many in the field support this (Chang & Smith, 2008; Legg et al., 2009; K. Murphy et al., 2005; E. Murphy & Rodriguez-Manzanares, 2009; Payne & Reinhart, 2008). One consideration is timing, that is, when students do their coursework. Most online courses use a format that allows students to do their assignments and interact with other students at times that suit them. This is referred to as asynchronous participation.

Other class work may involve voice or video conferencing or instant messaging (IM) through a chat room. This second form of involvement, which is real-time communication, is identified as **synchronous.**

Although it may be desirable, synchronous communication is used less frequently online, since most online learners expect they do not have to block out specific times for class meetings. Moreover, scheduling is problematic because students are often in different time zones and geographic regions or have jobs, other classes, or personal responsibilities. In our experience, all these demands make synchronous communication with a group of as few as four or five people difficult.

Most online courses rely on asynchronous communication. The individuals in the class participate in a **threaded discussion** on their own schedule. In addition, groups in the class can engage in separate discussions and work independently. This phenomenon is a good match for the constructivist approach. The student completes assignments to build meaning. This may include working with others to develop ideas related to the content.

The instructor helps students as a guide on the side. This is not to say that expert or instructor assistance and teaching are absent. For example, the instructor may ask students to view a video or listen to a lecture that the instructor or others have recorded. The student-centered aspect of such an assignment is the follow-up. The student chooses what to react to and in what manner.

Online, instructors need to model behavior by giving useful feedback, asking clarifying and probing questions, and intervening to maintain a supportive environment. Key to this is community building and an encouraging atmosphere so that students are not anxious about or overwhelmed by a learning experience.

The constructivist approach also involves having students assemble their understanding of a topic by building on previous knowledge. It is a process of knowledge acquisition (Henze, 2009), allowing the learner to organize information in a sequence that leads to meaning for that individual. Constructivism allows the inclusion of others' ideas and knowledge from the past and present as well. Two teaching strategies that can be used to support constructivism are project-based learning and authentic learning. The following strategies work well both face-to-face and online, since they engage students in meaningful activity:

- *Project-based learning.* Project-based learning aligns with constructivism and is compatible with the online environment (R. Kelly, 2005). In this approach, students are asked to develop a project based on a "driving," or essential, question (or more than one of these) that the instructor (or student) poses. The projects are designed to be interactive, so that the student devises a way of answering the question by engaging with others or with nonassigned material, and can be completed cooperatively. The instructor works as a facilitator (O'Sullivan, 2003) to help students find resources and serves as a sounding board as the student develops the project.
- *Authentic learning.* Another teaching strategy that is widely used online is authentic learning. Students investigate or learn about and engage with real-world issues so that their studies are relevant, interesting, and useful to them, as well as, potentially, to others (Donovan, Bransford, & Pellegrino, 1999). Students decide how they will design and complete the assignment (Herrington, Reeves, & Oliver, 2006) and answer their own and others' questions on a given topic (C. Miller, Veletsianos, & Doering, 2008). Project-based and authentic learning strategies may overlap. For example, a student could be asked to answer the question "How is the U.S. contending with global warming?" The project might include designing a solution for global warming. A project typically has several phases such as research, devising a plan for action, and evaluation. Authentic learning is about exploring relevant topics. The difference, however, is that project-based learning may involve action about the topic.

Using both or either of these support strategies does not mean that the instructor is absent. On the contrary, in an online setting, the instructor needs to structure the assignment carefully so that the student has a sense of direction without being too constrained. The instructor helps students stay focused. The lesson should be prepared so that the student is also learning skills related to information gathering, analysis, and synthesis, as well as how to communicate what has been learned. The instructor's availability to guide students, answer questions, and help them when they are stymied is essential.

The difference between face-to-face and online in this instance is that in online, preplanning is indispensable, and the instructor must be mindful and explicit when supporting students. An example of preplanning and structuring is making sure that students submit or share *chunks* of their assignments as they proceed. In our experience it is essential to have students complete a minimum of one assignment per week, especially if the project is large and complex. If this is not done, students tend to procrastinate and either submit low-quality work or ask for extensions. Online, there is no room for winging it.

Consider the assignment from our course, ECOMP 5007 *21st Century Teaching: Supporting All Learners on the Ability Spectrum*, presented here in Figure 2.4. This is an example of both project-based and authentic learning. Students, primarily K–12 instructors, are asked to do a case study of their school or district to examine how technology in special education is used in that setting.

The school or district case study is completed over a 2-week period and has four major components. The first is gathering data from a variety of sources. The student decides which resources to use. Listing the types of data that need to be collected provides structure for the assignment, but how that is done is left up to the student. For the second part of the assignment the student determines how to organize the data in a report that is posted on the class Discussion Board. The third component is to read two or three classmates' reports and take notes.

Finally students engage in a synchronous voice conversation using Skype to discuss the reports and similarities and differences and to learn from each other. (More information about conducting synchronous conversations is in Chapter 3.) Each group posts a summary of the synchronous conversation on the class Discussion Board as an additional part of this last component. The instructor coordinates the assignment by posing questions. The students must interact with individuals in their own settings, going beyond the usual way in which they relate. They speak with people and discuss topics they would not ordinarily talk about. Some students have stated that the experience exposed them to technology available for students with special needs that they had not known about. Others indicated that they were surprised by how little technology was available for these students.

One student starting a new job at a private school told us that at first he believed that the assignment did not apply to his situation, since none of his students were identified as having special needs. However, after giving this some thought, he transformed the assignment into developing a plan to address the needs of students he knew had learning issues. He sent a proposal to the headmaster based on the work he did on this assignment.

Our students often find that speaking with colleagues about technology for students with special needs stirs up some interest or builds some bridges to help their students. In many cases new and useful alliances are formed. This assignment addresses real-life issues. Students can shape it. They are primarily teachers in regular education classrooms and are interested in using technology to help students with special needs. They increase their ability to promote the use of technology for students with special needs and, by extension, for all students.

Figure 2.4. Constructivist Assignment (Project-Based/Authentic Learning)

Weeks 4 and 5: Assignment #4a—School or District Case Study and #4b—Skype Discussion

Week 4—#4a. Case study of special education implementation and use of technology

Purpose of Assignment: To become familiar with special education services in your school district and community. This knowledge will provide you with better access to resources and enable you to support the use of technology for students with disabilities. If you are not currently teaching, use your contacts in the district you live in or a nearby district to gather the needed information.

Individual Project: Conduct a study in your school or district with regular and special education teachers, principal, special education director, superintendent, computer coordinator and other appropriate individuals. In addition, reports and web-based information about your district may be useful.

Your case study report should include the following details. The main focus of the report should be on the use of technology. *(Components #1 and #2 should be brief.)*

1. Demographics of the community or school, types of students enrolled in special education services, and the approximate numbers served in each category.
2. Type of special education services provided for students and inclusionary practices.
3. The uses of technology in your district or school to augment learning for students with special needs. Provide specific information on the type of technology, support systems, access, and so on.
4. Based on your readings and the data you gather, discuss how well your community or school implements the use of technology for students with special needs.
5. Briefly describe how one or two students with special needs use adaptive devices or technology to facilitate learning.

Note: For the School District Case Study Assignment, you should form groups of four students and post the group membership in the Teachers' Room.

Due Date: This assignment is due on the date indicated, not before or after.

Week 5—#4b. School District Case Study Skype Conference

Purposes of Assignment: To become aware of other communities' experiences with special needs services and use of technology. This process will allow you to evaluate and make recommendations for your school district for the use of technology for students with special needs. Another purpose of this assignment is to experience using Skype, which can be used as an **assistive technology (AT)** device.

Figure 2.4. Constructivist Assignment (Project-Based/Authentic Learning, continued)

> ### *Group Project*
>
> 1. Schedule and hold a Skype conference with the course faculty member and three to four classmates to discuss the School District Case Studies.
> 2. Prior to the Skype conference you will need to read all the School District Case Study reports written by each person in your Skype conference group. Make notes as you read. Each person will share the following:
>   a. one feature you like about each classmate's school district or school's implementation of technology
>   b. one question or comment about each classmate's School District Case Study
>   c. comments should be "unique," so be sure to have a list of at least four items for both a & b
> 3. Each person will have a role during this discussion.
>   a. Note taker (during the Skype conference).
>   b. Note checker and poster (after the Skype conference).
>   c. Leader/organizer (before and after the Skype conference). Get group organized, post names of members and their roles (in the Teachers' Room), and coordinate the date and time of the conference.
>   d. Supporter (during the conference) to keep the discussion focused. After the conferences make sure the notes are posted.
>
> *Due Date:* This assignment may be completed during the week, but it is due no later than the end of the designated week.

After completing this assignment, one student, an instructional technology specialist, told us during a voice conference that she decided to become a member of the special education technology committee. Authentic learning can make a difference. Another student, who was not a teacher, conducted the case study in her place of business. As the culminating assignment, this student wrote and published an article based on her case study (Houck, 2004).

Programmed learning, teacher-centered, and constructivist approaches all have their strengths and weaknesses. Instructors need to consider how well each of these approaches aligns with their philosophy and with the subject. We prefer the constructivist approach for what we teach because we have found that it involves students more deeply and effectively. Whichever instructional approach is selected, integrating currently used technologies is central to engaging students and producing the best learning results.

Technology Decisions

The technology that is used in the delivery of online instruction influences how a course is taught and how students learn. It ranges from applications such as

Step-by-Step Course-Building Activity #4:
Developing Constructivist Assignments

This activity will help to develop assignments that are constructivist and includes project-based and authentic learning principles.

1. To develop this assignment you can refer to the websites listed below.
2. Select a content area and topic that you currently teach or plan to teach.
3. Develop a case study assignment for students to learn about the topic. (You may follow the steps listed in Figure 2.4.) The case study may include suggested readings, either texts or websites, possibilities of individuals to interview, or field studies.
4. In developing the assignment focus on allowing students to gather information based on their own environments and learning styles.
5. Devise a way for students to share the results of their case study through synchronous Skype or IM discussion, an asynchronous blog, Discussion Board, or Facebook conversation.

Web Resources

Project Based Learning

- The Buck Institute for Education and Boise State University, Department of Educational Technology. Designing Your Project, http://pbl-online.org/pathway2.html
- Houghton Mifflin Company. Project-Based Learning Space: Background Knowledge and Theory, http://college.cengage.com/education/pbl/background.html

Authentic Learning

- Lombardi, M. (2007). Authentic learning for the 21st century: An overview. Educause Learning Initiative. Retrieved from http://net.educause.edu/ir/library/pdf/ELI3009.pdf
- Mims, C. (2003). Authentic learning: A practical introduction and guide for implementation. *Meridian: A Middle School Computer Technologies Journal,* 6(1). Retrieved from http://www.ncsu.edu/meridian/win2003/authentic_learning/

Constructivism

- North Central Regional Educational Laboratory. (n.d.). Constructivist teaching and learning models. Retrieved from http://www.ncrel.org/sdrs/areas/issues/envrnmnt/drugfree/sa3const.htm
- Gagnon, G. W., Jr., & Collay, M. (n.d.). Constructivist learning design notes. Retrieved from http://www.prainbow.com/cld/cldn.html

learning management systems to instruments such as mobile phones. Instructors are somewhat constrained by what their institution offers or requires. Instructors can, however, supplement what is available to enhance their courses.

Learning Management Systems. A learning management system (LMS) or curriculum management system (CMS) is a Web-based space in which course content and communication reside. LMS developers try to anticipate the needs of students and instructors to create a secure and welcoming site for a course. There are many LMSs available. Two commercial LMSs that are widely used are Desire2Learn (http://www.desire2learn.com/) and Blackboard (http://www.blackboard.com/). Blackboard is the LMS used by Lesley University.

Moodle (http://moodle.org/) and Sakai (http://sakaiproject.org/), two other popular LMSs, are free and **open source**. Both commercial and free systems provide a framework in which a course can be organized. The systems are customizable by the individual instructor and the institution. Cole and Foster (2008) indicate that Moodle's foundations are based on the social **constructivism** philosophy of the original developer, Martin Dougiamas. There is an implication that other LMSs do not afford that opportunity. However, we have found that Blackboard does allow us to practice a social constructivist philosophy. We consistently ask students to work together to extend their learning and teach each other through conversations and projects using Blackboard.

Use of an LMS (Blackboard). Although we focus here on how Blackboard is configured and used, the same concepts, setups, and uses are available on most other LMSs. Figure 2.5 shows a snapshot of the instructor's view of a course in Blackboard. The left-hand side contains a list of menu buttons that can be customized for content, color, and shape. The boxes below the menu button links contain tools for the instructor. As can be seen in Figure 2.5, the Control Panel is a link in the middle box that leads to instructor tools for posting and modifying information on the Blackboard course site. All LMSs allow the instructor to have some control of the tools they want to use and the look of the space.

Overview of useful links in the Blackboard interface. The following is a list of Blackboard button links we use most often in our courses:

- *Announcements.* This area is typically the first item students see when they sign on to the course. We post general directions, advisories, and congratulatory and other explicit feedback to all students. We use Announcements for encouraging participation as well as staying in touch with students on a regular basis. We post a new announcement at least once a week. With some LMSs such as Moodle, postings in the Announcements area may automatically be emailed to those enrolled in the course. Figure 2.6 shows a sample announcement from the second week of ECOMP 5007 *21st Century Teaching: Supporting All Learners on the Ability Spectrum.*

Figure 2.5. Instructor's View of a Course in Blackboard

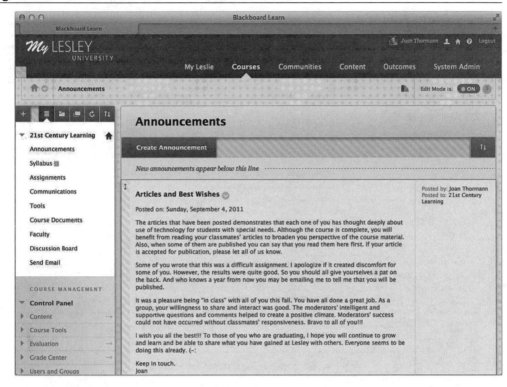

Figure 2.6. Sample Blackboard Announcement

Dear 5007ers,

We have a really interesting group of people in our class. I will post a summary of your introductions in the forum called "Teachers' Room," since everyone enrolled in the course has posted his/her introduction. Please check to make sure I got the information right and add to the information by replying to my message if you wish. Don't forget to complete the second part of the introduction assignment. Many of you have done this. So far there are lots of great questions, responses, and information sharing!!! What a wonderful group! If you have questions post them in the Teachers' Room or ask me.

Joan

- *Syllabus.* We post the syllabus as an attachment. This allows students to save it on their own computers for quick access and to print relevant sections easily.
- *Assignments.* Each assignment folder contains the title, week of completion, due date, and purpose such as in Figure 2.7. In many courses we teach, the first few folders contain information pertaining to the entire course. For example, we always post a summary table of assignments, due dates, and other crucial information. We provide this information in multiple places (Ragan, 2007). We place assignments in individual folders in weekly "chunks" so that they are easy to view and not overwhelming. The weekly arrangement lets students focus on one week at a time while having the option of

Figure 2.7. Sample Blackboard Assignment Page

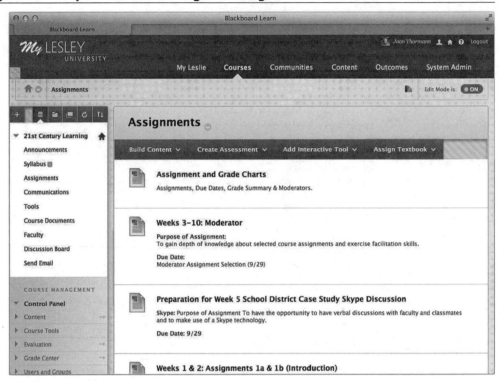

looking ahead to plan. Some students ask clarifying questions, which helps us and everyone in class. We use these questions to revise the wording of assignments.

- *Communications.* This link in Blackboard has some features that duplicate the list of button links on the left side of the page. The duplicates we use are the Discussion Board and Send Email links; because they are used so often during the course, we want to make them easily accessible. This is an example of how an instructor can customize a LMS. Other Communications links that we include are Collaboration, which is a chat tool; Group Pages, for small private discussions; and Roster, which contains a list of all students enrolled in the course.

- *Tools.* One tool used by students for looking up their grades during the course is MyGrades. There are other tools that we do not actively use.

- *Course Documents.* In our courses this space is used for important documents such as Course Guidelines. This document repeats some of the information provided in the syllabus but expands on it. We discuss details in Chapter 4. Journal articles that can be shared under copyright laws are in this folder also.

- *Faculty.* Blackboard provides a button to access Staff Information (which we have customized to Faculty) with name, email address, work phone, and office hours. We offer office hours by appointment. We tried having regular office hours but students did not use them. We also post our résumés. After reviewing these, some students ask questions about articles we have written or places where we have worked.

- *Discussion Board.* This is essentially our classroom. On Blackboard the Discussion Board is not a default link. We make it one, another example of how we tailor the LMS. We ask students to post all their work in forums on the Discussion Board and "speak" together there. This area of the LMS permits the structuring of activities so that students learn from each other, in keeping with our constructivist philosophy. Almost all our assignments require a distinctive product that is based on the individual student's situation and experience. By our having students post assignments publicly they all benefit from reading each other's work. An equally powerful reason to share assignments is that it raises the quality of work. It is one thing to submit an assignment to the instructor; it is another for students to know that peers will also be viewing their work. Even online students do not want to look ignorant or foolish in front of peers. (-:

Recently a student asked for an extension by writing the following:

Student Voice

I have struggled to find a person with the appropriate knowledge necessary to answer the questions in this assignment. During the past week, our special education director and special education department head were on vacation. Our building technology integrator and our district technology director were not familiar with the AT [assistive technology] devices being used by faculty/students utilizing special services. The special education faculty member that was available to speak with me has been playing phone/text tag with me for four days until last night. I have finally gathered the information necessary but fear that I will be presenting a product other than high quality to my group. Is there a way that you could allow a 12-hour extension for me to complete this assignment?

This was a reasonable and elegant request. (-: We were delighted that his concern for the quality of his presentation to his group contributed to an excellent product.

To promote camaraderie and share non-course-related ideas, we set up forums titled Coffee Shop and Teachers' Room on the Discussion Board. In the description of the forums we repeat the purpose for each assignment or forum. Including the due dates is extra work for us but it pays off by decreasing students' concerns and confusion about when an assignment is due. Figure 2.8 shows the instructor's view of a portion of a Discussion Board forum on Blackboard.

- *Send Email.* The last button link is Send Email. As with the Discussion Board link, this is not a default, but we change that. We want to make it easy for everyone to email each other with as little navigation as possible.

The way we organize Blackboard for our courses can be applied to most LMSs. However, instructors should *play* with the components of their LMS to derive the greatest benefit for their course. If the instructor is new to online teaching, it is a good idea to begin simply. Once instructors have achieved a level of comfort using a LMS, they can gradually add other features.

Figure 2.8. Sample Blackboard Discussion Board Page

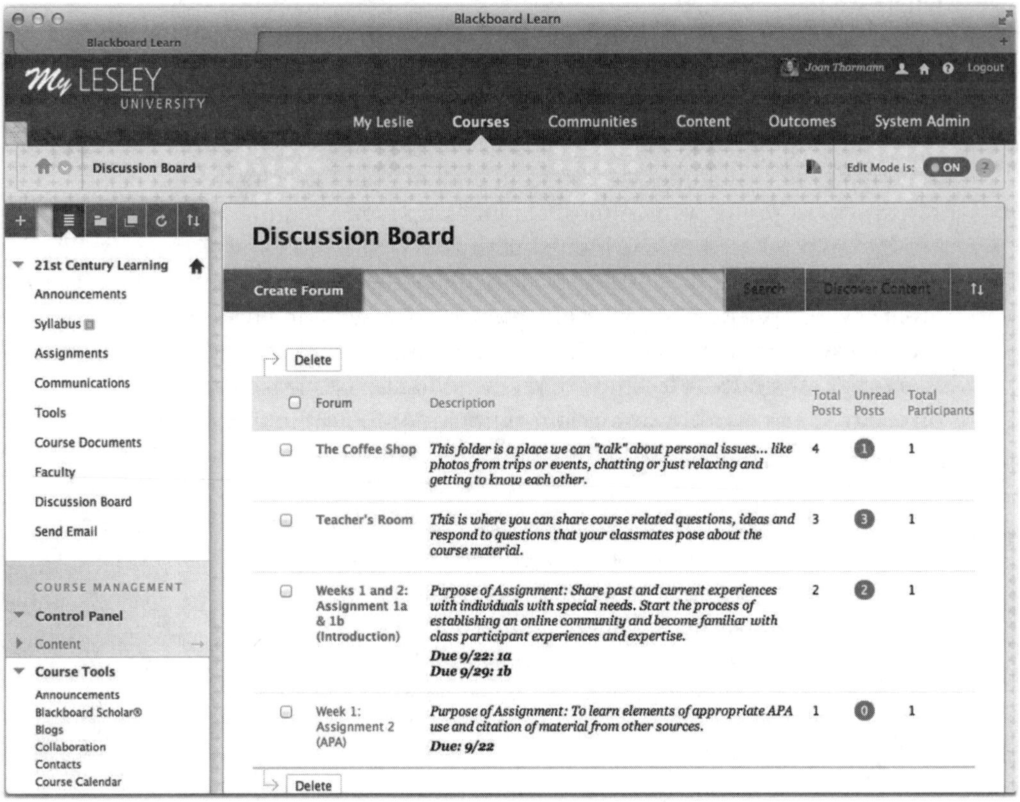

Step-by-Step Course-Building Activity #5: Constructing a Course on an LMS

The following activity assists in determining the elements of the LMS that might be used and in starting to construct a course on an LMS.

1. Locate and explore the LMS you may use. If an LMS tutorial or training is provided, enroll.
2. Talk with colleagues about how they use the LMS.
3. Based on your educational philosophy and the information you have gathered, determine the elements you will use.
4. List additional features or tools you might use that are outside your LMS.
5. If you have access to an LMS, start to build the online version of your course. If you do not have use of an LMS, use other software (word processor, graphic organizer, etc.) to build the course. Be sure to include the requirements of your institution.

All LMSs offer similar features that can be used in different ways. However, once familiar with one LMS, instructors only have to find the correct commands to set up a class that supports their teaching preferences in another LMS. Over time LMSs add features based on instructor and student demand. An example of this occurred as we were writing this chapter. Blackboard announced that it was buying Elluminate and Wimba, two real-time voice communication systems (Customers question tech, 2010). Blackboard's competitors will undoubtedly embed a similar tool soon. LMSs will continue to improve.

Figure 2.9 shows a table that we developed to compare features of various popular LMSs. It is not exhaustive, and since features are constantly changing, may not be totally current. For customizable and in depth comparison go to the EduTools site at http://www.edutools.info/item_list.jsp?pj=4

How we learned to love our LMS. Even though some of our colleagues find that using a LMS constrains their ability to shape their course exactly as they wish, we find the LMS helpful. We started teaching online before our university adopted Blackboard. We grumbled a bit when we started using it. However, once we learned how to use it, which did not take long, we realized that we could work around some of the constraints and live with others.

Prior to Blackboard, the university supplied us with a threaded Discussion Board. We had to create all other supporting materials by developing and updating our own websites, sending files as attachments, and communicating about all course issues using email. We had to create everything from scratch, including ways to communicate grades, assignments, and resources. During the course we spent time and energy on the

Figure 2.9. LMS Comparison

Feature	Blackboard	Moodle	Sakai	Desire2Learn
Announcements	X	X	X	X
Discussion Board/Forums	X	X	X	X
Email	X	X	X	X
Email archive		X	X	
IM/Chat	X	X	X	X
Wiki	X	X	X	
Blog	X	X	X	X
Voice conferencing	X			
Student home page	X		X	X
Roster	X	X	X	X
Syllabus	X	X	X	X
Assignments	X	X	X	X
Calendar	X	X	X	X
Automated assessments	X	X	X	X
Notes/Journal	X			X
Whiteboard	X	3rd party	X	X
Grade book	X	X	X	X

mechanics as opposed to course content and students. Although we do not find exist-ing LMSs to be perfect, they enable us to focus on teaching rather than on arranging our classroom. We are grateful for many of the current features, including the grading center that maintains privacy but allows students to view their individual grades.

We consider an LMS a replacement for our face-to-face classroom and thus *decorate* it. Sometimes we wish that other tools, such as videoconferencing, were available in the LMS classroom. Budget constraints can get in the way. In those cases, we go outside the LMS and find free tools or pay for them ourselves. Most instructors are familiar with this scenario, whether in a face-to-face or online class. We use tools outside the LMS with some reluctance, since, as with face-to-face classroom field trips, there is often a level of unease, additional navigation/challenges, and extra work for both students and instructor. Because Lesley University uses Blackboard, we refer to Blackboard throughout this book, but Moodle, Sakai, Desire2Learn, and others sup-port online learning equally well.

Mobile/smart phones. There is increasing use of mobile/smart phones as an instrument for conveying information. The use is limited by the power of the specific device and service. Currently the most ubiquitous use of mobile phone technology in distance education is **short message service (SMS),** also known as texting. In places where there is little or no access to computers, there are experiments with mobile phones to provide educational opportunities for students. (Hendrikz, Prins, Viljoen, & Du Preez, 2009; Islam & Doyle, 2008). Use of SMS is relatively inexpensive and thus may be a viable alternative. It still represents an added cost that students may not be willing or able to handle. Also, depending on the phone provider and the student's location, voice communication may be unreliable and financially prohibitive.

Some universities are incorporating mobile phones in online courses (Horton-Salway, Montague, S. Wiggins, & Seymour-Smith, 2008; Librero, Ramos, Ranga, Tri-ñona, & Lambert, 2007). In his face-to-face course, Bill Ashraf from Sussex University in the United Kingdom described an interesting use. He teaches a large introductory biochemistry course and has a mobile phone with an alternate SIM card in it (so stu-dents don't call him on his personal phone). During his lectures he tells students to text him questions that they have. He takes a break every 15 minutes or so, looks at the texted questions, and responds to some of them. He responds to the remaining questions via email later on. This tactic is good for shy students or those who might think their question is "stupid." It also gives students the chance to guide the direc-tion of the lecture (personal communication, 2009). Mobile phones can be used in online courses for students who prefer to leave voice messages. Mobile/smart phones are also used as a polling device with appropriate software which collects responses and shows them as graphs and pie charts (Kolb, 2007).

Voice conferencing. Voice conferencing is available with online systems such as Skype or Vyew at no charge. Other commercial versions, such as GoToMeeting, Wimba, and Elluminate (the latter two were purchased by Blackboard, as noted above), are also available. We use Skype in every course to hold small group conferences at least once a semester. The main challenge with synchronous voice meetings is finding a time when all group members are available.

We offer students the opportunity to have one-on-one Skype meetings with us. When students do projects in pairs or groups, Skype is useful. It eliminates long-distance phone charges and lets users speak while keeping their hands free to work on the keyboard. This is particularly helpful in researching content on the Internet or taking notes. One student wrote, "The ability to orally communicate with many people at once was very helpful." We share more student feedback and how we use voice conferencing in Chapter 5. It is essential to focus on course content and ensure that the use of the medium serves the purpose.

Matching instruments with methodology. With the advent of Web 2.0 applications or tools such as blogging, wikis, Facebook, and Twitter, instructors need to consider how and if these applications will enhance instruction. One example of how Twitter was effectively used was shared by Dan Lake, a Lesley University adjunct faculty member, whose student Lisa Hogan works as a technology integrator for Maine School Administrative District 75 in Topsham, Maine. In Figure 2.10 we present the communication she sent to Dan and her classmates. The example in Figure 2.10 demonstrates one way a Web 2.0 tool can be used.

Wikis and Google Docs are ideal tools for students to write and edit collaboratively (Blau & Caspi, 2009; Hudson, 2009; McPherson, 2009; Oishi, 2007). Facebook can also be used effectively to hold discussions. Although this can be done on the class LMS, the advantage of Facebook and other similar tools is that students are constantly accessing those applications. They maintain students' attention (Haverback, 2009; Secker, 2008).

Step-by-Step Course-Building Activity #6:
Matching a Technology Tool to a Learning Objective

This is an activity designed to help match a technology tool to a learning objective to improve instruction.

1. Choose a learning objective you have found difficult to teach.
2. Select a technology tool that may advance teaching that objective. It is preferable to choose a tool you are familiar with. However, if the tool is new to you, this exercise can be seen as more of a challenge.
3. Test the tool before using it.
   a. Obtain clear directions from the Web or your computer resource person or make up the directions for how to use the tool. Include these in your assignment or activity as appropriate.
   b. Ask a colleague, student, or friend to test the assignment and tool using your directions.
4. After using the tool in your course, ask students for feedback about how the tool helped or detracted from learning the objective.
5. Refine the process.

Figure 2.10. Student Use of Twitter to Conduct Research

For the past week now I have been actively researching Dean Shareski. My research has taken a very different path than any other research I have ever done before. I decided to use **social networking** tools to help me find out about Dean. Using Twitter I began to follow Dean's tweets. My friends don't think much of Twitter calling it silly and stupid, "Who cares about what someone is doing every moment of the day," they ask. Actually, my friends don't realize what a great tool Twitter can be for researching.

I read Dean's tweets often finding links to his blog, the blog entry of someone who had a post about a topic Dean found interesting, and URL's that sent me to look at Websites about his work or others' work related to his work.

After a few days of reading Dean's tweets, I began following a few people who follow Dean. Things got pretty interesting because the thoughts and ideas in their tweets sent me off again to places like UStream or Slideshare where ideas Dean wrote about in his blog post or in his tweet were once again illuminated. . . .

Where has this gotten my research? I have had to research other people before. It has always felt like "flat, factual" research. In this case, I feel like I have met a new person. . . .

I wonder how different research would feel to students if they were using blogs, Flickr, Twitter, UStream, Slideshare, and YouTube videos produced by their subject of research to gather information. I wonder if the plagiarism issue teachers sometimes encounter when students are asked to research a person would diminish leading students to analyze, synthesize, and evaluate as they used these tools for research. This assignment has made me think as much about changing the way I have students conduct research as about Dean Shareski. I am happy about this.

Note: Dean Shareski is a digital learning consultant with the Prairie South School Division in Moose Jaw, Saskatchewan, Canada (http://ideasandthoughts.org/).

In the early stages of online education, we asked students to prepare a PowerPoint presentation. PowerPoint had just been introduced. We thought it would be great to use this exciting new tool for our students to develop a lesson. Some were able to do this easily; others inserted so many pictures that the files could not be posted or emailed. We spent an inordinate amount of time assisting students to use PowerPoint appropriately. The objective of the assignment was lost in this technical digression. But we learned that we need to know our technology thoroughly, give specific and clear directions, and try to anticipate possible problems.

SUMMARY

In this chapter we have presented the elements of designing and developing an online course, from establishing a teaching philosophy at the conceptual end, to the use of appropriate technology tools for learning objectives at the practical end. These elements include preplanning; determining goals, objectives, and outcomes; syllabus development; and online pedagogy.

An important aspect of course development is alignment with standards and high-stakes testing. Decisions about technology tools are made by matching learning requirements to available tools. All these elements need to be thoughtfully addressed in order to provide the best online learning experience for students.

CHAPTER 3

Instructional Methods, Models, and Strategies

At the heart of all teaching and learning are instructional decisions. The online format requires instructors and students to engage with new and different approaches to learning. The curriculum we teach face-to-face has essentially the same content when taught online, but requires that we use strategies that are effective and feasible online. In this chapter we discuss the challenges confronted in making a transition from face-to-face to online delivery, including the selection of blended and totally online approaches, types of assignments, and interaction with students.

BLENDED VERSUS TOTALLY ONLINE: CHOOSING A DELIVERY METHOD

Two delivery methods/models are customary for online courses: totally online and blended (also known as *hybrid*). The choice to use one over the other will depend on student, instructor, and school needs and interests; the viability and appropriateness of course content for the format; and the capacity of the infrastructure.

Blended Method

The blended model consists of a combination of face-to-face and online instruction. This model has many variations, based on the balance between face-to-face and online activity.

Many instructors in a face-to-face classroom supplement their teaching with online resources and communication with and among students. In this case, face-to-face is the primary instructional format. This practice may not officially be considered blended, but it is a point on the blended-to-face-to-face continuum.

The following are examples of blended models:

- An intensive weeklong residency combined with online learning
- Face-to-face weekend classes supplemented with online learning
- An intensive weekend-format model, with one weekend of face-to-face class work and the remainder of the work conducted online
- Meeting face-to-face all day Saturday and Sunday for two weekends, a month apart, with the remaining class time online

Students enrolled in the Fulcrum Institute for Education in Science at Tufts University have a combination of a weeklong residency, online coursework, and several Saturday meetings. In K–12 schools, a typical blended model consists of meeting once or twice a week face-to-face, with the rest of the coursework online. These meetings sometimes take the form of tutorials.

Many instructors at all learning levels are taking advantage of what the online instructional setting offers and incorporating online into their repertoire. Increasingly, programs offer a mixed delivery method, with some courses completely face-to-face, some blended, and some conducted totally online.

Totally Online Method

Totally online instruction means that all interactions and teaching/learning experiences take place remotely. When we tell people that we teach courses totally online, they ask, "You mean you never meet your students?" We answer, "That's correct. However, we get to know our online students as well if not better than our face-to-face students."

Adapting Teaching Approaches to Blended and Totally Online Courses

In each format, a variety of strategies and approaches may be used. The programmed learning, teacher-centered, and constructivist approaches detailed in Chapter 2 can be effectively adapted to a number of totally online and blended classroom situations.

Programmed learning approach. The programmed approach can be used successfully in a blended course when the instructor wants students to do some prelearning or to review a skill that was taught in a face-to-face meeting. Programmed learning may also be used in a totally online course model to teach suitable topics or to match a student's learning style.

Teacher-centered learning. A teacher-centered approach can be used to ease the transition from face-to-face to online teaching. The topic can dictate when to use this method. As previously stated, some students and instructors prefer this strategy.

Constructivist approach. This approach enables the instructor to move from *sage on the stage* to *guide on the side* by allowing students to research and develop ideas and projects more independently or with other students. Although constructivism can also be implemented in face-to-face courses, the online and blended formats provide an environment that makes constructivist teaching easier to accomplish. The instructor is not physically present to oversee every step of a student's class work, resulting in students' having to take greater responsibility for their own learning.

INSTRUCTIONAL STRATEGIES

While the whole course needs to be carefully planned prior to launching, this is particularly true for assignments and activities. They need to be appropriate for the age, level, and experience of the students and they need to capture the students' interests. Moreover, the instructional method should have enough flexibility so that all students are able to pursue a special interest.

As earlier noted, in an online course, changing plans once the course has begun can be disruptive to both students and content flow. At the same time, the instructor has to be vigilant in enabling and integrating students' novel or unexpected contributions.

Visual cues and immediate interaction are not available to the online instructor. As a result, it is best to start out with a plan and follow through with it to maximize student involvement and commitment.

Learning Progression

In order to provide a logical sequence for student learning we believe that each class, week, or segment of a course must begin with a stated purpose. This is useful from both instructor and student perspectives because it keeps everyone focused and in alignment. The purpose needs to relate directly to the goals and objectives of the course. For example, an objective from ECOMP 5007 *21st Century Teaching: Supporting All Learners on the Ability Spectrum* is

> To explore ways of adapting hardware, software, and the classroom environment to enhance instructional effectiveness for students with disabilities.

A related assignment that explores software has as its purpose

> To become familiar with and evaluate software designed to support learning and to assess how it might be used with students with special needs.

As can be seen, the statement of purpose is simple and direct but focuses the assignment. It is also important when moving from one topic to the next. The instructor and students need to relate the new topic to what has been learned, to summarize key points, and to align those points to the course objectives. This can be achieved through questions and comments.

Students can also be required to incorporate previously learned knowledge as a part of a new topic. Students may be asked to write a reflection, journal, entry, or blog. In a face-to-face classroom, transitioning is normally done by the instructor's giving a brief summary at the beginning of class or a wrap-up at the end. The instructor may also walk around and chat with students. Online instructional progression must be more explicit and deliberate.

Variety in Assignments and Activities

A key to keeping students engaged in a course is to vary the assignments and activities. Following the same routine constantly can become tiresome for students even if they are interested in the content. Some students may even become completely disconnected. The same problem is potentially true in a face-to-face course; however, the instructor's and students' presence, personalities, and classroom interactions can counteract repetitiveness.

We use a variety of activities and assignments to keep students involved. We also present learning opportunities in ways different from those we would use in face-to-face. The following are three examples from two courses. We present these and others as templates that might be adapted and used in other content areas in Chapter 4.

Figure 3.1 presents an assignment from ECOMP 7104 *Technology in Education Thesis Project.* As can be seen from the assignment in Figure 3.1, we design activities so students work independently as well as together, building on each other's work. They also work directly with a variety of material. In the same course and on the same topic, the assignment in Figure 3.2 is completed individually and in a gamelike format.

Completing assignments in a variety of ways, as seen in Figures 3.1 and 3.2, helps students sharpen their skills and understanding of how to write a literature review.

The assignment in Figure 3.3 is completed by students in ECOMP 5007 *21st Century Teaching: Supporting All Learners on the Ability Spectrum* to familiarize them with web resources for special education and to have them develop a resource for local use.

Many students take this course toward the end of the program. As a result they know how to build their own website. Most of the students choose to develop a website that serves a specific purpose for their school or community. Others do a PowerPoint presentation or a text document.

The reason for including this assignment here is to illustrate how to offer students a variety of ways to do research and share their knowledge. As can be seen in the three examples above, the key is to use a range of assignments to keep every student actively engaged.

Guided Practice/Coaching

The instructor can be any or all of the following: a curriculum developer, a source of support, and a mentor. The instructor can help students by walking them through the steps needed to complete a task or study content. Online this is best accomplished with carefully planned assignments, activities, and checkpoints to make sure students are on track. As always, there is a delicate balance between guiding students and dictating what

Figure 3.1. Sample #1 of Assignment Variety

Assignment #2: Literature Review Investigation

Purpose: To review the structure and content of a literature review

1. Read at least two of this week's assigned readings to get an idea of how various universities describe what a literature review section should contain.
2. Read the literature review section of the research article that has been assigned to you by your faculty member.
3. Write and post a report describing and commenting on the components of the literature review of your assigned article. Give examples of the components (see list below) found in your research article. In addition, use some of the ideas found in #1 above to critique your research article's literature review. Post a report including the following:
   a. key features
   b. structure
   c. use of American Psychological Association (APA) writing and formatting rules
   d. length in relation to the overall article
   e. topics addressed in relation to the research being conducted
   f. number of different citations used
   g. type of citations used (i.e., research studies, opinion of experts, essays, etc.) and sources
   h. missing or extraneous information
   i. citations from some of this week's assigned readings
   j. other observations

Readings

Caputo, R. K. (2004). Advice for those wanting to publish quantitative research. *Families in Society, 85*(3), 401–404.

Christensen, C. (1996). *Guidelines for writing a review of literature*. Retrieved from http://www.sjsu.edu/faculty/christen/review_guidelines.html

Mongan-Rallis, H. (2006). *Guidelines for writing a literature review*. Retrieved from http://www.d.umn.edu/~hrallis/guides/researching/litreview.html

Taylor, D. (2006). *The literature review: A few tips on conducting it*. Retrieved from http://www.writing.utoronto.ca/advice/specific-types-of-writing/literature-review

University of Wisconsin–Madison Writing Center. (2006). *Writing a review of literature*. Retrieved from http://www.wisc.edu/writing/Handbook/ReviewofLiterature.html

Due Date: This assignment may be posted early but is due no later than the end of the designated week.

Figure 3.2. Sample #2 of Assignment Variety

Assignment #3: Literature Review Problems

Purpose: To become aware of potential problems with literature reviews

1. The literature review posted in the "Problems with Literature Reviews" forum is flawed. (I found a perfectly good literature review and changed it so that it is now flawed.)
2. Download and read the literature review, making notes of what you think the flaws are.
3. Using MSWord, turn "Track Changes" on. Edit the document to make comments and correct the flaws where possible.
4. Send the document to the faculty member as an attachment.

The actual published literature review will be posted at the end of the week so that you can compare your critique with the published document.

---

they should do. It is critical to let students have the freedom to be creative and shape their own vision of the assignment. However, it is essential to supply ample assistance and guidelines so that students do not flounder or lose focus.

Guided practice is a method for providing assistance to students. In a face-to-face classroom, the instructor can observe that students have grasped the skills, concepts, and modeling the instructor has presented. The instructor circulates and provides aid. Students demonstrate what they have learned and at what level they have learned it. The instructor gives feedback—correction, affirmation, further probing.

In an online course, this assistance can be provided quite easily by keeping track of successive copies of work and giving written or oral feedback through the use of Track Changes in MSWord, sticky notes, emails, chat rooms, Skype, and so on. In an online course, there is a record of student growth. It is easy to configure and then characterize online teaching as guided practice.

Coaching is another method of teaching people to develop specific skills and concepts. Usually associated with athletics, coaching has become a valued tool in academic instruction. Students practice the skills and apply concepts repeatedly until they master the skill or concept under the direct supervision of an instructor or classmates.

In an online course this is most effectively achieved by working with students one at a time or in small groups. It is also possible to establish peer coaching, whereby students support each other in learning new skills and concepts as well as practicing old ones.

Real-World, Authentic Learning

While we have already discussed authentic learning in the context of a constructivist approach, we feel that it is worth reexamining as part of selecting instructional strategies, assignments, and activities.

Figure 3.3. Sample #3 of Assignment Variety

Weeks 3 and 4: #5a Resource Manual and #5b Discussion

#5a Resource Manual

Assignment Purpose #5a: To research and locate Internet resources available on the topic of special needs and technology. To create a customized resource for your teaching practice or classroom.

1. Decide what kind of special education and technology resource you want to create.
   a. Ideas from previous ECOMP 5007 students include but are not limited to reference manuals for parents about technology use for students with **ADHD** (attention deficit hyperactivity disorder), technology guides for Windows PCs; a library reference guide, and a technology and special needs website for colleagues in a school district.
   b. The format may be a Word document, a website, a PowerPoint presentation with voiceover, or whatever medium serves you and your audience.
2. Visit and review at least ten sites relating to technology and special education to find information for your customized resource.
3. Develop your technology and special education resource by doing the following:
   a. Include information from some of the ten sites you reviewed.
   b. Find and include information from your state's technology and special education or assistive technology (AT) sites
   c. Cut and paste information you find on these sites for your resource. Be sure to cite your sources using APA format.
   d. You may add other sites.
   e. Include an introduction that describes the purpose of the resource and for whom it was designed.
   f. Describe the information collected *or* insert a table of contents.
4. Post the URL or attach the document of your resource on the Discussion Board.

Due Date: This assignment may be posted during the assignment week, but no later than the due date.

Week 4: #5b Resource Manual Discussion

Assignment Purpose #5b: To learn about additional resources from classmates and enhance your own "technology in special education resource."

1. Review at least one classmate's resource.
2. After reviewing the resource, write substantive comments about the resource and ask at least one question.
3. Reply to the comments and questions that your classmates and instructor post.

Due Date: This assignment may be completed at any time prior to the due date but must be completed by the due date.

Step-by-Step Course-Building Activity #7: Diversifying Assignments

This activity is about diversifying assignments to maintain engagement and meet student needs.

1. Make a list of the variety of ways you can engage students with the content.
2. Discuss your list with a colleague.
3. Choose the three most promising ways from the list and develop assignments.
4. For each assignment, write a purpose so that it aligns with your goals and objectives.

Students are asked to select a topic that relates to their own setting and interests within the context of the course. For the topic to be *real world* and authentic it needs to present a problem or challenge that students must investigate and address. Students extend their knowledge by interacting with classmates about their topics.

By having students select their own topic, the assignment becomes a part of the student's world and offers a way for students to use what they have learned. The real-world nature of the assignment ensures that students will remember the ideas and perhaps learn more about them in the future.

Learning that can be applied directly and immediately excites students and creates a greater involvement in learning. After doing an assignment relating to National Instructional Materials Accessibility Standard (NIMAS), we received an unsolicited email from a student who was teaching in Alaska and enrolled in the ECOMP 5007 *21st Century Teaching: Supporting All Learners on the Ability Spectrum* course:

Student Voice *On Friday I was sitting in the teacher's lounge and some of the [special education] teachers were discussing something and one of them said NIMAS and I was thrilled that I knew what they were talking about. I surely feel more confident and knowledgeable when it comes to discussions with the sped teachers.*

Learning Communities

The development of a learning community among students makes the educational process more compelling. When we teach a group of students who do not know each other, we start the course by having them introduce themselves. We ask for demographic information as well as information relating to course content. It is good for students to know where each person *is coming from* and what expertise each offers.

In every introduction or icebreaking assignment we make sure that this activity encourages students to think about the course content. This conveys from the beginning that learning the course content is the primary purpose of our meeting. Figure

3.4 shows the Introduction assignment for ECOMP 5007 *21st Century Teaching: Supporting All Learners on the Ability Spectrum.*

The demographic data in the assignment shown in Figure 3.4 helps all of us to place people in context. It is worthwhile to know if students work in a small or large school district and if and what they are currently teaching. Sharing personal information and interests creates a great deal of discussion. Students like to talk about their commonalities and learn about each others' lives.

Although students are required to communicate with only two other classmates for this assignment, most of them go well beyond this requirement, as can be seen on the Discussion Board screen under the Introduction assignment in Figure 3.5, where 231 in the upper-righthand corner indicates the number of posts (from a class of 15 students).

We model communication by posting a comment and question to each student and when the student responds, we reply as appropriate. One of the particularly interesting results of the Introduction assignment in this course comes from the reflection that students are asked to share about their experiences with individuals with special needs. They often write about family, friends, children they went to school with, or students in their classes. Students in our classes who have a sibling or family member with a disability rarely mention it in the Introduction. However, later in the course as they feel more comfortable, students gradually share anecdotes or events about a spouse, sibling, child—or themselves.

These personal contributions help to build strong ties and pull classmates into the course content. The Introduction is just the beginning of building a learning community.

We also use forums such as the Coffee Shop and Teachers' Room, student moderators, group assignments, online voice conferences, and shared assignments. These techniques will be discussed in greater depth in Chapter 5.

In a face-to-face setting, alliances and community can be fostered fairly easily. Online, the instructor needs to consciously build opportunities for students to relate to each other and the instructor. However community building is accomplished, it is clear that it keeps students more connected with the learning process (Chapman, Ramondt, & Smiley, 2005; Dawson, 2006; Shea, Sau Li, & Pickett, 2006) and should be planned in advance.

Skype Communication to Create Personal Connections

We use Skype at least once a semester. Our goals are to increase interaction with and among students, build community, and provide another communication tool. It also helps us match vocal use of language with written work, providing another way to ensure that students are doing their own work.

We use Skype because some students already use it, it is easy to use, and it is free. If students have never used Internet voice communication this is a good opportunity to acquaint them with this tool.

Figure 3.4. Sample Assignment to Develop a Learning Community

Weeks 1 and 2: Assignment #1a and 1b: Introduction

Individual and Group Project

Purpose of Assignment: Share past and current experiences with individuals with special needs. Start the process of establishing an online community and become familiar with class participants' experiences and expertise.

#1a. Introduction

Introduce yourself to all students in our online community. Include all components (items a through g) as follows:

a. The subject(s), grade(s) you teach or your position at work. If you are not currently working outside your home indicate your past work and aspirations.
b. Where you work (district name, city and state, and name of school or similar information). If you are not currently working outside your home indicate your past work and aspirations and where you currently live.
c. The number of courses or other programs you have completed and the courses you are enrolled in this semester.
d. Why you are interested in this course.
e. If you have had experience using technology with individuals with special needs, share the experience. If not, describe how you think technology could be used.
f. Introductory comments. In special education today it is believed that attitudes have played and continue to play a large role in the development and provision of services to children who are disabled. The type, amount, and location of these services are largely determined by the attitudes of the service providers, rather than by any test of efficiency or effectiveness. Write a reflection and include the following:
   • Describe any experience(s) you have had with someone with a disability, either recently or in your own education and childhood. For example: Did you know a child who stuttered? Do you have a friend who had or has a developmentally delayed brother or sister? Did you have an aunt, uncle, or cousin who wore a hearing aid or went to a special school? Do you yourself have a learning disability?
   • If you had any of these experiences or similar ones in the past or recently, describe them.
   • Reflect on your current and past experiences. For example: When you were a child, did you see a person with a disability who frightened you? What did your parents say about this, and how did they explain it to you? Is there one incident that stands out from the rest? Or is it possible that you cannot remember a single encounter with a person with a disability?

- If you had any of these experiences or similar ones in the past or recently, describe them.
- Write about how you think the experiences you describe affected your own attitudes towards individuals with special needs.
- How do those experiences shape your current attitudes and feelings?

g. Tell us about yourself, family, friends, interests, and so on. After the second week of class all personal communications should be posted in the Coffee Shop forum.

Due Date: This assignment may be posted any time during the first week but no later than the due date indicated on the syllabus, assignment chart, and Discussion Board.

Weeks 1 and 2: #1b: Introduction—Meet and Greet

Group Project

1. Read *all* your classmates' introductions.
2. Identify two students in the class whose introductions are posted before and after your own introduction posting.
3. Ask the two identified classmates a question about what they wrote in their introduction. Post your question in the Discussion Board directly under your classmates' introduction. Use the Reply button to do this. (I encourage you to converse with other students as well.)
4. Respond to *all* questions. Post your responses directly under your classmates' questions. Use the Reply button to do this.

Due Date: This assignment may be posted any time during the first 2 weeks but no later than the due date indicated on the syllabus, assignment chart, and Discussion Board.

Figure 3.5. Illustration of Discussion Board Activity for Learning Community Assignment

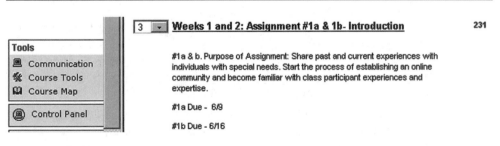

We introduce the idea of a Skype conference at the very beginning of the course and require students to install Skype on their own computers, if they have the capability. We are also careful to include those who are unable to use Skype on their own computers. Our introduction is shown in Figure 3.6 as an illustration.

To implement the use of Skype after students install the application, we have students post their Skype name in the Teachers' Room by replying to a message that we post. We fill in the student's Skype name in a table as shown in Figure 3.7. We place

Figure 3.6. Introducing a Skype Assignment

Purpose of Assignment: To have real-time voice discussions with your instructor and classmates about course content.

At least twice during the course you will participate in a Skype conference with a faculty member and a group of classmates. If you do not already have Skype, you will need to set up and test Skype to make sure it works. You will need the following:

1. High-speed connection (cable or DSL) for the computer
2. Skype software (downloaded from http://skype.org/)
3. A microphone and speakers.

Use of Skype is free, although there are services and products you can buy. If you do not have high-speed access at home, you can check to see if your school or library will allow the use of Skype or get together with a classmate or friend who does have high-speed access.

If none of these options are possible, we can use my Skype phone account, which allows me to contact you at no cost and include you in a group voice conference.

The ideal situation, however, is to get Skype so you can experience using it with your classmates, friends, and family. In the past many students who were introduced to Skype become Skypeaholics . . . a money-saving affliction at worst!

Figure 3.7. Skype Name Posting in the Teachers' Room

Dear Thesis Writers,

Please post your Skype name by replying to this message. Directions for the Skype assignment and setup are found under the Assignments button.

I will be updating the table below as you reply with your Skype name. I look forward to speaking with you.

Joan

Name	Skype Name
Karl Grogan*	Karl Grogan
Carol Haliday*	carol_grainger626
Sharon McLean	
Charlene Samson	
David Tabor*	Tabor3
Joan Thormann	JoanThor

*Added name to JT's Skype contact list.

> **Step-by-Step Course-Building Activity #8:**
> **Working Relationships Among Students**
>
> This activity helps to develop collegial working relationships among students.
>
> 1. Get together with some colleagues who are interested in online teaching, or do this activity independently.
> 2. Brainstorm a list of ways to start off a course to encourage the development of an online learning community. You may want to adapt icebreakers used in face-to-face courses or develop entirely new ones.
> 3. In these icebreaker/introduction activities include some elements that address or introduce course content.

an asterisk next to the person's name when we add it to our Skype contact list. It is beneficial for everyone to have all Skype names of those enrolled in the course, so students can build their own contact lists and speak with classmates independently.

To facilitate discussions we have students form teams of three or four. We found that four students is optimal; three is also fine. This ensures that each student has the time and opportunity to contribute to the discussion.

We ask for one student from each team to volunteer to be a leader/organizer. Sometimes students are reluctant, so we offer five extra points to the volunteers for this task. This usually does the trick and those who earn the extra points usually do not need them.

In a table in Announcements, we share times that we are available to meet. As team leaders notify us about when they can meet with us, we post this information, as seen in Figure 3.8.

We provide an agenda for meetings indicating the roles students should take during the Skype meeting. This is important. Its purpose is to focus the meeting on course content so that it does not turn into a general gab session.

However, at the end of every meeting, we always ask students if they have any questions or comments that are not directly related to the current assignment. They are then able to raise issues or concerns they may have. We also invite them to Skype us one-to-one if they wish.

We have been using Skype meetings for some time and have found it to be an excellent strategy for enhancing learning and building community. In the second part of the assignment in Chapter 2, Figure 2.4, we have an illustration of the directions for a Skype meeting.

Maushak and Ou (2007) found that using IM synchronous communication was beneficial for students. Others who teach online, such as Chen, Ko, Kinshuk, and Lin (2005), report that students found that "online synchronous live instruction mode and online 'office-hours' activities provide excellent learning outcomes and satisfaction for online courses." These researchers used a model in which the instructor lectured and managed discussions. As the technology for synchronous communication online becomes more stable and easier to use it will become ubiquitous in online courses.

Figure 3.8. Announcement Scheduling Skype Meetings

Dear 5007ers,

As you look at the assignment chart you will notice that the discussion about the Field Research and Alternative Assignments (#3b) will take place in small groups using a real-time Skype meeting. I'm looking forward to reading your reports and having a good discussion with each group.

Potential meeting times for the Skype discussion are below. I have included day and evening times. Your leader/organizer will work with you to coordinate the day and time. Then he or she will email me with what you have decided. This may be a little difficult due to the different time zones, but I know you will work it out.(-:

Two groups have established dates and times which are indicated below. The other groups should select times that are still available.

Date and Time	Group	Date and Time	Group
Wednesday 7/14		**Saturday 7/17**	
1:00–2:00 P.M. EDT	Eric's group: Jim, Terry, Jan	9:00–10:00 A.M. EDT	
2:00–3:00 P.M. EDT		10:00–11:00 A.M. EDT	
3:00–4:00 P.M. EDT		11:00 A.M.–12:00 P.M. EDT	
4:00–5:00 P.M. EDT		1:30–2:30 P.M. EDT	
7:30–8:30 P.M. EDT		2:30–3:30 P.M. EDT	
8:30–9:30 P.M. EDT		3:30–4:30 P.M. EDT	
Thursday 7/15		4:30–5:30 P.M. EDT	Stella's group: Kim, Barb, and Oscar
9:00–10:00 A.M. EDT		7:30–8:30 P.M. EDT	
10:00–11:00 A.M. EDT		8:30–9:30 P.M. EDT	
11:00 A.M.–12:00 P.M. EDT		**Sunday 7/18**	
1:30–2:30 P.M. EDT		1:30–2:30 P.M. EDT	
2:30–3:30 P.M. EDT		2:30–3:30 P.M. EDT	
3:30–4:30 P.M. EDT		3:30–4:30 P.M. EDT	
4:30–5:30 P.M. EDT		4:30–5:30 P.M. EDT	

There is currently an interest in improving the use of synchronous voice and video communication, as indicated by a student survey about how to enhance implementation that was conducted by Groen, Tworek, and Soos-Gonczol (2008). Thormann's research indicated mostly positive student comments about synchronous communication using Skype. A few of the student comments serve to illustrate the point:

 In an online course, I think the Skype helped us in refining our work through verbal communication rather than through emails.

 I liked the whole concept of Skype . . . it was fun!

 It was helpful to hear classmates' opinions and suggestions during the conferences. It was easy to make the suggested changes in the final thesis.

We continue to refine the strategic use of synchronous communication through our own research and by reading about what others experience. We are convinced that online instructors should use this medium in an innovative way.

Online Collaboration

Online collaboration, both synchronous and asynchronous, is a way to help build community, but it has other benefits. Behavior in each mode can be different. Online students can share their strengths without worrying about being ostracized or ridiculed. In face-to-face, students often compete for the instructor's time-limited attention and, if successful, can be considered a *teacher's pet*.

Online there are few time limitations, so all those who want to participate fully and share their knowledge can. Online the exchange of information is easier to achieve and individual students as well as the entire class can solidify and increase their learning.

Collaboration might occur naturally but we typically orchestrate it. We encourage students to post questions in the Teachers' Room forum and suggest that anyone in the course may answer them. We usually wait before responding to give students an opportunity to answer first. All this gives them a sense of belonging to a group with a common purpose.

The major difference between collaboration in face-to-face and online courses is that most online communication is asynchronous and in written format (although more vocal and visual avenues are being used). Therefore communication needs to be carefully prepared to ensure that others understand what is intended. The asynchronous nature of most online interaction permits students and faculty the time to think through what they want to say.

It is commonly agreed that asynchronous online written discussions are potentially more coherent than face-to-face discussions (Palloff & Pratt, 2001; Tinker and Haavind, 1996). While such asynchronous communication may lose some spontaneity, it gains depth. Furthermore there is a written record of the discussion, so everyone can refer back to it.

Depending on the students' level, they may need more or less help getting organized when asked to work together in groups or pairs in an online course. Whatever the level, especially for group work, it is key to build in checkpoints, timelines, and due dates for assignment components. For any level we recommend no fewer than one assignment per week. The younger or less experienced the student, the more frequent the contact should be.

We ask students to do one or two collaborative projects each semester. The reason to limit the number is that producing a deliverable with one or more persons adds time and logistical challenges to the assignment. Collaborative work is time consuming. It is important to keep the focus on the course content.

Unless the goal of the course is working together, collaborative projects should be assigned sparingly and directed at knowledge building. Sometimes we assign students to groups. At other times we allow them to choose their partners or group members.

We always plan a collaborative assignment later in the course so students choose their collaborators with some knowledge of the strengths and weaknesses of potential partners. We also use Skype as a vehicle for synchronous voice communication before assigning a group project. This enables group members to be familiar with and able to make use of this additional tool. We assist students by giving the selection of a partner and topic as an assignment.

Interactivity Features and Learning by Doing

It is advisable to take advantage of as many of the interactivity features provided by the LMS such as a threaded discussion board, chat capabilities, ability to email everyone in the class, and wikis. This helps students stay connected and allows them to learn from each other. The instructor must guide and structure activities as well as student interaction (Coffey, 2009). In our courses we develop assignments that are structured but rely on the individual or groups of students' own perspective of a topic.

For example, in the Literature Review Investigation Assignment #2 (Figure 3.1) we assign an article to read that addresses the topic that each student plans to research. They use this article as a model (or anti-model) to examine how a published research study is written. Students are asked to critique their article independently and post a list of strengths and weaknesses.

As Part 2 of this assignment (not shown), they compare what some of their class-mates found. To help students put it all together, selecting the most salient items, we develop a list drawn from all the students' lists. This *groupthink* occurs throughout the research paper process so that students have guidelines to follow, generated by their own group.

The value of doing this on the Discussion Board is that students can easily access their classmates' lists and articles. Moreover, the online environment allows contri-butions from everyone, not just those who are articulate and enjoy public speaking. The instructor and groups of students read successive versions of each section of each paper to give and get feedback to ensure proper synthesis.

Student Choice

To maintain students' interest it is useful to give them choices within the con-text of the topic and an assignment. Structuring assignments is necessary so that students do not flounder or miss learning opportunities. Students take greater own-ership and are more motivated if they have some control over what they do and how they do it.

For the Literature Review Investigation assignment (Figure 3.1), we describe how students in the thesis-writing course are assigned research articles. Although we select the articles, they are determined by the topic the student chooses to study. In addi-tion, students are offered the option of finding their own research article.

Step-by-Step Course-Building Activity #9: Choosing an Assignment

This activity is designed to give students choice in assignment completion.

1. Select a topic that you plan to teach online.
2. Develop two different assignments that include the following features:
   a. interactivity
   b. structure
   c. meaningful choices
3. Test these assignments with students or share them with colleagues.
4. Getting feedback:
   a. If you used the assignments with students have them complete an anonymous online survey (SurveyMonkey.com) to get feedback. This will help refine the assignment.
   b. If you shared the assignments with colleagues ask for feedback or ideas to improve them.

Interestingly, so far, no one has opted for his or her own article. Many students are pleased to be given an additional article for their literature review. This assignment illustrates how a narrow structure allows for student interests. It does take time on our part to find articles that meet our criteria and all students' thesis topics.

In some courses we want students to experience or examine specific ideas. Figure 3.9 shows an assignment from ECOMP 6008 *The World Wide Web as an Educational Resource*. Students are free to select any site they wish to experiment with or one that we have preselected.

Another example of student self-determination is the culminating project in ECOMP 5007 *21st Century Teaching: Supporting All Learners on the Ability Spectrum*. The student writes an article and is free to choose the topic and journal for publication. The only limitation is that the article must focus on use of technology in special education. As one student wrote,

Student Voice *I like that a lot of things are pretty open-ended, so you can focus on the things you want to focus on.*

The online instructor is engaged in a delicate balance between guiding and structuring the learning and allowing student choice and freedom to deviate. It is up to the instructor to find this balance. It may be easier to do so by incorporating the tactics we suggest, seeing how they work with students, and modifying as needed.

Tailoring Assignments for Diverse Learners

We have argued that it is important to give students some choice in selecting the content of their assignments. It is also important to enable students to complete

Figure 3.9. Sample of a Student-Determined Assignment

Week 3: Assignment #5a—Online Projects

Purpose of Assignment: To consider some new resources and ideas about how you can use the Web in the classroom.

Individual Project

1. Read at least one of the articles in this week's readings. (See below.)
2. Locate at least one more article relating to online projects.
3. Use the Resources, below, or research your own, to find classroom Internet projects.
4. Select two online projects from the Resources list.
5. Post information about your selections in the appropriate Discussion Board folder. The subject line of your posting should include the names of the online projects you wrote about. Include the following in your report:
   a. A description of the projects with details like URL, grade levels, time frame, costs, and materials.
   b. Why you selected these projects.
   c. How you would use them in a classroom.
   d. The strengths and weaknesses of the projects.
   e. Include any pertinent information from the articles you read.

Due Date: This assignment may be completed prior to but no later than the due date.

Week 4—#5b: Projects Discussion

Purpose: To extend knowledge of online projects and delve more deeply into the online project that was reviewed.

1. Read at least two classmates' posting of online projects you did *not* explore.
2. Make substantive comments and ask a question.
3. Respond to all the questions that you are asked.

Due Date: This assignment may be completed early but no later than the due date indicated on the syllabus, assignment chart, and Discussion Board.

Resources

Global SchoolNet, http://www.globalschoolhouse.org/
They had a Dream Too!, http://www.teachersfirst.com/share/mlk/proj-open.html
The Jason Project, http://www.jasonproject.org
Journey North: A Global Study of Wildlife Migration, http://www.learner.org/jnorth/
Scholastic Online Projects/Field Trips and Lesson Plans, http://teacher.scholastic.com/activities/
Take Your Students on a Virtual Field Trip, http://www.field-trips.org/index.htm

Other Virtual Field Trips and Web Museums, http://midgefrazel.net/fieldtrip.html;
http://www.virtual-field-trips.com/
The Underground Field Trips, http://teacher.scholastic.com/fieldtrp/socstu/explore.htm
The Teacher's Guide to Field Trips, http://www.theteachersguide.com/virtualtours.html
"How Everyday Things Are Made," http://manufacturing.stanford.edu/

Online Tours

http://www.virtualfreesites.com/museums.html
http://www.theteachersguide.com/virtualtours.html

Teacher-Created Virtual Field Trips

http://www.tramline.com/trips.htm
Wright Flyer Project, http://quest.arc.nasa.gov/aero/wright/
Friendship Through Education Consortium, http://www.friendshiptrougheducation.
org/about.htm
The Project Center, http://www.k12science.org/currichome.html
Letterboxing, http://www.letterboxing.org/index.php

Online Projects

Virtual Architecture, http://virtual-architecture.wm.edu/
Monster Exchange, http://www.monsterexchange.org/about/about_msdescription.
htm
Earth Day, http://www.earthdaybags.org
TeachersFirst, http://www.teachersfirst.com/matrix.htm

Readings

Leu, D., Jr. (2001). Internet Project: Preparing students for new literacies in a global
village. *Reading Teacher, 54*(6), 568–573.
Siegle, D. (2005). Six uses of the internet to develop students' gifts and talents. *Gifted
Child Today, 28*(2), 30–36.
Troutner, J. (2005). Educational activity sites for high school students. *Teacher Librar-
ian, 32*(5), 40–43.

work based on their abilities. Students enrolled in online courses are diverse and some have identified special needs.

Schools at all levels have specific regulations about eligibility for special services and support. For those who have identifiable and eligible special needs, it is best to work with the special education or disability services office. There may also be students who are English language learners (ELL), gifted, or at risk.

Within the parameters of the school administration's guidelines the instructor is often asked to make accommodations for students with diverse needs. We discuss techniques of addressing student diversity in Chapter 7.

SUMMARY

In this chapter, we have explored instructional methods and strategies for delivering courses online. Many elements are not very different from face-to-face teaching, so anyone interested in online instruction should feel competent to make the transition. A clear vision of the teaching approach and instructional strategies prior to launching a course is essential. Delivery and facilitation are significantly different aspects of teaching online courses. In online courses students learn almost entirely through activities and assignments. The manner in which these are structured is critical to the learning experience.

In addition, teaching a diverse student population online presents both challenges and rewards. Teaching online offers instructors the opportunity to extend their repertoire and emerge with additional approaches to meet the needs of our 21st-century students.

CHAPTER 4

Assignment Templates and Examples

When we plan a course and develop assignments we first determine course goals and objectives. Based on these, we craft interesting and challenging activities to assist students in learning content and skills. We have designed assignment templates and use some of the same templates for various courses but, naturally, change the content. In this chapter we offer 20 templates for instructor use with some examples of how we and others infuse content and skills into these templates. The first ten templates have examples that have been used in courses. The remaining ten templates do not have examples associated with them, but instructors will find them useful.

TEMPLATES FOR INNOVATIVE EXERCISES AND EXPERIENCES

Students find the process of learning more appealing when they are presented with varied activities. Two of the key features that most of our assignment templates include are (1) making assignments sufficiently open-ended so each student or small group creates a unique product and (2) having students interact with each other in a follow-up discussion. In addition, many of the templates are designed so that students can, within boundaries, make choices about what they do. Wherever we have students post written material, they may also post PowerPoint files, **vodcasts** (video podcast), **podcasts** or other appropriate media. In some cases our templates focus on the use of a particular medium. This break from writing a paper can be a refreshing change for students. Most of the assignment templates can be applied to any content area.

Assignment Template 1: Video Viewing

Each student views the same video with local colleagues for group knowledge development and discussion of the local situation with classmates.

a. Select a video that is pertinent to the course content.
b. Require students to view the video with two or three colleagues or interested individuals in their community.
c. Develop guidelines. The following is a suggested set:

      i. Discuss the video with the group.
      ii. Take notes during the discussion.
      iii.Post a report capturing the reactions of group members.
    d. Require students to read classmates' reports, compare, comment about their own group's work, and ask questions.

Another version of viewing the same video is to have students add a segment of a video that they all view and then discuss what classmates have added.

1. Select a video that addresses issues in the field of study.
2. Challenge students to think of additional issues missing from the video that could be included.
3. Have students develop a script or additional video to add coverage of the issues identified by student analysis.
4. Have students discuss the pros and cons of adding other issues.

Figure 4.1 contains an example from ECOMP 7017 *Teaching Online: Issues and Design*. This assignment engages students by having them think about all the course materials and activities that have been completed and challenges them to synthesize in a creative way the ideas they have been exposed to. Additional reading is assigned and they follow up by viewing and discussing classmates' ideas.

Assignment Template 2: Online Artifact Jigsaw

Students use online artifacts to learn about an aspect of the content area. They then present the information they have learned for classmates to read, discuss, and reflect on.

a. The instructor or students locate artifacts, such as online videos, websites, and articles, that illustrate different aspects of a course topic.
b. The instructor develops guidelines for examining the artifact. These might include having students list elements of their artifacts and how these elements can be applied in the students' practice.
c. The instructor assigns an artifact to each student or a group of students or has students select their own artifact from instructor's list or one they develop on their own.
d. Students read each other's reports, discuss, and ask questions.

The example for this template, presented in Figure 4.2, is from ECOMP 6008 *The World Wide Web as an Educational Resource*. This assignment template lets students explore and learn about various aspects of an issue of their choice and learn from others' explorations. In the assignment presented, students review websites that examine different aspects of Web 2.0. This allows our students to be exposed to an issue within

Figure 4.1. Video Viewing

Assignment #7a Video *The Bottom Line in Education: 1980 to the Present—Online Learning Segment*

Group and Individual Project

Background: This assignment provides an opportunity to synthesize ideas that you have reviewed, read, and discussed up to this point. The assigned video presents a view of the road that public education has traveled in the past 30 years. In this assignment you will describe how online learning is starting to affect K–12 public education and also project into the future and predict online learning's impact.

1. Independently, with a partner, or in a small group, view the video *The Bottom Line in Education: 1980 to the Present* by going to http://vimeo.com/19452881
2. Do the assigned readings so that you can use information as potential background for developing an additional segment to this video.
3. Independently, with a partner, or in a small group, develop a 3- to 4-minute segment that could be added to the end of this video about the use of online learning in the K–12 environment. You may "do" interviews with spokespeople, politicians, historians, business people, or teachers and raise points both pro and con. The format of the segment may be submitted in a number of formats:
   a. a written script
   b. PowerPoint
   c. any medium, as long as it can be uploaded to the myLesley Blackboard site
4. Post the segment

Assigned Readings

Davis, N., & Roblyer, M. (2005). Preparing teachers for the "schools that technology built": Evaluation of a program to train teachers for virtual schooling. *Journal of Research on Technology in Education, 37*(4), 399–409.

Huett, J., Moller, L., Foshay, W. R., & Coleman, C. (2008). The evolution of distance education: Implications for instructional design on the potential of the web. *Tech-Trends: Linking Research and Practice to Improve Learning, 52*(5), 63–67.

Rice, K. (2006). A comprehensive look at distance education in the K–12 context. *Journal of Research on Technology in Education, 38*(4), 425–448.

Rice, K. (2009). Priorities in K–12 distance education: A Delphi study examining multiple perspectives on policy, practice, and research. *Journal of Educational Technology and Society, 12*(3), 163–177.

Due Date: This assignment may be posted any time but no later than the due date indicated on the assignment chart and Discussion Board.

Figure 4.1. Video Viewing (continued)

Assignment #7b

Group Project

1. View or read at least two of your classmates' segments.
2. Ask one question and offer substantive additional ideas regarding your classmates' topic and report.

Due Date: This assignment may be posted any time but no later than the due date indicated on the assignment chart and Discussion Board.

---

a limited period of time. Some students are so inspired by their classmates' reports that they delve more deeply into the topic.

Assignment Template 3: Compare and Contrast Case Study Findings

Students conduct an informal case study about a topic from their own setting that is related to the course content. Students write a report and then compare and contrast findings of their studies with classmates.

a. The instructor defines the topic that will be studied, either developing parameters for the case study or having students develop them and submit them for approval.
b. Students post the findings of their case studies and then compare and contrast their findings.

Assignment Template 4: Project Work

Students carry out a project structured by the teacher or another student and then share it.

a. Students develop a proposal for their project using online resources.
b. Once approved by the instructor, students design and implement the project.
c. Students write and post the project.
d. In small groups or with partners, students evaluate and comment on each other's project.

The assignment shown in Figure 4.3 is from ECOMP 8000 *Advanced Professional Seminar in Technology in Education*, the first course in Lesley's post-master's Certificate of Advanced Graduate Studies program. Part of the program is directed at developing students' leadership skills. To do this we ask students to engage in tasks that many will be called upon to implement once they have earned their degree. Thus it is an authentic learning experience.

Figure 4.2. Online Artifact Jigsaw

Weeks 4 and 5: Assignment #6a Web 2.0
and #6b Discussion About Web 2.0

Week 4—#6a Web 2.0

6a. Purpose of Assignment: To explore one example of Web 2.0 use in depth and consider how it can be used as an educational tool.

1. Below is a list of some Web 2.0 applications and websites. Select one of these applications. Be brave and select one that you have never used before. No more than two people per Web 2.0 selection category. Post your selection in the Teachers' Room with the name of the selection in the subject line. The list includes (1) social networks, (2) **virtual worlds**, (3) photo-sharing sites, (4) video-sharing sites, (5) blogging resources, and (6) **RSS** resources.
2. Experiment with the application and a few of the websites.
3. Think about how you might use these Web 2.0 concepts in your classroom. Do some reading to get some ideas about uses. See readings below.
4. Write a brief report about what you experienced and discovered with your Web 2.0 selection and how you might use it in your classroom.

1. Social Networks

Myspace, http://www.myspace.com
Facebook, http://www.facebook.com
Bebo, http://www.bebo.com
Classmates.com, http://www.classmates.com
Hi5, http://www.hi5.com
Friendster, http://www.friendster.com

TagWorld, http://www.tagworld.com
43 Things, http://www.43things.com
Sconex, http://www.sconex.com
Orkut by Google, http://www.orkut.com
IMBEE, http://www.imbee.com

2. Virtual Worlds

Second Life, http://secondlife.com
Active Worlds, http://www.activeworlds.com
Habbo, http://www.habbo.com

Hive7, http://www.hive7.com
There, http://www.there.com

3. Photo Sharing

Picasa, http://picasa.google.com
Flickr, http://www.flickr.com
Zoto, http://www.zoto.com

Fotki, http://www.fotki.com
Photobucket, http://photobucket.com
Shutterfly, http://www.shutterfly.com

4. Video Sharing

Vimeo, http://vimeo.com
Google video, http://video.google.com
YouTube, http://www.youtube.com

Vsocial social, http://www.vsocial.com
Jumpcut, http://jumpcut.com
Eyespot, http://eyespot.com

Figure 4.2. Online Artifact Jigsaw (continued)

5. Blogging

Edublogs, http://edublogs.org

Blogger from Google, http://www.blogger.com/start/

LearnerBlogs, http://learnerblogs.org

Class Blogmeister, http://classblogmeister.com

Movable Type, http://www.movabletype.org

Blosxom, http://www.blosxom.com

6. RSS (Really Simple Syndication)

Radio UserLand, http://radio.userland.com

Mac OS NetNewswire, http://netnewswireapp.com

WindowsFeedDemon, http://www.newsgator.com

SharpReader, http://www.sharpreader.net/

Ampheta Desk, http://www.disobey.com/amphetadesk/

Yahoo!News RSS, http://news.yahoo.com/rss

RSS–CNN.com, http://www.cnn.com/services/rss/

Resources and Readings

News Readers: collecting RSS feeds, http://en.wikipedia.org/wiki/News_aggregator. This article shows how to use an RSS news aggregator

wrichard's Blogs: a comprehensive list of educator written blogs from Will Richardson, http://bloglines.com/public/wrichard

RSS Feeds in Education: conquer info clutter, http://www.techteachers.com/rss.htm

FirstGov even has RSS info: http://www.firstgov.gov/Topics/Reference_Shelf/Libraries/RSS_Library/Education.shtml

Stephen's Web: "An Introduction to RSS for Educational Designers"—very technical article, http://www.downes.ca/files/RSS_Educ.htm

Trackbacks: keeping track of who is commenting about your blog on their blog, http://en.wikipedia.org/wiki/Trackback

Adam, A., & Mowers, H. (2007). YouTube comes to the classroom. *School Library Journal, 53*(1), 22.

Brydolf, C. (2007). Minding Myspace: Balancing the benefits and risks of students' online social networks. *Education Digest, 73*(2), 4–8.

Foust, R. (2007). Techno-klutz meets the blog. *Library Media Connection, 25*(4), 56–57.

Hutchison, D. (2007). Video games and the pedagogy of place. *Social Studies, 98*(1), 35–40.

Karrer, T. (2007). Learning and networking with a blog. *T+D, 61*(9), 20–22.

Kennedy, S. (2007). The time/space continuum: You are here. *Information Today, 24*(5), 17–19.

Long, C. (2007). Educators got game. *NEA Today, 26*(2), 42–43.

Losinski, R. (2007). Patrolling Web 2.0. *THE Journal (Technological Horizons in Education), 34*(3), 50–52.

Figure 4.2. Online Artifact Jigsaw (continued)

Talab, R., & Butler, R. (2007). Shared electronic spaces in the classroom: Copyright, privacy, and guidelines. *TechTrends: Linking Research and Practice to Improve Learning, 51*(1), 12–15.

Van Horn, R. (2007). Web applications and Google. *Phi Delta Kappan, 88*(10), 727–792.

Due Date: This assignment may be completed before or prior to but no later than the due date.

Week 5—#6b Discussion About Web 2.0

#6b. Purpose of Assignment: To expand knowledge about Web 2.0 uses and experiences.

1. Read at least two classmates' postings. Make sure that they are about two different Web 2.0 applications and different from the one that you wrote about.
2. Write substantive comments and questions about their suggested use of Web 2.0. Based on what they wrote and your own knowledge suggest additional ways to use their Web 2.0 application.
3. Respond to all comments and questions posed by your instructor and classmates.

Due Date: This assignment may be completed during the week but is due no later than the end of the designated week.

Assignment Template 5: Research Paper

Students write a research paper independently or with a classmate.

a. Provide a list of potential topics for students to select from.
b. Students select topics or identify their own and work individually or with a partner.
c. Develop a sequence of assignments and due dates. The sequence must include subassignments such as bibliography, outline, first draft, second draft, and final version.
d. Have students support each other as partners or small groups by reviewing subassignments for each other. The instructor also provides corrective feedback.
e. Students share final drafts with the entire class to discuss what they have learned.

In our ECOMP 7104 *Technology in Education Thesis Project* the entire course follows the format described above as we guide our students through the process of writing a thesis. We have also assigned research projects in other courses such as ECOMP

Figure 4.3. Compare and Contrast Case Study Findings

Weeks 6 and 7: #14a Examining a District Technology Plan and #14b Discussion

Examining a District Technology Plan

Purpose of Assignment: This activity provides the opportunity to review your local technology plan and compare it with other communities.

1. Background: District technology plans require a great deal of time and energy to prepare. An approved plan is often needed for state funding. If correctly written it is a blueprint for success in a school system's approach to technology.
2. Read the following article online: *Critical Issue: Developing a School or District Technology Plan*, http://www.ncrel.org/sdrs/areas/issues/methods/technlgy/te300. htm. Explore five additional links relating to the development of a school district technology plan in your state.
3. Examine your own school district's technology plan. Make a list of the components that it contains.
4. Search the web for at least two other district technology plans from comparable-size districts. Write a report differentiating between the two plans, contrasting vision, mission, strategy, goal, target, measure, and so on. In addition, compare the two plans with your own district's plan addressing the following questions:
   a. Are there missing components?
   b. Are there components inadequately detailed?
   c. How broad is the group that developed the plan?
   d. Is there an appropriate role for all the constituent groups?
   e. Has the plan been approved by the proper authority?
   f. Is the plan a *shelf* document or it is actionable?
   g. Does the plan indicate how its success will be measured?
   h. What leadership skills might be applied to reach the plan's goals?
   i. Finally, when you are not near the plan, how much of its contents do you recall?

Due Date: This assignment may be posted anytime but no later than the due date.

Week 7—#14b Examining a District Technology Plan Discussion Group

Purpose of Assignment: To develop an improved version of your school district's technology plan.

1. Read at least two classmates' reports of the school district plan.
2. Based on the information gathered from your own and others' reports, make a list of suggested revisions that would strengthen your district's plan. Work with a partner.
3. Post the list along with a description for how you might share this information with your district.

Due Date: This assignment may be posted anytime but no later than the due date.

5007 *21st Century Teaching: Supporting All Learners on the Ability Spectrum* in which students write a paper about a disability category focusing on how technology can assist students. This assignment can be seen in Figure 4.4. Two assignments precede this. The first assignment is to select a partner and special education category, which can be found in Chapter 5, Figure 5.17, and the second is developing a bibliography the week prior to writing the research paper.

A research paper requires students to examine a topic in depth and become an authority for other students in the class. Students also learn about the opinions of experts in the fields, studies conducted by researchers, and how to write about research. The discussion that follows may entail additional research on the students' part.

Figure 4.4. Research Paper

#8a Investigation of Special Needs Categories and Use of Technology

#8a. Purpose of Assignment: To gain an in-depth understanding of one specific special needs category focusing on the use of technology. To acquire a common understanding of several special needs categories.

Group Project: You have 3 weeks to complete this assignment. You should start working on this project with your partner by posting a bibliography in the Bibliography forum and reading the articles you have found. You should get started writing your report.

Readings in your bibliography (Assignment #6b) will provide you with a sufficient number of resources. However, you will probably need to do additional research. Use the Lesley Library online databases for at least six sources (Wilson Omnifile, Expanded Academic ASAP, etc.), our class Web Resource area, search engines, and interviews. Also check out organizations dealing with your special needs category and library resources to investigate the special needs category you have selected.

Your investigation should include the elements listed below, a through e (However, the focus and major portion of your report should be on elements c and d, which relate to technology use):

a. A definition of the special needs category.
b. A description of observable behaviors.
c. How technology is used by students in this special needs category and by professionals to address students needs (academic and/or social). Include brief descriptions of studies or anecdotal reports you read or other information you have gathered from other reliable sources.
d. From your investigation *each* partner should indicate how he or she would modify and teach a student with this disability in his or her class. Discuss both technology-based and non-technology-based modifications. Be sure to label each partner's modifications in your report.
e. *Note:* When referring to students with disabilities it is important to avoid defining the child by the disability. Thus when writing or speaking about students with

Figure 4.4. Research Paper (continued)

disabilities the phrase "students with a speech impairment" or "students with a learning disability" should be used rather than a "speech-impaired student" or a "learning-disabled student." Likewise use phrases such as "students who have an emotional impairment" rather than "students who are emotionally impaired." Appropriate use of language is important, since it relates to the use of labeling and the potential for a self-fulfilling prophecy.

Reminders

1. Cite a minimum of 12 different sources you used to complete this assignment. Remember to use APA format for *all* citations (in the document and the reference list) and no more than 30% of the references may be works written before 2000.
2. You will work on this project collaboratively and write a report with your partner. One partner will submit the report. Be sure to put both names of the authors on the report.
3. Post the report on Turnitin to catch potential citing errors. Fix errors before posting on the Discussion Board.
4. All assignments submitted as attached files should have a file name that includes an abbreviation of the assignment name and the students' name or initials. Examples: spedcat_jt_bw.doc or spedcat_joan_bill.doc

Due Date: This assignment is due on the date indicated in the assignment chart, not before or after.

Readings

Bull, G., Bull, G., Dawson, K., & Mason, C. (2001). Evaluating and using web-based resources. *Learning and Leading with Technology, 28*(7), 50–55. Scanned.

The Bull et al. (2001) article is assigned as a guide to help you evaluate quality web-based materials. You are not required to cite this in your reference list. However, you do need to cite sources that you have used to write your report.

#8b Extending Categories

#8b. Purpose of Assignment: To build awareness of additional special needs areas and do additional research on your specific topic.

1. Read at least one other report.
2. After reading the report(s), write substantive comments about the report and ask at least one question.
3. Respond to the comments and questions. Report partners should divide up the work of responding.

Due Date: This assignment may be completed anytime during the week prior to the due date but must be completed by the due date.

Assignment Template 6: Writing an Article for Publication

Students write an article about the content area being studied as a culminating activity in the course.

a. Instructor helps students define a topic by focusing on previous class activities or assignments, extending work done, summarizing aspects of the course, and so on.
b. Instructor lists potential publications. Students may select their own.
c. Students find and read submission guidelines for their targeted publication.
d. Instructor suggests a potential outline for the article.
e. Students submit a cover letter, outline, and the article.
f. The instructor and classmates provide feedback to help enhance the likelihood of publication.

This assignment serves both as a culminating activity and as a way to validate students as knowledge creators. From one of our courses 11 student articles have been published, to date. Publications range from an online journal to a widely distributed educational technology magazine. An example of the assignment we use to guide students in writing an article is shown in Figure 4.5.

The impact can be seen in the following comments from former students, elicited through research conducted by Thormann.

Students feel empowered:

I have never even considered myself an 'author,' but now that I understand the process, I find myself thinking about writing another article to submit for publication.

Students also understood how knowledge can be imparted:

I am now in awe at the thought of how our efforts have combined to potentially result in someone somewhere—someone whom we will never know or see—receiving some type of assistive technology software or hardware device that will significantly change their life.

Assignment Template 7: Real-Time Meetings

Instructor and students use Skype, Elluminate, GoToMeeting, or other real-time conferencing tool to hold a meeting.

a. Students and/or the instructor determine(s) the meeting topic in advance.
b. A student leader takes responsibility for scheduling a small-group meeting of three to four classmates.
c. Students, or the instructor, develop(s) and share(s) a protocol, including an agenda for the meeting interaction.

Figure 4.5. Writing an Article for Publication

Week 8: #10a Article and #10b Discussion

Purpose of Assignment #10a: To synthesize and apply the knowledge you have gained in this course. Potentially to publish an article about using the Web to contribute to the field and help students and teachers.

Purpose of Assignment #10b: To gain additional information about use of the Web from classmates' perspectives. To assist classmates in enhancing the articles they have written.

Individual or Group Project

You will write an article based on what you have learned in this course that is suitable for publication. You may use information gathered in your other assignments. If you do this you must extend and reshape what you have written. You may write the article with a partner from our class or someone in your school district or you can write independently.

Include all three components in one file. Submit the following:

1. A letter of inquiry to the journal you plan to submit the article to
2. An outline of your article
3. An article with the primary focus on the use of the web in education

Your article should be targeted for publication in a specific journal such as *Learning and Leading with Technology, Instructor,* or a similar a journal in your discipline. Locate and examine submission guidelines for the journal you plan to submit your article to before writing. You should be able to find the guidelines on the Web or in the journal. Your article should comply with the guidelines of the journal for which you are writing:

a. Articles written based on your own experience should be written in the first person. If you co-author the article make sure it is clear which author is reporting his or her experience.
b. Read a few articles from the journal you have selected to make sure to write an article with the appropriate level and tone for the journal.
c. Target a specific audience such as teachers or administrators, parents, or others.
d. Focus on practical ideas about use of the Web and how to employ it in the K–12 curriculum or activities of daily living.
e. You might include lesson plans, reproducible pages of student lessons and worksheets, and teacher-to-teacher advice on the best ways to use the Web.
f. Include appropriate references and citations in APA format *if* the targeted journal requires APA.
g. Read and follow submission guidelines.
h. Include a brief biography.

i. It's a good idea to wait until you receive feedback from your 6008 classmates and instructor before submitting the article. The suggestions may increase your chances of getting your article published.

Reminder: APA, file naming, and Turnitin.

Week 8— #10b Article Discussion

Group Project

Purpose of Assignment #10b: To gain additional information about use of the Web in education from classmates' perspectives. To assist classmates in enhancing the articles they have written, do the following:

1. Read at least one classmate's article. Although it is the end of the course, I encourage you to read more than just one. (-:
2. Post a response to your classmate with
   a. at least two aspects of the article you liked and think would be useful for others to read
   b. at least two ideas that you think will improve the article
3. Respond to your classmates' comments and edit your article as appropriate.

Due Date: This assignment may be completed anytime prior to the due date but should be completed by the due date.

d. The instructor facilitates the first conference but may want to delegate facilitation for later meetings.
e. One student from each group takes notes summarizing the meeting and posts them on the Discussion Board.

In Chapter 3, Figure 3.6, we have an assignment that illustrates use of voice conferences. In that chapter we also describe the procedures we use for arranging a Skype voice conference. Other voice conferencing systems such as Elluminate, Wimba, or GoToMeeting, can be used. We like Skype because it is free and relatively reliable. Having at least one voice meeting with students in an online course helps to build community, which we discuss in depth in Chapter 5.

Assignment Template 8: Attending a Webinar or Virtual Conference

Students attend a virtual conference.

a. The instructor finds a national or local conference relating to the course content. The conference program must include presenters and the titles of the presentations on the web.

b. Students find a presentation that is interesting to them, read what is available from the conference website, and then contact the presenter to request the paper or PowerPoint.

c. Students post a summary of the presentation and their interactions with the presenter.

d. Students read classmates' postings and discuss the presentations.

Alternately, students attend a webinar.

a. Webinars in the content area are found by students or instructor.

b. Students each sign up to attend a different webinar or limit the number that may attend each webinar.

c. Students post a summary of the webinar highlights.

d. Students read summaries and discuss.

We have used the assignment shown in Figure 4.6 in a number of courses to encourage students to reach out to professionals in the field and to obtain access to the most recent research and thinking in our field. The assignment shown in Figure 4.6 is from ECOMP 7017 *Teaching Online: Issues and Design.*

We received an email from a student at a distant university requesting the slides from a conference presentation. We sent the slides and also questioned the student about why he was requesting them. He explained that it was for an assignment in his online course. We realized that turn about is fair play!

Figure 4.6. Webinar or Virtual Conference

#4a and 4b Conference Attendance Report and Discussion

#4a Purpose of Assignment: To become aware of the wide scope and the most recent activities, research, and developments relating to technology and e-learning.

Individual Project

In this assignment you will be a virtual attendee of the DevLearn\10 conference held in San Francisco, November 3–5, 2010.

The following website contains a list of presentations given over the 3-day period. The conference provides a broad spectrum of topics: http://www.elearningguild.com/ DevLearn/concurrent-sessions/?event=64&selection=doc.1676

You will do the following:

1. Visit the website, select the Program menu, and select Concurrent Sessions from the pull-down list.
2. Read through the session titles and select ten sessions that you would have liked to attend. Be sure to

    a. read the presenters' bios.

    b. read the description of the presentation.

3. Select three of the ten that you would like to "attend."
4. As soon as you have decided which presentations you will "attend" post the names of the presentations and presenters that you have selected in the forum titled Session Attendance. You are posting these selections so that you won't "attend" the same presentations as your classmates.
5. Now the detective work starts. The goal is to ask each presenter to send you his or her presentation slides or paper. Here is a simple Web-based strategy for tracking down your presenter:

    a. Note the person's name and employer/affiliation (university, business, or organization).

    b. Find the site of the employer and locate the presenter's email address.

    c. Send a polite email to the presenter requesting his or her slides or a paper about the presentation topic.

4. Read through the materials each presenter sends you.
5. Write a summary of each of the sessions you attended. Include the following:

    a. The title and presenter of the paper/session

    b. A brief summary of the session

    c. What the most interesting aspect of each session was

    d. A question you would have asked the presenter if you were physically present at each session

    e. The slides or papers that the presenter sent you so that your classmates can view them

Optional: If the presenter seems receptive, send her or him a question. Whenever and if you receive a reply, share the question and response with the class.

Due Date: This assignment is due on the date indicated in the syllabus, assignment chart, and Discussion Board, not before or after.

#4b Conference Attendance Discussion

#4b Purpose of Assignment: To broaden your perspective of e-learning based on classmates' interests.

1. Select and read two presentations and your classmates' reports from two different classmates.
2. Reply to your classmates, including

    a. What you thought was the most interesting aspect of each session.

    b. A comment or question about your classmates' reports.

3. Respond to your classmates' comments and questions.

Due Date: This assignment may be posted a week in advance of the due date indicated in the syllabus, assignment chart, and Discussion Board, but not after.

Assignment Template 9: Case Study Analysis

Students are asked to develop a solution to a case study about a problem situation and to compare their solutions.

a. The instructor prepares a case study about a problem situation.
b. Students develop solutions individually, in pairs or groups.
c. Students compare their solutions with classmates and discuss the pros and cons.

We developed a detailed case study for our students in ECOMP 8000 *Advanced Professional Seminar in Technology in Education*, presented in Figure 4.7. In this assignment we asked students to practice their problem-solving skills.

The use of a case study is an opportunity for students to analyze a problem situation that they may encounter and devise a reasoned solution. It is a common teaching tool in many fields.

Figure 4.7. Case Study Analysis

#10 Case Study for Technology Leadership

Rationale: In your leadership roles you will be asked to assist the people you supervise to solve problems. Real-life problems are not neat and it takes practice to unravel the important issues and figure out how to address them. Using case studies can help those you work with hone their problem-solving skills. Thus learning to write and use case studies will add to your skills. In addition, writing a case study is itself an exercise in problem solving. When you have to compose a short narrative, you are forced to think clearly, plan, and polish.

1. We will discuss the following case study as a group on the Discussion Board.
2. In small groups you will develop a case study that deals with technology issues that your group might use to help school personnel think about challenging problems.
3. The case studies will be shared and reacted to by the class.

Teaching Case Studies

The following case studies are based in the Arlstone School District and Arlstone/Boilton Regional School District. The town of Arlstone has five K–6 schools with 2,500 students, and the Arlstone/Boilton Regional School District has two schools, 7 and 8 and 9–12 with 2,200 students from both towns. Two of the elementary schools and both secondary schools are situated in Arlstone in a campus arrangement. The remaining three are some distance from campus, although two sit next to each other, separated by a field. Boilton has one elementary school and is a separate school system for that one school. At the elementary level in Arlstone parents can choose which school in Arlstone their children will attend but must also indicate a second and third selection.

As with all school districts in this state, there is local control of education. The state provides direct financial support to cities and towns and regional school districts through a formula that reflects the property wealth of a community, and it offers grants that generally come from federal funds. The rest comes from local taxes.

By state law, voters need to approve any additional tax levy above a 2.5% increase in the annual budget. Open town meeting is the form of local government.

This is a community of highly educated townspeople, many of whom work in the technology industry, and the districts have a technology plan, approved by both the school boards and the state (required to get any grant funding).

The school districts, despite spending less than many comparable communities on education, get surprisingly good results academically, on the high-stakes tests, in college admissions, and on the playing field.

Case 1. The Challenge of New Leadership

Patricia Kolman has just been appointed director of instructional technology for the Arlstone and the Arlstone/Boilton Regional School District. Her duties include planning, policy recommendation, budgeting, purchasing, and supervising the use of instructional technology and the network and the people who are the support personnel in her office.

Patricia has lived in Arlstone for many years (her two boys went to the local schools). She was working as a technology aide in a neighboring community when the superintendent, Irene Kenmore, offered her the position of curriculum and technology integration specialist for the Arlstone schools. This position was one of the first of its kind in the state. The convenience of being in town with her children and the reputation of the schools made the decision no challenge at all for Patricia. She was an early supporter of technology as a tool for learning. She has seen the effects on her own children. The phrase "passionate about technology" applies to her.

As the curriculum and technology integration specialist, she worked with elementary teachers, planning units with them, modeling teaching with technology, troubleshooting, and providing official professional development opportunities, among other tasks. Patricia also served on both the Citizens Technology Advisory Committee to the Superintendent and the small K–12 technology leadership team inside the school districts. At the end of her fourth year, Irene Kenmore, who had hired her and who was a supporter of technology in the schools, retired. After Irene left, Patricia remained in her position for 3 years but just now has been promoted. She accepted the promotion because despite the challenges and stresses, she felt she would be in a position to influence and direct the use of technology in the school districts. Patricia is certified as a teacher in the state but not as a director of instructional technology. At the same time she is in a doctoral program at a nearby university, finishing her last two courses.

During the intervening 3 years, several important events have occurred. The new superintendent, Warren Rose, who had been the assistant, while not hostile to the instructional role played by technology, has no particular passion for it. Warren sees its

Figure 4.7. Case Study Analysis (continued)

value for data collection and reporting, payroll, and all the other managerial functions such as attendance and communication.

But with regard to the curricular use of technology (professional development, integration into teaching practice), he leaves the leadership to the person in the technology director's position, which Patricia now fills.

Patricia's mentor, Jeffrey Conant, the man who held the director position during the incumbency of Irene Kenmore and the intervening 3 years has just unexpectedly died. So Patricia is new to the position, although a veteran in the school districts. She has watched support decline both in terms of centrality to the superintendent and also financially, given the economic downturn. She has also lost Jeffrey, a person with whom she could share concerns and potential solutions.

Patricia now supervises three curriculum and technology integration specialists, a secretary, and a technical network coordinator who also maintains the districts' website and intranet. All these people (except the secretary) were her peers.

Her current budget for both school districts, including technology personnel salaries (providing both technical and instructional support to educators) and all other technology functions, maintenance, new and replacement equipment, and software, is $800,000, which may or may not be increased by 5% ($40,000) in next year's budget.

The town of Arlstone is looking to the electorate for a $4,000,000 override, that is, an amount supplementary to the annual budget request, an unusually high amount to be requesting at any time. Of that $4,000,000, $500,000 is earmarked for technology, as a result of pressure on Superintendent Rose from one segment of the community and some members of the board. The money, following the trend in the state to support one-to-one wireless computing, is for students in grades 7, 8, and 9 and represents the start of a plan to give every student (and educator) ubiquitous access. The $500,000 will be supplemented by grants and gifts from the corporate community and parents and other residents, a model being used in other parts of the state and supported by many legislators.

Success is not guaranteed; what is certain is that there will a great deal of campaigning, both pro and con, with many night meetings, at which Patricia will have to defend the request for funding that she firmly believes in. She will have to answer detailed financial questions and technical questions, write some newsletter articles and reports, and contribute to Superintendent Rose's preparation for his presentation to the town voters at the annual town meeting. She will have to make the case that one-to-one computing contributes significantly to student achievement. Further complicating but actually ameliorating this process is that the town of Boilton will also need an override but a much smaller one, and this town has a history of approving school expenditures with very little controversy. On the other hand, the town of Arlstone usually has contentious town meetings.

There are labs in all the schools, there is an elementary technology curriculum, and some classrooms have multiple computers. The new high school renovation included several stationary labs. The same is true of the new elementary building. Complicating

Figure 4.7. Case Study Analysis (continued)

---

the issue is that technology practice is not consistent among schools, grades, and teachers and the funds, if approved, will address only some of this inequity.

Patricia knows that without the $500,000 listed in the ballot question, all her plans to reinvigorate the school districts' technology resources and programs and once again position Arlstone and Boilton as leaders in technology integrated education in the state will fail.

For the instructor:

The objectives of this case are

1. To understand the multiple and competing demands of leadership.
2. To learn to think strategically.
3. To make decisions based on professional priorities.

Some questions to consider:

1. What are the key issues in this case? Whose issues are they? Why?
2. What constraints and opportunities are there? Why?
3. Who are the key players and with whom should Patricia collaborate?
4. How should she characterize to the various constituencies the potential losses and gains (pros and cons) the school districts face if the override succeeds or fails?
5. What additional information would you have liked in order to analyze this case?

Assignment Template 10: Conduct an Inquiry

Students conduct a science inquiry and discuss it with each other, the class instructor, and a science specialist.

a. The instructor provides a specific scientific phenomenon for the students to investigate.
b. Students post their data and results of their investigation. Each student also posts possible explanations of his or her data and results.
c. Online, small groups of students discuss similarities, discrepancies, and explanations. Discussions are facilitated by students in the group, who take turns facilitating.
d. The facilitators for that week meet online with the instructor, who suggests provocative questions and follow-up activities.
e. The instructor summarizes the week's discussion, highlighting what the students felt was new in the week's work, what if anything surprised them about the phenomenon they investigated, and what they wanted to know more about.
f. A science specialist reviews the instructor's summary and comments about possible links to related concepts and phenomena (J. Schwartz, personal communication, February 3, 2011).

Step-by-Step Course-Building Activity #10: Using Assignment Templates

The following is an activity that inserts content into the templates to develop assignments or activities.

1. Review the templates and sample assignments in this chapter.
2. Using the content you teach, select three of the templates that you think you could use.
3. Add content to each template to build an assignment for one of your courses.
4. Field test this assignment with colleagues or students.
5. Revise the assignment based on performance and feedback.

Assignment Template 10 is from Tufts University's Fulcrum Institute for Education in Science, where inquiry-based learning is stressed. Classmates discuss why the results turned out the way they did and why there were variations in the results. A sample assignment from the Fulcrum Institute (2007) course, *Some of What Matters About Matter*, is presented in Figure 4.8.

The assignment shown in Figure 4.8 was excerpted to provide a sense of the format that is used throughout the Fulcrum Institute online science courses. More background information, challenges, and other materials are part of this assignment not included here.

SAMPLE SUCCESSFUL ONLINE ASSIGNMENT TEMPLATES

The remaining assignment templates in this chapter do not include examples. However, we have used most of them in our online teaching. Those that we have not used were repurposed assignments from our face-to-face courses. All assignments in this chapter are those that we found to be particularly effective in engaging students and that resulted in deep learning.

Assignment Template 11: Simulation

Students use a simulation about a topic and discuss the outcomes.

a. The instructor develops or finds a simulation. For example, PhET(originally standing for Physics Education Technology), developed at the University of Colorado at Boulder, is free, interactive, research based, and for high school students. Another is River City, a multiuser virtual environment, or MUVE, developed by Chris Dede at the Harvard Graduate School of Education for middle school. The Concord Consortium site has many modeling and simulation activities that can be downloaded.
b. Students manipulate variables, ending up with different results.
c. Students as a group discuss the alternative outcomes and why various variables affected the results as they did.

Figure 4.8. Conduct an Inquiry

Session 2. Salt Water Versus Fresh: A Puzzle

Session Overview

When you think about matter, water probably isn't the first thing that comes to mind. Why on earth would we choose to focus on water? Why on earth, indeed. If you take a step back to look at the earth, way back, you see land and water. But above all else, you see water. Water is essential to life and it is one of the most distinctive characteristics of our "blue" planet. For this reason, it makes sense to focus our study of matter around a substance that arguably "matters" most. This week you consider a puzzle about fresh water and salt water. You'll each have a chance to bring your experiences and your thoughts to the table and to raise questions that you'll investigate in the weeks to come.

Here's what's in store for you this week: inquiry-based science. This week you explore what happens when ice is placed in fresh water and salt water. Through first-hand investigations and discussions, you'll raise questions about some of the properties of fresh water and salt water.

Understanding Goals

- Raise questions about two types of material: salt water and fresh water.
- Begin to understand how investigations can provide insight into complex puzzles in the world around you.

What you need

- A paper notebook that will serve as your course journal
- 2 identical, clear, straight-walled glass tumblers (or plastic cups from your kit)
- 4–6 similarly sized cubes of ice
- Tap water, at room temperature
- Salt
- A stirrer or spoon
- A timer, or clock
- Digital balance scale
- Graduated cylinder, 100 ml
- Tricornered plastic beaker, 1,000 milliliters

Exploration: What happens when ice is placed in fresh and salt water? (about 2 hrs.)

The vast majority of the water on Earth is the salt water residing in the seas. . . . This week, we begin to investigate the differences between fresh water and salt water by using tap water, salt, and ice cubes to explore. What happens to ice when it's in salt water? Is it the same as when it's in the fresh water of lakes and rivers . . . or in drinking water?

Figure 4.8. Conduct an Inquiry (continued)

Part A. Your Journal

A science journal can be a powerful tool. . . . You can sketch out ideas for the reports and messages you post online. . . . Read about how Darwin used his notebooks in Learning from Darwin's Journals. . . . Think about how you'll use and organize your journal.

Part B. Predict

. . . Turn your attention to a puzzle: Imagine that you have two glasses of water. One is fresh water and the other is salt water. Now imagine that you add the same number of same-sized ice cubes to each glass. What do you think you'll observe over the next hour?

You might be wondering how you could possibly be expected to answer this question without actually trying it. Don't worry; you're not expected to get a "correct" answer. This is a chance for you to explore your ideas.

Why Predict?

Prediction serves a number of purposes: It provides you with an opportunity to articulate prior assumptions and it also helps you consider how your previous life experiences and your ideas might be valuable in puzzling through new problems. The prediction focuses your attention and helps you become invested in the outcome of the investigation. It's crucial to predict the outcome of the investigation prior to performing it. Then afterward, you'll be able to compare your outcomes with your predictions.

In your journal: Take 15 minutes to write your present understanding and ideas about what might happen over an hour to the ice cubes in fresh water and salty water. What do you think you will see? Do you think that the ice will melt at the same rate in both glasses? Why or why not? Sift through your ideas and memories of any experiences that seem related. Take notes, draw pictures, and record the reasoning that informed your prediction.

Part C. Investigate

Measurements Matter—Use the mass balance and the graduated cylinder from your kit to measure the salt and the water. In your journal, record the amount of salt and water that you use.

Measuring the salt and the water with some care allows you to describe and control the amount of matter you're using. You'll be able to come back to this data to make sense of your results, to share information with your class colleagues, and to repeat, or vary, your tests.

First, you'll need to mix up some salt water. To create water that has approximately the same salinity as the ocean, add 8 grams (g) of salt to 250 cubic centimeters (cc) of water. Keep in mind that measurements may help reveal what can't be seen. After you mix the salt in the water and it all dissolves, measure the mass of the salt water. Also check the volume of the salt water and record any increase in volume.

Figure 4.8. Conduct an Inquiry (continued)

Then, pour the same volume of fresh and salt water into two identical clear glasses or cups. Allow both salt and fresh water to sit on a counter for a while so that they are both at room temperature. Gently slip two or three similarly sized ice cubes into each glass.

Watch the glasses carefully until all the ice has melted, recording your observations in writing. In addition to making qualitative observations, keep track of quantitative observations (e.g., How long has the ice been melting? At a given time, what is the shape and size of the ice cubes?). You may find it helpful to draw sketches of the details that you observe.

In your journal: Record your observations, sketches, thoughts, and questions. Any surprises? Based on your observations, what questions do you have? At this point you might want to explore some more, to retest some of your ideas. Go right ahead!

Report and Discuss (about 2 hrs.)

Go to your group's Science forum and post a concise message reporting on your exploration this week. In your report, address the following questions:

- What was your prediction and the reasoning behind it?
- What actually happened when the ice melted in the two glasses? Please be descriptive so that your colleagues will have a mind's-eye view of what you observed. Include measurements where appropriate.
- How well does your evidence support your prediction and the reasoning behind it?

Three Questions

Add a paragraph reflecting on your experience. In your reflection, respond to the following questions:

- What do you think is the most important thing you learned from this week's exploration?
- What surprised you? Why?
- What questions are you left with?

Post your report in the Science forum by Tuesday.

Between Tuesday and Thursday return to the Science forum and read and respond to your colleagues' posts. "Listen" to your colleagues and build on their responses. Please contribute at least three substantive posts to the discussion this week.

Here are a few questions to keep in mind as you formulate your responses:

- What patterns emerge across these preliminary reports? Are there differences across reports—if so, what might account for them? Are there similarities?
- Do your group's findings make sense? What experiences or understandings do you have that might be relevant to this discussion?
- Were there any surprises for you? Did the exploration raise any questions or issues for you? In what ways have the group's findings challenged or

Figure 4.8. Conduct an Inquiry (continued)

changed your thinking? What additional tests or explorations might help you address your lingering questions?

Pulling it Together (about 0.5 hrs.)

There follows a section relating the issues explored in this investigation to larger global considerations of polar ice cap melting. . . .

What's the Big Idea?

Interpreting what happened in this investigation involves a number of different issues and we won't completely unravel the whole story until later in the course. For now let us just note that the salt water and the fresh water behaved very differently.

Salt water is obviously different from fresh water. How do they differ?

When you started this investigation you took two identical containers with equal masses and volumes of fresh water and added salt to one of them. Reflect on what your measurements begin to reveal. Go back to your notes and ask yourself:

- What volume of water (in cc) did you use in each container?
- What was the mass (in gm) of salt that you added to the water in one of the containers?
- What was the volume (in cc) of the salt that you added to the water in one of the containers?
- How did the mass of the salt water compare with the mass of the fresh water?
- How did the volume of the salt water compare with the volume of the fresh water?

As you poured salt into the water, you managed to pack more mass into the same volume as the fresh water. In other words each cubic centimeter of salt water has more mass than a cubic centimeter of fresh water.

The amount of mass that a cubic centimeter of a substance has is a measure of the density of that substance. It is measured in gm/cc (read as grams per cubic centimeter).

Assignment Template 12: PowerPoint

Students develop a PowerPoint slide show about a topic.

a. The instructor defines a topic that would be appropriate for sharing in a PowerPoint format. Students have the option of deciding what topic they would like to present in a PowerPoint within boundaries that are stated below. (Part of the challenge is for students to explore what topics are appropriate and learn what constitutes an effective PowerPoint presentation.)

b. Students conduct research about a segment of the topic or the whole topic that might be presented to colleagues or a targeted audience.

c. Students develop and post a PowerPoint file.

d. Students and the instructor give feedback and ask questions to enhance the effectiveness of the PowerPoint presentation.

Assignment Template 13: Online Publication

Students produce an issue of a newspaper or a journal together, each taking a different role, such as editor-in-chief, copyeditor, and column writer.

a. The instructor defines the overall topic of the newspaper issue and lists the jobs, such as editor in chief, copyeditor, production manager, reporters, and columnists.

b. Students select jobs.

c. The newspaper is produced, published, and shared with an audience.

d. Students seek feedback from the audience and debrief about content and how the newspaper might be enhanced.

Assignment Template 14: Review of Articles, Videos, Podcasts and Other Media

Students write reviews of work done by others about topics like current news events, new social networking sites, and nuclear power to learn content and how to develop their own communication skills.

a. The instructor develops and shares a list of articles, videos, podcasts, and other media resources.

b. The instructor develops a list of parameters for students to use when reviewing the articles, videos, podcasts, and other media.

c. Students are asked to select media resources from the instructor's prepared list to review.

d. Students post the reviews.

e. Students and the instructor discuss the content of the media resources and the student reviews.

Assignment Template 15: Developing a Podcast

Students develop a podcast or vodcast on a topic like a science experiment, a historical debate, or a literary improvisation.

a. The instructor defines an area for the podcast or vodcast.

b. Students select a topic, develop a podcast or vodcast, and post it.

   c. Students listen to classmates' podcasts or vodcasts, comment on them, and ask questions.
   d. The podcast or vodcast developer responds to the comments and questions.

Assignment Template 16: Developing a Blog

Students develop a blog to teach content, such as assistive technology, to describe a technical process, a novel, or the American Revolution. The instructor defines a topic for students to select.

   a. Students develop a blog to teach or discuss a content area.
   b. Classmates are required to read and comment on two or three classmates' blogs.

Assignment Template 17: Try a Technique or Tool

Students try a technique or tool such as developing an animation video (xtranormal.com) or a slide show (Prezi.com) related to the course topic and share results.

   a. The instructor provides a list of tools or techniques for students to use.
   b. Students select one from the list, use it, and report about the use.
   c. Students read each others' reports and discuss issues raised by the use of the technique or tool.

Assignment Template 18: Role-Play and Debrief

Students adopt a role such as that of a famous scientist or mathematician or historical figure in a real-life situation relating to a course topic and debrief about the outcome of the role-playing. Some students act as observers.

   a. The instructor defines a topic for the role-playing and the roles students may select.
   b. Students select a role and prepare the content based on their role.
   c. Students engage in a discussion based on their role either in an online Discussion Board or using VoIP.
   d. Observers summarize the issues raised during the interaction and debrief about the discussion.

Assignment Template 19: Student Developed Activities

Students research a topic like security on the Internet, Nathaniel Hawthorne, or the Chinese economy and develop activities to teach classmates about the topic.

a. Students select a topic from an instructor's list (with or without resources) or based on a student's interest.
b. Individually or in a small group, students research the topic and develop an activity or assignment for their classmates.
c. Classmates engage in one, two, or more of the activities or assignments their classmates developed.
d. Students debrief and discuss the content they learned in the activities or assignments.

Assignment Template 20: Developing a Website

Students learn about a topic and develop a website to disseminate information. Instructors can direct students to a number of sites that host sites and offer online help for development. A few of them are http://www.weebly.com, http://iteach.org/hosting/, http://www.fatcow.com, and http://www.ipage.com.

a. The instructor defines the topic students need to address.
b. Students choose the audience, content, and format of their website.
c. Students conduct research on their selected topic.
d. Each student develops a website about the topic selected.
e. Students view each other's websites to gain additional information for their own website and give feedback to help classmates improve their sites.

In ECOMP 6008 *The World Wide Web as an Educational Resource* we have students develop a website that addresses an educational need. Over a number of weeks students engage in assignments that inform them about how to build an effective website, including Web accessibility for individuals with disabilities, reviewing similar sites, developing story boards, and selecting a Web-development tool. The ultimate goal is to have students learn how to develop a useful and well-designed site. This provides an occasion for students to complete a project that involves research, planning, designing, and implementing. It can be authentic learning at its best, since it requires students to be knowledge creators and develop a website that they are able to use. This skill and understanding can then be used repeatedly.

Step-by-Step Course-Building Activity #11: Developing a Template

The following is an activity that allows you to develop your own assignment/activity templates:

1. Make a list of activities that you typically utilize in your face-to-face classroom.
2. Select two or three activities that would, with some reshaping, work online.
3. Using the activities you selected, design some templates.
4. Add content to each of the activities.

SUMMARY

In this chapter we have presented 20 assignment templates that can be used and reshaped to meet our changing content and student needs. Developing different ways of presenting material online sparks our creativity and is one of the reasons we enjoy this format. It also creates enthusiasm and interest in learning on the part of students. It is a challenge to think of ways to help our students learn without face-to-face classroom contact. These templates can be adopted as is or adapted to match teaching and learning styles and requirements. New approaches may also be turned into templates. We do this all the time.

CHAPTER 5

Facilitation and Building Online Community

In a conversation, our colleague João Fernandes, author of *Moodle 1.9 Multimedia*, indicated that being a student in an online course can be lonely and unmotivating (personal communication, 2010). However, a better way is possible. By creating a learning environment that is personal, students become more engaged in their learning. Many students need guidance and support to interact effectively in an online course. Consciously building an online community is part of the instructor's role. Creating interactive situations with and among students avoids isolation and helps them learn (Baran & Correia, 2009; Havard, Du, & Olinzock, 2005; Merrill & Gilbert, 2008). Some techniques to create useful interactions have been discussed in this book in another context.

In this chapter we discuss two distinctive aspects of teaching online: building an online learning community and facilitating discussions. The first part of this chapter deals with getting started and setting the tone for the learning and teaching. The second part of this chapter addresses the nitty-gritty of teacher-to-student and student-to-student interactions and techniques for promoting effective communication and learning. Finally we present techniques for being clear with students about course and assignment requirements and responsibilities.

STUDENT AND FACULTY INTERACTION

Although we have been teaching online for many years, occasionally we teach a course face-to-face. This occurred recently and reminded us of some of the similarities and differences between the two types of teaching. In our face-to-face course we use the same constructivist philosophy and similar supportive remarks to encourage students to participate during class. However, we also use other techniques such as the *power of personality* to engage students. When lecturing, we are spontaneous, using examples or including the names of students sitting in front of us. We walk around the room, smile, frown, and use humor to connect with our students and, in turn, connect the students to the content. As many face-to-face instructors know, teaching is similar to acting. (-:

After the refreshing experience of teaching face-to-face again, we realize that online we make connections with our students in different ways. We rarely get the opportunity to use humor in written communications in our online courses. The risk of being misunderstood is too high. Online, all the personal connections that are automatic in face-to-face classes need to be carefully orchestrated to gain students' attention, confidence, and participation. It is a challenge but we think we have found some good techniques to substitute for the immediacy of spontaneous body language and verbal responses.

Personal Connections

Personal connections among all participants should be established from the beginning of the course. This sets the tone and expectations and allows students to recognize that the instructor knows who they are and cares about them as individual learners. Online this is done by replying to students' postings, sending emails, having voice conversations, and doing vodcast or podcasts. These modes of contact should be encouraged to go several ways: between student(s) and instructor and among students. However, we find that only the more confident students initiate contact without explicit encouragement. The instructor needs to be the instigator and facilitator. One of our classes was particularly reticent, which we recognized was inhibiting their learning. Discussions were perfunctory and sluggish. Our solution was (1) to contact individual students who showed some initiative and encourage these students to post their comments more often, (2) to reply publicly to selected strong student postings with a positive comment and probing question, and (3) to post an announcement promoting deeper and more frequent responses. Using these interventions a few times resulted in students' responding more thoughtfully and more often on the Discussion Board.

It is necessary to plan and let students know in advance when and how contact will be made, as well as to establish the minimum number of contacts. Moreover, student-to-student contact should be required through joint projects, discussion of student projects, and debates about course issues. We strongly suggest focusing primarily on the student as learner and on the student's involvement with the course content. Although personal exchanges can take place, such as interests, hobbies, family and friends, we recommend keeping such exchanges to a minimum and in a confined area, since the principal goal of the course is learning the content. On the other hand, sharing personal information that supports and facilitates learning is a good way to establish a positive course environment. In one of our online courses about special education issues, a student told the group that her husband had a learning disability and struggled through school. Despite this, he became a successful building contractor. We suggested she talk with him about what helped him the most to get through the challenge and then to inform the rest of the class. Because of this her classmates became more involved, asked many questions, and were more forthcoming themselves.

To See or Not to See

Some instructors ask students to post a picture of themselves. This has pluses and minuses. It helps to put a face to a name or voice. On the other hand, it may result in stereotyping and can affect the attitudes of both instructor and students. We recently attended a seminar in which one of our adjunct faculty members was shown in a video. We knew her well from many email communications, contributions to coursework revision and student evaluations. Oddly we had never met her in person. Her name always conjured up a specific image in our minds. After viewing the video of this lovely person talking, we are still trying to reconcile our mental with the real image. Part of us prefers the *image* that was created by a long-term verbal interaction. This experience confirmed our policy. We do not require students to post pictures, since we prefer everyone to interact without any pre- or misconceptions, as reflected in innumerable psychological studies (Croxton, Van Rensselaer, Dutton, & Ellis, 1989; Dion, Berscheid, & Walster, 1972; Eagly, Ashmore, Makhijani, & Longo, 1991; Hatfield & Sprecher, 1986).

Fostering Peer Relationships

Online, students are not able to saunter out of the classroom or turn to a classmate and ask if he or she understands the course material. They are unable to drink coffee and talk about a particularly interesting idea. In online courses instructors need to create opportunities for students to support each other and discuss ideas that are meaningful to them. Here are some ways to do this, including group work, peer mentoring, encouraging appropriate participation, and serving as a role model.

Group work. Students can be asked or required to select a *study buddy* to discuss individual assignments and help each other understand course material. The buddy system may also become an informal relationship in which students check in with each other periodically for support and to validate learning.

It is important that students find their buddy, partner, or group relationship mutually beneficial and that they get along. If there are problems, the instructor needs to be ready to help resolve issues that arise. This rarely occurs, but when it does we have private communications with individuals to help smooth over problems. In our conversations, via email, IM, or Skype, we focus on learning and content. We reassure individuals who are conscientious that their grade will not be affected by a classmate's failings. Also, group assignments last no longer than 2 weeks, so students know that the problems are time limited.

We usually allow students to select their own partners or group members. With younger students for most group activities it is advisable for instructors to arrange groups based on what they know about the students' strengths and challenges. We start group work after students have had a chance to read each others' postings or talk with each other on Skype.

Peer mentoring. We use many informal mentoring techniques. We direct students to post general course-related questions in the Teachers' Room forum. When possible, we let students respond to each others' questions. The Teachers' Room description

---

Step-by-Step Course-Building Activity #12:
Techniques for Online Interaction

This activity is designed to assist in developing techniques for online interaction.

1. Think about and make a list of the ways you develop personal relationships with your face-to-face students and how you show them that you care about them as individual learners.
2. Put in parentheses items on the list that you are *not* able to do online.
3. Decide which, if any, of the interactions on the list can be adapted to an online environment.
4. From your list, select at least two ways that you will create an ongoing connection with every student. For example, you observe a pattern that indicates some students are having difficulty. Decide if you will send individual messages or a group message.
5. Decide if you want students to post photos or not. If you do, decide where and how. Write directions, including the purpose for having students post photos.

---

encourages students respond to and discuss questions that their classmates pose about course material. We wait a while (a day or two, depending on the urgency of the question) before answering in order to allow classmates to respond. For example, a typical student exchange was

Student Voice

STUDENT A: *I do not understand what the phrase "discuss ALL of the assigned reading" means.*

STUDENT B: *I took that to mean the Supporting Publication link at the bottom of the page. Hope that helps.*

After we develop a better understanding of our students' strengths and expertise we use an additional method. We ask individuals to share their knowledge with classmates. In ECOMP 5007 *21st Century Teaching: Supporting All Learners on the Ability Spectrum*, we often have a couple of students who are teachers of students with special needs. We urge them to share how they use technology with their students. Usually there are at least two students whose family members have a special need. Once a comfortable online *classroom climate* is established, these students always find some topic that compels them to "step forward" to help everyone understand many of the emotional issues and other barriers facing individuals with special needs. This peer interaction serves to motivate our students. The informal mentoring increases our students' interest in learning about and using technological solutions to support their students with special needs.

In a number of activities students conduct their own studies or research their own areas of interest. By completing an assignment like this, they come to know more about their topic than do most of their classmates. Students thus become de facto mentors as discussions occur. We require students to ask each other questions about postings and to respond to one another.

Formal mentoring systems are also implemented. More knowledgeable students may be assigned to work with less informed students. Students are trained to help peers with content and to improve writing or study skills. At Lesley University's Center for Academic Achievement many of the tutors are students who have strong academic and study skills and are trained to support other students. When teaching face-to-face it may be easier to determine when to intervene with a student. Online teaching requires different approaches to evaluate when students need help. We discuss these in Chapter 6.

Leaders and followers. Allowing students to stay in their comfort zone, by either taking a leadership role or being a follower, can assist them in focusing on learning the content. We have seen leaders and followers emerge on our course Discussion Boards. Typically, leaders respond quickly to questions classmates post in the Teachers' Room forum; they go beyond the required number of interactions by asking more questions and expanding discussions. These leaders help us in developing a positive learning community. We encourage and support them by sending personal emails thanking them for their active class participation. If a leader provides misleading information or is disruptive, we intervene. When responding to a student's posting, we may quote the leader or praise a leader for a contribution. We also recognize the followers but do not push them individually beyond the participation requirements. We assume that they are reading discussions and hope our praise of more "vocal" students motivates the followers to speak up. Our observation is that this reinforcement works to increase participation for some but not all students. In part we attribute the less participatory students' behavior to motivation, time limitations, and learning style.

By using a cooperative learning paradigm we ensure that students are participating in group assignments. We prefer to let them choose a role that fits their learning style. In some of our Skype meetings we ask students to take the following roles: organizer, note taker, note checker/poster, or supporter. This gives everyone responsibility but also lets individuals select their own type of participation. We usually facilitate during these Skype meetings and make sure that everyone contributes.

For a portion of most courses we require students to take a leadership role by moderating and summarizing a discussion for one assignment. We engage with moderators differently from leaders who emerge. We describe specific moderating expectations and our interactions with them below.

Most students appreciate peer moderation but a few do not enjoy moderating and believe the instructor should assume this role all the time. We have conducted surveys about student moderating. On the positive side, the following were typical student responses:

 It allowed me to be completely engaged in the assignment, and allowed for a real exchange from the class. In distance learning, real communication can be an "interesting" concept. Moderating "forced" the conversation in a good way.

 It really helps to get feedback from your peers. It is a different kind of validation that is important. I did, however, find that I really had to be on top of my game in order to comment on the work of others. It stretches you to know more.

The few students who did not like taking a leadership role wrote comments such as

 I didn't like moderating, I think that should be what the teacher does, not the student.

From our experience and that of others (Baran & Correia, 2009; Rourke & Anderson, 2002; Thormann, 2008) we believe that student moderation provides a significant learning benefit. We share details about the process of implementing student moderating later in this chapter.

Attitudes and behavior. Encouraging peer relationships involves more than arranging group interaction. It includes modeling attitudes and behaviors. Posting a list of **netiquette** rules or course participation rubrics is useful and necessary. However, we believe that the strongest influence that the instructor can have in an online course is modeling how to interact.

All communication with students should demonstrate tolerance of divergent ideas. Writing questions and comments in a supportive way is essential. We always make a draft of our feedback, usually writing the substance of our comments or questions first. If we have not done so already, we go back to the beginning and add a thank you or some laudatory comments. Occasionally it is difficult to think of positive comments, but there is always a kernel of an idea that we can help our students to build on. The effort that writing positive comments takes pays off many times over. First, it keeps our students involved in the course, feeling good about the learning process and the instructor. We always have to remember that in the online environment we cannot smile, nod, or have eye contact to support students in the learning process. Second, being supportive sends a direct and indirect message to students: This is the way we communicate with each other in this course. Some of the opening remarks we use in response to a question are, "Thank you for asking this question" and "Thank you for raising an important issue."

Timely responses are also part of establishing positive attitudes and behavior. Haavind (personal interview, 2009) commented that she is *"very* present" during the first few weeks of a course. She is at her keyboard, responding almost 24/7. This helps to reassure students that she is available and attending to student needs. We do the same.

While it is essential to be supportive, it is equally important to interact in a constructively critical way. If the response to students' work is only congratulatory, students do not learn from the instructor or classmates. Honest, clear, nonjudgmental feedback and questions are needed. We ask students questions about their work and make comments to promote a meaningful conversation on the Discussion Board. However, we do not post corrective feedback directly associated with the student's name in public places. If appropriate, we send a separate generic comment about an issue to the whole group. Our overall goal is to make learning safe and inviting and free of the fear of embarrassment. The latter usually shuts down conversation and learning.

We had the experience of being enrolled in an online seminar in which the instructor was sarcastic, did not thank participants for their contributions, and publicly, by name, corrected participants' postings. The 25-plus participants all taught at the college level. However, even with our strong academic and professional experience, the forum interaction quickly decreased. During the final Elluminate conference when the instructor asked for someone to speak up, no one volunteered. The instructor then said, "You're all chicken," and continued her lecture with PowerPoint. It appears that her nonsupportive behavior created an environment in which participants did not feel safe to contribute. She then confirmed our reluctance by referring to the group in a lighthearted but derogatory way. This seminar was eye opening for us primarily because it demonstrated how subtle and outright negative comments and lack of support can affect even a group of professionals. Such behavior cripples learning. Although we participated fully, this uncomfortable interaction is the only *content* we remember from the seminar.

Another key to encouraging student participation is remaining silent or *listening*. This may sound odd in an online setting but asking students to discuss a topic among themselves on the Discussion Board forum first empowers students and gives them control of the content. If, at the beginning of a discussion, an instructor comments and asks questions, students tend to think that the instructor has addressed all the important issues. Students then participate only to fulfill requirements, the communication becomes forced, and students are not engaged.

But there is a delicate balance. The instructor should listen for a while but also needs to join in so that students do not feel abandoned. It is sometimes difficult to determine the right time to jump in. Of course, following the students' conversation closely helps us figure this out. We also keep notes on the conversation to post later.

An instructor's enthusiasm is reassuring to students because it demonstrates that he or she is knowledgeable, enjoys the topic, and takes pleasure in teaching and communicating with students. Also, being enthusiastic about students' work and their participation encourages relationship building with and among students. We sometimes use the technique of congratulating students as a group. If students are told that as a group they are progressing well, those who are doing less well often increase their participation and contributions.

Figures 5.1 and 5.2 show two examples of encouraging communications that we posted as announcements for the whole group. The first announcement from ECOMP 7104, *Technology in Education Thesis Project*, is a summary with snippets from assignments to highlight something interesting or important that each student observed. At least once a semester we post this type of communication to motivate students to read each others' postings. We also publicly recognize the individual contribution each person has made. The second example congratulates all students for doing good work.

DEVELOPING ONLINE COMMUNICATION AND FACILITATION SKILLS

We have already mentioned the importance of the instructor's modeling good communication. Another critical feature is making sure that the content of the communication is substantive and relates to the course. We have several techniques to help keep us in line with these objectives. They involve feedback templates, communicating directly with each student and with the entire class, and tracking communications.

Feedback Templates

We learned about feedback templates many years ago at a conference when a faculty member from Golden Gate University in San Francisco introduced the idea. As we listened to the presenter we inwardly gasped, "How could an instructor do such a thing?" However, the idea rolled around in our heads and we started to incorporate feedback templates. We conserve time and are able to focus more on the unique aspects of each student's work. Feedback templates save us from retyping some of the same comments. They also help us standardize the feedback so that we do not shortchange anyone.

> **Step-by-Step Course-Building Activity #13:**
> **Orchestrating Peer Relationships**
>
> This activity helps you plan how you will orchestrate peer relationships.
>
> 1. Select the most successful ways in which you encourage students in your face-to-face courses to interact or select from the ideas presented in Figures 5.1 and 5.2.
> 2. Decide which of the interactions can be used in an online environment (at least three).
> 3. Write directions or develop a plan for those selected to promote peer interaction in your online course.

Figure 5.1. Summary Announcement

Dear Thesis Writers,

I had a great Skype conference with three of your classmates last night. I let them know (and want all of you to know) that you are all doing a great job and have been doing so since the beginning of the course. As I explained to them, you either learned more than other groups, knew more when you started, work harder, or are smarter than most other groups I've had in this course. (-: This was apparent to me from the beginning and has held true so far.

I have read most of the literature reviews you posted and all the comments you have made. Below are some comments and ideas that I pulled out from your interchange. I have posted them to whet your appetite and encourage you to read through the comments, since you have a lot to offer each other. I will also be sending each one of you my reactions to your literature review so that you can incorporate both your classmates' ideas and my comments in Assignment #5a Thesis Draft.

Many of you addressed the format and writing style used for the literature review and provided some helpful input. Barbara pointed out that Suzanne did a nice job reporting about what she found about her topic. Cindy wrote that in Anne's literature review she *"used intelligent wording in your ideas, but you made the review easy to understand for the common reader."* Roberta suggested that slang should not be used by the author and that a lead-in to what you are going to research is useful. Rob supported the idea of using subheadings to guide the reader and help define themes.

Al expanded the conversation and suggested the need for additional studies to be done. In a discussion with Al, Lane wrote, *"Only after I was well down the road of my own project did I discover open-source games."*

Jane made a good connection between Lisa's and Cindy's studies.

Lisa wrote about the impact of reading George's research: *"It was great! (I don't think I would have considered letting them listen to their music [on an MP3 player] before hearing about your research.)"* George responded by describing his experiences letting students use MP3 players in class and wisely wrote, *"I think each class will react differently and given enough time, problems will surface, but they will do that with or without the MP3 player present."* Kim also found George's research relevant. She wrote, *"I have participated as part of our school's science textbook adoption and Harcourt Publishers has included podcasts as part of their teacher resources."*

Anne had some great suggestions about to how to convince the administration that teachers should learn about technology and students should use it in the schools. She wrote the following in response to a comment that Jane made, *"Maybe you could share Celeste's research and some of the research on the Millennials and how they learn."*

In response to Jennifer's literature review, Suzanne wrote, *"I think the key is to get students to have a realistic perception of their abilities and then to understand that progress comes with time and effort."* In looking at Robin's literature review Jennifer had a few questions about other topics relating to Jennifer's main topic that she might want to review.

This discussion is thoughtful and thought-provoking.

Joan

Figure 5.2. Congratulatory Announcement

Dear Thesis Writers,

As some of you know, I am in the process of reading your drafts and am sending you detailed feedback on what you have written. So far everyone has incorporated ideas about writing a scholarly paper that we have discussed during this course.

The theses are looking very professional!!!

Joan

We develop a feedback template for each assignment, addressing each component of the assignment. The crucial point is that in each template there is a place to personalize the feedback and, of course, we change the template itself as appropriate for individual students. The following examples illustrate our two template formats.

The first type is a checklist, as seen in Figure 5.3. We use this at the beginning of the course to emphasize the importance of addressing every component of the assignment.

There is a code in the checklist template to guide the student. The code indicates whether a component of an assignment is complete, missing, or only partially complete. We include additional text for students so that they can understand how to interpret the code, points they earn, and how to improve their work and think more about the content.

The second feedback template, in Figure 5.4, is a narrative. We use this template more than the checklist despite the fact that it takes us longer, since students respond more positively to the narrative.

The words in both templates that are capitalized, separated by slashes, or both to indicate where we make a decision about what the student has done. For the narrative feedback template we have alternative sentences to indicate which components are complete or missing.

For both template formats, after reading the assignment and taking notes, we do some basic editing of the template, such as including the student's name, filling in blanks, and selecting appropriate descriptors. Once that is done, we do in-depth personalization of the feedback. We make substantive comments and expand on ideas the student has presented and ask a question or two based on our notes. We have a standard sentence in both feedback templates stating, "Please respond to the above question, comments, or both, which I will post on the Discussion Board so everyone in the class can benefit from your response." We post our individualized comments and questions to students on the Discussion Board so that we can engage in a conversation in which the entire class can participate. Opening it up to everyone expands potential learning similar to what happens in a face-to-face course.

In the past when we sent email feedback and students replied we ended up engaging in extended conversations with that one student. It was clear that our animated correspondence deserved a wider audience. It took a little while to come up with a satisfactory way to redirect students' responses to our questions and comments by asking for a reply on the Discussion Board. However, as mentioned, in public postings we do not post corrective feedback. This is sent and discussed privately via email, IM, or Skype. For example, a student published a website titled *Pimp Your Computer*, to complete an assignment relating to assistive technology. The website title was a takeoff on a popular TV program that this student indicated many of her middle school students watch. We pointed out, among other things, that none of her classmates had chosen her website to discuss. After a few days of emailing she wrote, "I have renamed it, because although my students would get a kick out of the title, and most teachers, but probably not most parents. So, since the site is for everyone,

Figure 5.3. Checklist Feedback Template

Dear _____,

  You have completed the following required components of the Online Project Assignment #4a. "X" indicates that you have fully addressed the assignment item; "/" indicates that you have partially addressed the assignment item; "?" indicates that you have not addressed the assignment item.

  _X_ a. A description of the projects with details such as the URL grade levels, time frame, costs, materials, etc.
  _X_ b. Why you selected these projects.
  _X_ c. How you would use them in your classroom or another classroom.
  _X_ d. What you see as the strengths and weaknesses of the projects.
  _X_ e. Included pertinent information from the articles you read.

THE CLASSROOM USE YOU DESCRIBED WAS GOOD/EXCELLENT/THOUGHTFUL/INTERESTING/ XXXXXXXXXXXXXXX

  I will post some of my questions and comments on the Discussion Board. Please respond there so that your classmates can benefit from your response.

                                                                                              Joan

Figure 5.4. Narrative Feedback Template

Dear _____,

  You have shared your thoughts about the usefulness and the concept of a Webquest for Assignment #5a.

  You have provided basic information (e.g., URL, name, topic, and grade level) about the Webquests you reviewed. You have *not* applied the information from assigned and researched articles and cited these articles.

  Your description of what you liked and disliked about each Webquest is very HELPFUL/USEFUL/INSIGHTFUL. You presented some GREAT/EXCELLENT/GOOD ideas about how to improve those elements of the Webquests that you disliked. You bring up some good points such as _____ for the _____Webquest and _____ for the _____ Webquest.

  IT IS GOOD THAT YOU LOOKED AT THE QUESTGARDEN SITE TO HELP YOU DEVELOP A WEBQUEST IN THE FUTURE.

  IT IS GOOD THAT YOU LOOKED AT VARIOUS WEBQUEST DEVELOPMENT SITES AND FOUND SOME THAT WILL WORK FOR YOU.

  You have/have *not* included citations from your readings to support ideas in your report.

PERSONAL COMMENTS XXXXXXXXXXXXXXXX

                                                                                              Joan

P.S. I have posted my question in the discussion area. Please respond to my question there so that your classmates may benefit from your response.

I changed the title." After the change one student did review her website. We do not allow students to leave inappropriate or incorrect material on the Discussion Board but we do not air problems to the community. Students need to feel it is safe to make mistakes and learn from them.

Interaction with Every Student

  The literature supports the idea that instructors play a key role in the students' learning process (Saphier, Haley-Speca, & Gower, 2008; Treacy, 2007). For this reason and based on our experience, we send students individualized feedback as promptly as possible. In this way, we communicate respect and concern implicitly. We want to let students know that we appreciate their completing the assignment and posting it on the due date. Although we are flooded with assignments on that date, we read and send the feedback no later than 3 or 4 days after the assignment is due. We vary who gets feedback first and also wait until we have read a representative number of assignments before we send the feedback. The latter is especially important when we give a new assignment. In this case we need to gauge how well the students have grasped what we intended them to learn. We want to be as prompt as possible to indicate that we as instructors hold ourselves to a similar standard as that to which we hold students. We also want students to receive feedback and engage in the Discussion Board conversation while they still have the content of their assignment in mind. Once students have moved fully on to the next assignment it is difficult for them to go back and think about what was done 2 or 3 weeks prior.

Feedback on assignments is one constant form of student communication that we use to create a relationship with our students. As noted, we post portions of the assignment feedback as a reply to their postings on the appropriate forum. When students reply we respond to their messages with substantive comments. Moreover, we engage in discussions that the students have started with each other, carefully weighing in with our knowledge of a topic, opinions, or ideas. We send them individual messages, congratulatory and also corrective in cases where there may be problems with an assignment. If appropriate we ask them to revise what they posted.

We are especially careful when communicating about problems, since we are aware that written communications can lead to misunderstandings. The most common problem is that a student has missed posting an assignment. An example of what we write is found in Figure 5.5. We sometimes use the subject line "Is everything OK? —James" or "Missing Assignment #5 Polly."

We keep these emails brief, only stating the facts we know. We end the message with a question to prompt the student to respond. In addition, with all individual emails, we include the student's name at the end of the subject line, whether it is the student's assignment feedback or individual emails, so we can locate the communication easily. We are compulsive about keeping all correspondence with students in a folder on our email system. We have two course folders, one for general communication and the other for assignment feedback.

Keeping all communications may seem excessive. However, we find this useful for a number of purposes. For example, recently a student was slow to participate in the first couple of assignments. We emailed her asking if everything was OK. She wrote that her father was ill and that her teaching load was difficult. We repeatedly and gently suggested that she might want to drop the course before the deadline and take it another time. She demurred and emailed back that she would be able to handle everything. Shortly after this she "disappeared." At the beginning of the next semester, we were contacted about this student and were able to share the emails we

Figure 5.5. Sample Email About a Missing Assignment

Hi Danielle,

Assignment #3a was due on Monday 9/24. You have not posted your assignment. Is everything OK?

Joan

had regarding her participation. The saved emails meant that we did not have to spend hours explaining what had occurred. We had supporting evidence. The result was that the student needed to repeat the course.

We also use saved communications to remind us about students' special requests such as vacation time or being paired with a classmate. Sometimes what we have written in the assignment feedback to one student is appropriate to tell another and we can easily find the text and copy it. We even use some of these communications from one course to another, editing as appropriate.

Interaction with the Whole Class

We generally use announcements to encourage students, share scheduling information, and provide additional material of interest. Announcements serve as another consistent tool for communication. At a minimum, we post a new announcement once a week. This is an unobtrusive way to keep in touch with students and let them know that they are on our radar screen.

When an individual student emails us with a question or comment that might be pertinent to the whole class, we use it as a means of communicating with the entire class. We remove the student's name and identifying information and include the student's question and our response. An example of a question posed by one student that we sent to the whole class is presented in Figure 5.6.

We consider this exchange similar to a student's raising a hand in the classroom with a question and our responding so the whole class can hear. The questions that we send to the whole class are those that we anticipate more than one student may

Figure 5.6. Sample Question and Response to the Whole Class

Dear 5007ers,

A classmate asked:

I'm a little confused about the letter I need to write for the journal. What should this letter be about?

The letter is a cover letter for your article. I suggest that you include a one- or two-sentence summary of your article. You may also write a couple of sentences indicating why your article would be appropriate for the journal you are submitting it to.

I hope this helps to clarify.

Joan

have. We do not use the student's name, so that he or she does not feel embarrassed or singled out. We guess that there are sighs of relief from some students. On the other hand, after sending out one of these group messages, we received the following reply from a student, "Good grief. I've lost count of how many times you've told us this and someone asks yet again? How ignorant can my classmates be? . . . I'm sorry you had to address this again for someone, who is pursuing an advanced degree, and just can't get it." We laughed out loud.

Tracking Communications

It is difficult to keep track of all the communications when we are teaching multiple classes, or even one! It is particularly important to keep track of communications that are related to grading. We monitor the *traffic* by creating a table, to which we also refer in Chapter 6. We have reproduced a table and key from ECOMP 7104 *Technology in Education Thesis Project* in Figure 5.7.

For ease of understanding, the table given in Figure 5.7 is an abbreviated version of our tracking system and includes only 6 of the 18 students and 3 of the 14 assignments. In the case presented in Figure 5.7, Mary received 9 out of 10 points for assignment #1 and #3 and 8 of 10 points for #2. This was based on the quantity and quality of her postings.

Once the table and code are developed and we use the table for a while it looks less like the Rosetta Stone. (-: We can glance at the table as the course progresses to track what we have read and whether we have sent feedback to a student, as well as his or her level of participation in a discussion.

Figure 5.7. Assignment Checklist

Name	#1 Literature Review Research	#2 Methodology Research	#3 Annotated Bibliography
Lee	rrr*10	rr*9	OK*10
Tom	rr*9	rr*9	OK*10
Randy	rrrr*10	rrrr*10	OK*10
Pat	r*8	rr*9	OK*10
Kirk	rr*9	rr*9	OK*10
Mary	rr*9	r*8	OK*10

KEY

Symbol	Meaning
r	responded to a classmate
repeated letters	multiple responses made to classmates
*	instructor feedback sent
numbers	points earned
OK	assignment accepted

> ## Step-by-Step Course-Building Activity #14: Interacting with Students
>
> These activities assist you in creating a plan for giving feedback and interacting with individual students and the class.
>
> 1. Choose at least two assignments and develop feedback templates for those assignments. Use them to give feedback to your students.
> 2. In an anonymous survey ask students if the feedback was useful, and why or why not.
> 3. Develop a plan for how you will communicate with students individually.
> 4. Think of ways that you will be able to reach out to the entire class. Make a list of the ways you can do this and develop a plan for how you will communicate with the class.

Guidelines for Online Course Communication

Students need to understand communication standards and the rules of the course. We put some of this information in the syllabus. But we do not want the syllabus to be so long that students will be overwhelmed and discouraged. We post course guidelines under a Course Documents link and, at the beginning of the course, urge students to read the guidelines. We repeat some of the information that is in the syllabus such as rubrics for online discussions and use of APA. We also elaborate on these in the guidelines. For example, we include information concerning participation on the Discussion Board, as shown in Figure 5.8.

We have a standard course guidelines document that we tailor as appropriate for each course. Further discussion of this can be found in Chapter 4, and a sample is in Appendix B.

Online Communication Conventions

At times in email messages we use abbreviations or **emoticons** to overcome the lack of a visual and physical presence. Many are familiar with how these help to

Figure 5.8. Discussion Board Postings

A portion of the points earned on each assignment or discussion will be allocated to participation. Participation is defined as writing and posting substantive comments, critiques, or questions relating to classmates' submitted assignments. Positive comments are encouraged, but the content of the comments or questions should contain thoughtful ideas and responses. Your comments do not have to be lengthy, but they should be meaningful. Avoid just responding with statements such as *"Good job"* or *"I agree."* Instead, make statements such as *"I agree because . . ."* or *"I disagree because . . ."* or *"Your comments reminded me of . . ."* You should also ask questions for clarification or as a gentle challenge.

dispel the formality of the printed word. We use abbreviation standards like *BTW* (by the way) or *TTYL* (talk to you later) or *LOL* (laughing out loud). A list of web abbreviations, including acronyms, and their meanings can be found at http://www. webacronyms.com/.

Emoticons can help to convey emotions that the printed word does not express. Some systems such as Moodle have a built-in emoticon-generating system. However, we have found that not all email systems can interpret graphic-based emoticon symbols. There are keystroke-based emoticons such as a smiling face, as in "(-:", or a frowning face, shown as ")-:". A list of keystroke emoticons and their meanings is available at http://en.wikipedia.org/wiki/List_of_emoticons.

Student/Peer Moderating

We introduced the idea of student moderation in Chapter 2. Here we share a detailed description of the reasons for student moderation, how we implement it, and research about instructors' and students' reaction to it.

Reasons for student moderation. Years ago we started to think about how to increase the level of student participation in online discussions. Around that time, we had a meeting with colleagues during which Sam Gladstein made a casual remark about having students lead discussions. A lightbulb went on in our heads. We did some research to find out how others organized and managed student moderators/facilitators in online courses. We found literature about what successful moderators/facilitators should do and have used those ideas to formulate our directions for students.

We thought that if students led discussions, the interaction would increase, and it did. We also realized that this supports a constructivist approach. An added bonus was that the responsibility for keeping a meaningful conversation going would no longer fall entirely on our shoulders. This turned out to be a relief. We also observed additional positive benefits, which we share.

Implementing student moderation. We introduced student moderating into our courses slowly and found that it worked well for some courses and not at all for others. Initially we asked for students to volunteer to moderate. When we found that student moderating worked well, we made it a requirement for some courses. We decided that students should moderate in groups or pairs, since it lightened what students saw as a heavy workload. Welcome to our world. (-:

One of the first assignments in many of our courses is for students to sign up to be a moderator. The assignment as students see it in ECOMP 6008 *The World Wide Web as an Educational Resource* is shown in Figure 5.9.

Along with the assignment titles listed in Figure 5.9, students can read what the assignment is under the Assignment link. This lets students decide in advance which topic they will moderate. As can be seen from the assignment, students are asked to select an assignment to moderate on a first-come, first-served basis. As instructors we post a table in the Teachers' Room forum with the names of the students who have

Figure 5.9. Student Moderation Assignment

Moderator—Purpose of Assignment: To gain depth of knowledge about selected course assignments and exercise facilitation and leadership skills in an online environment.

Each student will have the opportunity to moderate an assignment during this course (individually or with a partner). The moderator will not be required to post the regular assignment that he or she moderates. In cases where the assignment is a two-part assignment, the moderators will *not* have to do Part 1 and Part 2. The moderators will, of course, need to be familiar with the content and read classmates' postings.

Moderators will do the following:

a. Focus the discussion on course content and encourage new ideas.
b. Initiate deeper discussion through questions or observations.
c. Find unifying threads and communicate them.
d. Draw attention to opposing perspectives, different directions, or conflicting opinions and encourage debates.
e. Summarize and post a report about the discussion by restating the ideas and controversies, as well as clarifying misconceptions. The summary will serve to pull ideas together. It is best to post the summary in the Teachers' Room Moderator Summary forum so that classmates have a central place to find summaries and discuss them.

Many of you will work with a partner. If you have a partner, the two of you should figure out a way to divide the work equitably. For example, each person may be responsible for being moderator for half the postings, or one person may respond to the initial posting and the partner will do the follow-up. Similarly, writing the summary may be split. The moderators may want to confer with the instructor to clarify the assignment or issues relating to classmates' contributions.

Moderators should select one of the following assignments. Post your selection on the Discussion Board in the Teachers' Room forum by replying to the message titled Moderator Selection. Selections will be honored on a first-come, first-served basis. Post the name of the assignment in the subject line. You will need to review the choices that have already been posted *before* you post your own assignment choice.

#5a Online Projects and #5b Projects Discussion
#6a Web 2.0
#7a Security, Acceptable Use Policy (AUP), and Ethics; and #7b School Web Use Discussion
#8 Information Validity and Domain Names
#9 Educational Web Page Review
#10i Using a Web Page Accessibility to Evaluate Web Page *or* #10ii Alternate Accessibility

Due Date: Select a topic to moderate no later than the end of the second week of class.

> ## Step-by-Step Course-Building Activity #15:
> ## Organizational and Communication Details
>
> These activities help to develop organizational and communication details such as tracking assignments, course guidelines, and communication conventions.
>
> 1. Think about how you will track assignments and participation to supplement your grade book. Develop a table and coding system.
> 2. Review the sample course guidelines in Appendix B. Start building your own guidelines for course procedures that will supplement your syllabus and assignments. Add to it as you develop your course.
> 3. Make a plan for using text abbreviations and emoticons.

signed up for each week. This helps students keep track of when they moderate and who is moderating each assignment. Students are therefore not surprised, upset, or confused when they see a few classmates become very active and start asking questions and making comments.

In the course above, moderating starts with the sixth assignment. This is purposeful, so that we can model how to moderate and summarize a discussion. Generally students follow our example but occasionally they branch out and try something different, which can prove interesting.

A week before students start their moderating, if the student has not contacted us, we send an email repeating most of what is written in the initial assignment. We do this to remind students of their responsibilities and to reach out and reassure them that we are available for consultation.

Once students start to interact, we follow the discussion closely and "listen" for 1 or 2 days. If we find that the moderators have not started a discussion with students in that time, we send them an urgent reminder. This happens rarely. Students almost always take the moderating assignment seriously. After a waiting period of about 3 or 4 days, we post the personal comments that we have written in our individual feedback to students and also add to other parts of the discussion. When student moderators are active we explicitly let students know that we are letting moderators take the lead and change the feedback template to reflect this, as seen in Figure 5.10.

We learned that giving students a chance to take the lead by remaining silent was essential. This was pointed out to us by a student when we surveyed students' perceptions about moderating. Every time we make a major change in our course that has not been documented as beneficial in the research literature, we send a survey after the course is completed, to help us decide whether to keep the change or how or what to revise.

Figure 5.10. Feedback Template with Active Student Moderators

PS I will post some of my comments or questions on the Discussion Board in a few days to give the moderators a chance to orchestrate the discussion. Please respond to my comments and questions there. Thanks.

Students' reaction to student moderation. Thormann conducted research concerning students' perception of moderating. Six classes taught at Lesley University and one class taught at Tufts University's Fulcrum Institute participated in the study from 2006 to 2009. Most students responding to the Lesley questionnaire found student moderating beneficial (80%). They indicated that moderating helped them learn new skills, gave them a broader perspective, and immersed them further in the content.

Comments from these students support the idea that taking control of their learning is valuable. A student who was initially apprehensive about the prospect of leading the class discussion wrote,

 Somehow, conversations took on a whole new meaning and a different level.

Another student reported staying engaged longer as moderator and wrote,

 I think that the week that I moderated the discussion was one where I gained a tremendous amount of knowledge. Not only did I have an opportunity to research the topic, I was also afforded an opportunity to thoughtfully engage in conversations with each of my classmates.

Taking charge of the learning process by moderating seems to have helped many students get into the topic at a deeper level, as indicated by the following comment: "I read more on the topic so that I would have interesting information to offer." One student implemented student moderation in her face-to-face classroom. In this research students shared many useful insights. Providing differing perspectives seemed to be a central theme that many students agreed upon.

A small number of the students felt that the instructor should be the primary leader. This opinion is reflected in these two comments:

 The professor needs to keep the lead role.

 I think that the professor has more knowledge on topics than the students. So when students are moderators, I feel like we miss out on that knowledge that the professor could be sharing.

Student moderating at Tufts University's Fulcrum Institute was implemented somewhat differently from Lesley University's and some of the comments reflect this. The primary difference was that Tufts students wanted instructors to model the process and give more guidance before students were asked to take on the role. Some students requested real-time communication. The Lesley version of moderating includes modeling and some real-time conferencing. Some Tufts students felt that being excused from doing the assignment (typically a science experiment) was counterproductive. With feedback from the Fulcrum students, adjustments in student moderating have been instituted. We continue to monitor how it works with students and modify the process.

Creating a Presence with Technology

An important element in online learning is developing an online presence. We define presence in this context as a way for students and instructors to *know about* each other for learning purposes. Technology tools should be chosen to advance learning and not simply for their own sake. If students are already on Facebook, Twitter, or other social networking sites, incorporating these tools to create presence can be fruitful.

For some individuals who have a predominant or preferred auditory learning style, listening to or making their own podcasts or vodcasts is valuable in developing presence. Lee, McLoughlin, and Chan (2008) conducted a study focusing on student use of collaborative podcasting. The researchers wrote, "Podcasting also holds great potential for allowing students to articulate their understanding of ideas and concepts, and to share the outcomes with an audience they value, such as their peers"(p. 518). Others have successfully experimented with or written about having students make podcasts or using instructor podcasts (Beldarrain, 2006; Garrett, 2006; Hew, 2009).

We have found that Skype also helps students get to know each other, feel comfortable, and be connected with the instructor and classmates. Research conducted by Thormann and discussed later in this chapter indicates that including real-time voice communication is worth the effort. Students' appreciate immediacy and clarity of feedback. They also like the personal interaction. Programs such as Elluminate and GoToMeeting can help create a similar effect.

BUILDING ONLINE COMMUNITY

Much has been written about building online community (Cavanaugh & Cavanaugh, 2008; Edelstein & Edwards, 2002; Hudson, Hudson, & Steel, 2006; Jewell, 2005; McInnerney & Roberts, 2004). We have found that this is a vital part of making the online learning experience successful. We present three categories of community building: social and academic presence online, required exchanges, and embedding community building in deliverables.

Online Social and Academic Presence

Introduction and getting acquainted. We start each online course with some sort of icebreaker or warm-up activity. This is to let students get to know each other and the instructor. This initial activity also helps students start thinking about the course content and rhythm. We tailor the introductory exercise to the content of the course. In Figure 5.11, we ask students about their experiences using the Internet for ECOMP 6008 *The World Wide Web as an Educational Resource.* (In Chapter 3, Figure 3.4, we include an introduction assignment from ECOMP 5007 *21st Century Teaching: Supporting All Learners on the Ability Spectrum*, but with a different emphasis.)

Our exchange with students in the activity shown in Figure 5.11 usually focuses on their comments about the content. In this way we start to model the type of

Figure 5.11. Introduction Assignment (Part A) for ECOMP 6008

#1a. Part 1. Introduction Assignment

Introduction:

#1a and #1b Purposes of Assignment: Share past and current experiences with the use of the Internet as an educational tool. Start the process of establishing an online community and become familiar with class participant experiences and expertise.
   Introduce yourself to all students in our online community. Include the following:

a. The subject(s), grade(s) you teach, and how long you have been teaching. If you are not teaching, indicate where you work.
b. Where you work: school, city/town, and state.
c. Share some of your favorite educational sites and how you use them to support your own work and with students.
d. Describe your use and your students' or child's use of social networking sites such as Facebook and Twitter.
e. If you have a website please include the URL, give a little background about the site, and discuss how you developed it.
f. Tell us about yourself and your family, friends, and interests and an unknown fact about you. After the 2nd week of class all communications about personal matters should be posted in the Coffee Shop forum.

Due Date: This assignment may be posted anytime during the 1st week but no later than the due date indicated on the syllabus, assignment chart, and Discussion Board. (Assignment #1b is the same as in ECOMP 5007, which is in Chapter 3, Figure 3.4.)

---

interaction we expect students to engage in. Our comments are supportive and complimentary. We always include questions to indicate that students need to ask questions as well answer them. We require students to respond so they interact with classmates who post before and after their own posting.

We use this type of introduction in most of our courses. However, there are other icebreakers that may be used. For example, in a course taught by Kristen Bourgault, former instructional designer in elearning and instructional support at Lesley University, she asked participants to do the assignment, shown in Figure 5.12, at the beginning of the course.

This icebreaker can be amusing and revealing. Another technique is to ask students to partner with a classmate and have the two interview each other. We have them respond to similar questions, as in the introductions presented in Figure 5.12, adding course-specific questions, and some for fun, such as "What is a fact that most people do not know about you?" Students use IM, Skype, or email and then the interviewer posts the results of the interview. This process can set up a special bond between partners. If students are required to interact they get to know each other. A word of caution: We learned early that students are not eager to introduce

Figure 5.12. Icebreaker Using First-Name Initials

Write your name vertically to create an acronym, using each letter to write a word to describe yourself. For example, here's mine:

Knitter of socks, hats, and baby sweaters
Resourceful
Instructional Designer
Simmons College Alum
Tall
Energetic
Never Sleeps

When you've completed your acronym, read through the other posts and respond to a classmate with whom you share a common interest, skill, or attribute!

themselves when they already know each other, since they feel it is busywork. However, in the typical online course, using icebreaker activities created for online situations or adapting them from face-to-face structures help students to feel more comfortable, easing the way for them to learn from each other. This is our ultimate objective in building community.

Coffee Shop forum. In every course we have a Discussion Board forum titled Coffee Shop. We want to avoid having the course assignment forums cluttered with personal communications and non-course-related material. However, we do want students to be able to share events that are happening in their lives or things that interest them outside course content. Some groups use this Coffee Shop a lot, others only minimally. We promote the conversation by directly encouraging individuals to post personal information in the Coffee Shop. For example, students will often let us know about the birth of a grandchild or a trip that they plan to take. In most cases we email the student and suggest that he or she post a photograph of the grandchild, a description of the trip to Disney World, and so on. These postings get responses from supportive and interested classmates. We place the purpose of the Coffee Shop on the Discussion Board forum, as seen in Figure 5.13.

To further encourage postings in the Coffee Shop, we occasionally post something ourselves. We have not as yet figured out why some groups use the Coffee Shop a lot and others do not. We do have some observations. The students in groups that know each other use it more than groups of unacquainted students. Also, we see active use by groups in which one or two students initiate on their own and seem to enjoy making nonacademic connections. We read all Coffee Shop postings to make sure that nothing inappropriate is included.

Teachers' Room forum. In addition to the Coffee Shop we have a Teachers' Room forum, which we use to exchange communication about course-related topics such as schedule changes, assignment sign-ups, and questions posted. A description of the purpose is presented in Figure 5.14.

Figure 5.13. Coffee Shop Forum Purpose

The Coffee Shop

This forum is a place where we can chat, share personal information, or just relax to get to know each other. We can post photos of trips, events, newborns, and family.

Figure 5.14. Teachers' Room Forum Purpose

Teachers' Room

In this forum we share course-related materials, questions, and ideas. Please respond to and discuss questions that your classmates pose about course material. In addition, schedules, sign-ups, and changes will be posted here.

Once students are acclimated to our *classroom life*, they post messages in the Teachers' Room, including asking for help with finding readings, sharing course-related material, and posting comments about past assignments. We also ask student moderators to post summaries of each week's assignment in the Teachers' Room, so discussion about these can and do occur.

If a student posts a message on an assignment forum that we deem is more appropriate for the Coffee Shop or Teachers' Room, we send an email to the student asking that the message be moved. This happens infrequently, and, if it does, students do not seem to have a problem with moving the message.

Starting the course with introductions or an icebreaker assignment sets the tone of the course as a friendly and positive experience. It is also easy, since students know the subject. (-: It allows students to make personal connections and to discuss course content informally. The amount of time spent on introductions should be just sufficient for people to get to know each other. We attended an online seminar that was 2 weeks long and spent about 5 days (over one-third of the seminar time!) with introductions. Building community and engaging in social activities are necessary activites, but these should not dominate the course. The Coffee Shop and Teachers' Room are places to continue conversations that are outside the assignment forums.

Step-by-Step Course-Building Activity #16: Building a Learning Community

This activity is designed to assist in creating *student and instructor presence* and to contribute to *building a learning community*.

1. Think about how you and your students should "be present" in your online course to facilitate learning.
2. Make two lists:
   a. Ways for you and your students to have a personal presence.
   b. Ways for you and your students to have an academic presence.
3. Select at least one way of being present from each list for your students and at least one way for yourself and plan how you will implement this.
4. Write directions to share with students based on your selections to be included in your assignments, syllabus, or both.
5. Write notes for yourself about "how" you will be present.

Required Exchanges

As indicated, building an online learning community entails advanced planning. It is essential to think through how much required interaction is necessary to deepen learning. We incorporate various types of required exchanges in our courses and are constantly looking for new ones.

Jigsaw method. We described a number of assignment formats in Chapter 4. Many of them require students to comment on and ask questions about what each person has posted. These assignments create interdependence or a need to interact to acquire a broad understanding of the topic being addressed. The **jigsaw method** is an example of how students are able to learn from each other.

In the jigsaw, each student examines specific material or an item within a category or topic. For example, we have students examine Web 2.0 in ECOMP 6008 *The World Wide Web as an Educational Resource.* The first part of the Web 2.0 assignment (Chapter 4, Figure 4.2) involves reviewing various Web 2.0 sites. Students become knowledgeable and reflect on how a specific type of Web 2.0 site might be used in a classroom. The second part of the assignment is interactive.

By reading their classmates' postings, asking questions, and making comments, students are able to learn about more than one Web 2.0 site. Those who are intent on expanding their knowledge read and reply to more than what is required. Although it seems like common sense, we also let them know they need to read comments and questions that have been posted prior to making their own posting. The result is that a discussion about Web 2.0 and its uses gradually expands and builds with each person's reply. After waiting a few days for the conversations to get going, we add our comments and questions.

We use required exchanges during the first two-thirds of a course. Later in the course when we decrease the interaction requirement, at least half the class continues to ask questions, respond, and leave substantive comments. We infer that these students find the exchanges valuable or got into the habit of interacting.

Voice conferences. We use voice conferences with small groups of students at least once during a course to increase interaction with and among students, to build community and introduce an additional communication tool. We described how we implement Skype conferencing in Chapter 3. Here we share some results of research that was conducted by Thormann concerning students' perception of using Skype.

A survey indicated that 88% of the 58 students who responded to Thormann's survey found the Skype conferences very useful. Students were split over whether Skype should be used more or used the same amount of time, but 88% indicated that they would not change how Skype was used. The majority of students (67%) did not have technical difficulties with Skype. But we did, on a number of occasions, experience calls dropping or noise that was annoying or made it difficult to hear. When there is noise we ask all conferees to hang up and we initiate the call again.

Based on Thormann's continuing research about the use of voice conferencing, we maintain it in our courses and adapt use based on the feedback. We resolved the divided opinion about how much Skype time should be required by making additional Skype meetings in groups or individually optional. We think that Skype will become more stable in the future and that less technically volatile systems will also be available.

Comments students made include the following:

 Online is the wave of the future. However, Skype allows students to have an "almost" in-person connection with the instructor.

 Instant responses to questions allow a more human sense of contact to the distance learning experience.

 Feedback with tone of voice is much more useful and comforting than text.

In many courses you have to chat via typing. . . . It is difficult to get your questions answered effectively when they are interpreted differently than you intended. The ability to clarify remarks and comments.

 Everything was positive.

The responses to the positive and negative aspects of using Skype were instructive. The negative comments focused primarily on technical issues. The positive comments confirm our sense that Skype creates human connection and immediacy, which students appreciate.

Deliverables

Community building can be easily integrated into assignments. We deliberately include ways to promote interaction in all our courses. One obvious way is to require interaction. We share other ways below.

Sharing all assignments. Almost all assignments are constructed so that students can learn from each other. We typically ask them to investigate or research or practice something and then post a reaction. All assignments are posted on the Discussion Board in a specific location so that classmates' thoughts and ideas get maximum exposure. In traditional classes, students submit assignments to the instructor, as we did when we first taught online. We quickly realized that our students' reports were very informative. It seemed a shame that all our students did not have the learning opportunity we had. The online environment makes sharing very easy. Rather than our having students send their work to us, they post it for everyone. Students may paste their assignments in the textbox or include

---

Step-by-Step Course-Building Activity #17

The following is an activity designed to plan for student interactions.
Develop a plan for promoting student interaction. Consider the following:

1. Will you require interaction? If yes, how much? Will you assign grades for the interaction?
2. What techniques will you use to promote positive and growth-inducing interaction?
3. Will you allow for social interaction? If yes, how will you design it so that it helps rather than interferes with learning?
4. How will you measure the usefulness and impact of the interactions?

---

them as attachments. In the course guidelines presented in Figure 5.15, we offer advice about posting assignments.

We require students to give unique names to their attached files, since it can be frustrating for us or for classmates to download 15 attachments with the title Assignment_5.doc and figure out to whom they belong. Students are asked to both post and attach assignments to make class work as accessible as possible.

For the students who are especially eager to learn, sharing assignments is a positive experience. We expand the learning further with student moderators who must read many of or all the postings during their assigned week.

Group assignments. Group assignments bring students together and provide another way to alleviate potential isolation. In all our courses students work in pairs or small groups a few times a semester. We typically allow them to choose their own group members and have worked out the logistics by having them post partnering or group member information in the Teachers' Room. Partnerships sometimes present challenges such as disagreements, scheduling conflicts, or differing levels of expertise. Because we have established a relationship with all students, they are comfortable asking us for guidance. And we oblige. (-: Forming partnerships or groups is part of the assignment, as illustrated in Figure 5.16.

Figure 5.15. Posting Assignments

Format for Posting Assignments

All assignments must indicate the title in the subject line and be posted on the Discussion Board in the appropriate forum.

To make it easier for your classmates to access your assignments (decreasing the number of clicks and difficulty opening files), please write the assignments with your word processor and then copy and paste the assignment in the text box in the appropriate Discussion Board forum. In addition, for formatting purposes, you may attach the document.

All assignments submitted as attached files *must* have a file name that includes an abbreviation of the assignment name and the student's name or initials. Examples: apa_joan.doc or apa_thormann. doc or apa_jt.doc. Blackboard will not accept symbols in the file name, such as # or &. So it is best to use only the underscore or period symbols as part of the file name. Repeated failure to follow file-naming guidelines will result in points being deducted from your grade.

In the assignment shown in Figure 5.16 we make finding a partner an element of the assignment itself and give directions about how to do this. We also make sure that selecting partners occurs far enough into the course so that students have some time to get to know each other and have a sense of the other person's work ethic.

We occasionally are asked to intervene when students are not working well together. In Figure 5.17 is an email exchange that illustrates how we dealt with one such controversy.

As it turned out in this case and most others, the errant student started to contribute shortly after Carol followed my suggestion. They completed their group work together.

When asking students to work in groups of more than two people, it is a good idea to have them use a cooperative-learning approach. The second part of the assignment

Figure 5.16. Partner and Category Selection

Weeks 4 and 5: #5a Investigation of Special Needs Categories and Use of Technology and #5b Bibliography

Purpose of Assignment: #5a. To establish a partner and topic in preparation for completing the Investigation of Special Needs Categories and Use of Technology assignment.

Purpose of Assignment: #5b. To identify 12 or more resources as references or background reading for your Investigation of Special Needs Categories and Use of Technology report. To apply APA format.

Assignment #5a Investigation of Special Needs Categories and Use of Technology

1. Review assignment #6a Special Needs Categories and Use of Technology.
2. Use email, IM, Skype, or the Chat area to find and communicate with a classmate to find a partner. Do *not* post inquiries about partnering on the Discussion Board.
3. With your partner select a special needs category (e.g., educable mentally retarded, visually impaired, speech and language impaired, physically impaired, hearing impaired, learning disabled, emotionally disabled, autism) to investigate.
4. To avoid duplication of special needs categories, inform everyone in the class by having one partner post your category choice on the Discussion Board in the designated forum. Include the following in the subject line:
   a. The first *or* last names of both partners.
   b. The special needs category you and your partner will investigate

Please Note: Category selection will be honored on a first-come, first-served basis. You will need to review the choices that have already been posted *before* you and your partner make your choice. If your category has already been posted, select another one with your partner. If an odd number of students are doing this assignment, one group of 3 will be formed, or the assignment can be completed by one individual.

Due Date: This partner and topic selection assignment may be completed early, but it is due no later than the date indicated on the syllabus, assignment chart, and Discussion Board.

Figure 5.17. Group Controversy

-----Original Message-----
From: Ms. Carol N.
Subject: partner concerns
Hi Joan,

   I am emailing because I am a bit concerned and frustrated. Lisa put out an email looking for a group to work with and Michelle and I asked her to work with us so that she did not have to write the paper alone. Since that time we have received no communication from her. Michelle and I researched and put together a really good list of references for what I think will be a really good paper but Lisa has not responded to any of our emails or assisted in the process. What should we do? Any suggestions?
Carol

Hi Carol,

   Thank you for letting me know about this problem. You and Michelle should focus on doing your paper. I suggest that you send another message to Lisa and cc me so that she is aware that I know she is not contributing. If she responds and starts working with you that would be good. If not, I will discuss other options with her.
Joan

in Chapter 2, Figure 2.6, provides an example of how we use cooperative learning during a Skype conference. We recommend that students take roles for all group assignments. However, whether or not students take specific roles, group work supports affiliation and enriches the learning experience, since it broadens students' perspectives by taking into considerations classmates' views.

   Including participation in the syllabus. As we have repeatedly stated, clarity and forewarning are essential for student engagement and sense of fairness. Since participation in an online course is distinctly different from what occurs in a face-to-face environment, the more clearly the students understand what is required of them the better it is for their learning and the instructors' teaching. The syllabus should contain information about participation and expectations, including quality expected and grading procedures. Additional information about participation can be specified in individual assignments and course guidelines.

SUMMARY

In this chapter we have described various techniques for communicating with and engaging students in their learning in an online environment. Facilitating the exchange of ideas and concepts by building community is accomplished by creating a personal connection, fostering peer relationships, interacting with each student, and experimenting with new technologies. Incorporating and adapting the best aspects of face-to-face while leveraging the advantages of online education are key to successful learning online.

CHAPTER 6

Evaluation and Assessment in Online Teaching

Evaluation is a critical issue in any educational setting. For many years student evaluation in online courses was viewed with skepticism. Critics were concerned that students could not be evaluated effectively in an online environment because instructors felt they were unable to build a trusting relationship with students who did not sit in front of the instructor to take tests. However, based on our and others' years of experience, we know there are many valid ways to evaluate student learning in online courses. We describe these in this chapter. In addition, we share some technology that can be used, evaluation of various types of assignments, grading and high-stakes testing.

TESTING FOR LEARNING

There are two kinds of tests for learning. The first is diagnostic, which as the name implies, is a way to determine what students know in order to provide them with the appropriate level of instruction. The second is designed to measure progress. The latter is not simply an evaluation of performance but also an indication of whether the student is learning.

Instructors and students can use a variety of tools as feedback devices to help adjust instruction; these tools can also determine what and how students are learning. Multiple-choice, true/false, fill-in-the-blank, and standardized tests are the easiest to use, since numerical scoring and graphically presented data are possible. Other types of evaluations, such as journaling, discussions, or reflecting on the work, although more complex to use, provide important and deep information. If instructors examine test items or review written material carefully, they can see trends. As necessary, instructors can reteach or clarify areas that students seem to find difficult to grasp.

Students can use their own results from numerically scored tests to correct their errors and review problem areas. If written evaluations are shared among students as well as the instructors, students can learn from classmates' observations and also engage in discussions about areas that are confusing or unclear.

The online environment supports feedback loops well, since the most often used interactions are asynchronous in nature and thus give participants time to think about tests, written results, and postings. Reteaching, however, can be more challenging. Gauging the misunderstandings without having a conversation with a student or watching the student work calls for creative interventions such as using real-time voice conversations, asking students to produce their notes or having them explain in writing the process they used. However this is determined, it is essential to view and use evaluation as an occasion to improve teaching and learning.

Students in ECOMP 7104 *Technology in Education Thesis Project* complete activities to help them gain an understanding of how to write their thesis projects. The assignments they post are informative and serve as an indicator of their knowledge. For example, one of the assignments involves each student's reading the literature review of an article that relates to his or her research topic. Students are asked to analyze the literature review and make a list of salient features based on criteria we share with them. We put together a larger list from all of the students' postings, which serves as a guideline for writing their own literature review. One student posted quickly and we could see immediately that he missed some significant features. When we posted the compiled list, this student responded enthusiastically by writing

Student Voice *Wow, did I ever miss the boat!!! I'm glad that my classmates could see things that I TOTALLY missed. It was useful to compare what I did with the comprehensive group list.*

FORMATIVE AND SUMMATIVE EVALUATION

Formative evaluation involves using results to adjust teaching and learning while these are in progress. With formative evaluations students are typically part of the process of modifying how and what they are learning (Garrison & Ehringhaus, 2009).

Summative evaluations are given periodically to find out what students know and do not know in a particular content or skill area. However, since summative tests are given infrequently, they are able to check knowledge only for a portion of the learning that has occurred. This type of testing is also often used to assess the overall performance of the student and instructor and sometimes the institution (Garrison & Ehringhaus, 2009).

Formative and summative evaluation can and should be incorporated in an online course. Too many times evaluation occurs as summative when the course is completed. Although the information gathered about instructional techniques can be useful for teaching the next group of students, it is even better if students and the instructor can make teaching and learning accommodations while the course is in progress.

**Step-by-Step Course-Building Activity #18:
Developing an Evaluation Process**

This is an activity to *develop an evaluation process* to gain information about student learning and the impact of instruction.

1. Read three articles about testing for learning and formative and summative evaluation.
2. Based on your reading, formulate an evaluation process that will help to inform you and your students about what learning has occurred in your online course.
3. Your process should include at least five elements, such as
   - a precourse inventory,
   - midstream evaluation,
   - culminating evaluation/project,
   - evaluation schedule,
   - student and instructor journaling, and
   - various types of evaluation tools.

You will want to keep this plan available to revise as you read through this book.

Readings

Garrison, C., & Ehringhaus, M. (2009). Formative and summative assessments in the classroom. Retrieved from http://www.nmsa.org/Publications/WebExclusive/Assessment/tabid/1120/Default.aspx

Kim, N., Smith, M., & Maeng, K. (2008). Assessment in online distance education: A comparison of three online programs at a university. *Online Journal of Distance Learning Administration, 11*(1) Retrieved from http://www.westga.edu/~distance/ojdla/spring111/kim111.html

Sims, R., Dobbs, G., & Hand, T. (2002). Enhancing quality in online learning: Scaffolding planning and design through proactive evaluation. *Distance Education, 23*(2), 135–148.

WAYS OF EVALUATING STUDENT LEARNING

As already stated, there are many ways to evaluate student learning. We discuss each method listed below in the context of online teaching and learning:

- self-evaluation
- peer evaluation
- authentic assessment
- continuous evaluation
- pre- and post-testing
- use of observational data (coding methods and informal observation)
- Weekly reflection (journals and postings)

It is beneficial to use a variety of these methods throughout a course. Some students will be more successful using some and not others. In addition, we have found that it is useful to vary evaluation procedures to keep students engaged and motivated.

Self-Evaluation

Having students evaluate their own work using rubrics or a scale that the instructor or students generate motivates students and helps develop greater ownership of the learning process. Furthermore, it can assist students in focusing closely on what the course requirements are and what students want to learn. An alternative to instructor-developed rubric or scale is having students build their own self-evaluation tools.

Self-evaluation complements the constructivist concept of placing more responsibility for learning on the student. The self-evaluations can be maintained in private online areas. Ironically we often use Blackboard's group pages as a private area in which we communicate with students, enabling the maintenance of a permanent record. We create a group that only the student and instructor can access. Students can then post self-evaluations. Keeping this record online makes it easier for students and the instructor to see cumulative growth.

Haavind, an advocate of online education, uses a student self-evaluation technique to help strengthen their Discussion Board postings. She refers to the midterm self-evaluation as a *midstream* evaluation to indicate that improvement is continuous.

Shown in Figure 6.1 are the questions that students are encouraged to ask themselves about their contributions to class discussion. In the self-evaluation assignment Haavind asks students to identify postings of their own that they consider good.

Haavind finds that when students engage in self-evaluation they reveal that they could not find good discussion postings of their own. Some students admit that they need to improve. Haavind remarked that this is a "powerful way of improving the quality of dialogue for the rest of the semester" (personal interview, 2009).

Peer Evaluation

We use peer evaluations in an informal and subtle way. Students are required to post all assignments on the Discussion Board, which means their work is visible to all classmates as well as the instructor. No formal peer evaluation occurs. However, students are clearly aware that their peers will be reading their assignments. Most students do not want to appear inadequate or foolish in front of classmates even if they have never met them face-to-face. We have found that by using public posting the quality of student work improves. This is due in part to the students' self-evaluation and also because of their concern about what their peers might think of their work. Driscoll (2007) also reports to have found this to be true.

Figure 6.1. Guidelines for Participation in Discussions for Midstream Self-Evaluation

Guide for High-Quality Participation
in Weekly Discussions

Participants in high-quality discussions take a stance on collaborative inquiry and are active contributors to a knowledge-building community.

- Support the development of the sense-making understanding of the group.
- Be willing to share ideas that may not be fully formed.
- Find ways of presenting differing points of view that support shared development of understanding and approach difference with curiosity.
- Strive to understand and celebrate different approaches.
- A knowledge-building community works to build discussions in which the posts contribute to and support the deepening of the conversation and moving the discussion and everyone's understanding forward.
- The posts help move the discussion beyond brainstorming or simply saying, "I agree," or "Great work," or "You're wrong." A discussion characterized by collaborative inquiry is successful when the result is learning that is greater than the sum of the individual first posts.

Examples: When you participate, do you . . . ?

- raise new questions
- share and explore confusion
- pose hypotheses or conjectures
- take risks by sharing incomplete ideas
- share new insights gleaned from the discussion
- respond to the questions of others
- build on the ideas of others
- move beyond brainstorming
- ask for clarification
- use questions to stimulate thinking
- appropriately challenge assumptions
- support or challenge assertions or explanations with additional data, evidence, or counterevidence
- support findings and conjectures of others with explanations

- support the learning of others
- make cogent summaries
- point out commonalities or differences
- note and compare differing approaches/answers/perspectives
- find connections between ideas
- consider and celebrate multiple approaches and explanations
- help to resolve differences (when appropriate)
- suggest a focus
- evidence genuine interest in understanding the ideas of others (vs. just determining whether they agree or disagree with you) and see this as a source of learning for themselves

(February 2010)

Adapted from Scoring Guide by Professor Sarah Haavind shaavind@lesley.edu and Professor Ricky Carter, rcarter@lesley.edu

One group of students was wary of sharing work publicly. We heard about this from an instructor who taught the group face-to-face. We almost had an uprising. However, with a little coaxing and some reassurance, students lost their initial trepidation and found that their classmates' support and feedback were valuable.

To ensure that students discuss issues relating directly to the assignment we require that students comment on and ask questions about classmates' assignments. This is an informal mode of peer evaluation. Classmates often ask challenging questions about the substance of the posting. We also promote supportive and constructive interaction by modeling it. As we have indicated before, we ask probing questions and comment in an encouraging manner.

In the ECOMP 7104 *Technology in Education Thesis Project* course we have students work with a partner to give each other feedback. In Figure 6.2 we present the assignment we give students as guidelines for collaborating.

In all instances when we ask students to comment on a classmate's assignment we ask them to give substantive feedback publicly on the Discussion Board to extend everyone's learning. In the thesis course, students often report that by reading a classmate's draft and giving feedback, they learn more about writing their own thesis, including new perspectives and approaches. Another example of learning by reading a peer's posting is in an ECOMP 5007 *21st Century Teaching: Supporting All Learners on the Ability Spectrum* assignment. Students write an article as a culminating project addressing different aspects of the course. (See Chapter 4, Figure 4.5.) In the discussion that follows, students compare and contrast their observations and reactions.

Figure 6.2. Assignment About Feedback to and from Peers

Assignment #6b Feedback

Purpose: To review a colleague's work, learn new content and gain experience of critiquing a work in progress. To improve thesis projects by giving and receiving feedback.

1. Each student will read the draft of at least one classmate's thesis and give positive and constructive critical feedback.
2. Classmates select the thesis they want to read on a first-come, first-served basis and indicate their selection by posting a message in the Teachers' Room. Reply to the message with a subject line titled "6b Thesis Feedback." Post your colleague's name in the subject line to indicate whose thesis you will read. Each person should give and receive feedback from at least one classmate.
3. After reading your colleague's thesis draft, post substantive and constructive feedback.

Due Date: This assignment may be posted early but is due no later than the date listed on the assignment chart.

Additional peer evaluation occurs with our practice of using student or peer moderators to lead discussions with classmates. The impact of this leadership role is typically positive. Peer feedback and exchanges lead to a deeper and varied understanding of the material. We discuss implementation of student moderating in Chapter 5.

Student moderating, working with a partner, and sharing assignments are not what is traditionally thought of as peer evaluation. However, we believe it is in this category, and it has the added feature of being an effective way to extend learning for everyone.

Haavind uses peer evaluations regularly. Students read a number of their classmates' assignments and evaluate them before they are submitted to the instructor. Haavind finds that when students help each other by reading others' work they can see their own strengths and weaknesses. This peer evaluation arrangement results in having assignments that are greatly improved. Others who spoke up at a conference presentation given by Thormann indicated that they were not successful with peer evaluation/grading by saying, "They just all give each other A's." If peer evaluation is used it should be structured to produce real and positive learning outcomes.

Whatever peer evaluation method is used, the instructor needs to prescribe and model how evaluations are conducted. Moreover, the activity should be monitored to ensure that students are engaging appropriately. An occasional supportive comment from the instructor about peer evaluations can help to boost performance and keep students on track.

Authentic Assessment

We have discussed authentic assignments and activities in Chapter 3. However, it is worth addressing this topic in relation to evaluation. As with course content, evaluations should reflect real-world experiences or content that is relevant to the students' circumstances. Authentic assessment actively engages students and demonstrates to the instructor that students not only understand the concepts but also can apply them in real-life scenarios (Mueller, 2006). In our courses, assignments serve as evaluations of our students. We attempt to maximize the usefulness of assignments by making them pertinent to the student's situation. For example, in ECOMP 5007 *21st Century Teaching: Supporting All Learners on the Ability Spectrum*, students select a disability category to investigate, and as part of their report they present a brief case study of a student in their school. Many select a specific disability category because they work with students in this category and the assignment allows them to learn more about working with these children. In another assignment, we have our students use adaptive software with a student. To make the assignment truly authentic, we ask our students to indicate whether there has been an observable change in their student as a result of using the adaptive software. We have a general rubric for each assignment. In addition, we list the components that are needed. Assignments are evaluated for thoroughness, for accuracy, and for addressing each component of the assignment. The rubric helps to gauge the quality of the work submitted.

Continuous Evaluation

Ideally, evaluation should occur continuously. By checking on student progress and on how effective the teaching assignments are, we ensure high-quality teaching and learning. We combine assignments with evaluation. Each assignment achieves a piece of the larger purpose of the course. Examples from ECOMP 6008 *The World Wide Web as an Educational Resource* clearly illustrate how each assignment can build on another. About 4 weeks of the course focus on the development and publication of a website. Students complete a variety of assignments, including

- reviewing other websites and building a list of positive and negative attributes—the former to emulate and the latter to avoid;
- learning about Web accessibility to incorporate in website development;
- developing a **storyboard**;
- becoming familiar with and selecting Web-development tools;
- developing a site;
- publishing the site and revising it; and
- sharing the site and giving feedback to classmates.

Each assignment provides background and is a step in building the site. Students get feedback and discuss each step so that when they publish the site it is a compilation of what was learned from previous assignments. Not all assignments fit so neatly into a progression. However, by getting feedback regularly, students are able to improve their submissions. One student summed it up nicely by writing,

Student Voice *I like that you send the emails and give us feedback about our assignments. It means a lot and it helps to know when I've turned in assignment that is the quality you are looking for, and if it's not, it would give me an idea of how to do it better next time.*

Continuous evaluation and feedback as well as touching base with each student are particularly useful for online students, since there are no other cues to let them know how they are performing. In a face-to-face course the instructor's and students' body language usually indicates how the class is progressing. Continuous evaluation and steady improvement serve as motivation for all and provide concrete indicators of how teaching and learning are proceeding.

Pre- and Post-testing

Pre- and post-testing is often thought of in connection with conducting research. However, it can also be used to great advantage to collect data about what was and was not learned during a specific period of time. It helps everyone know the impact of the instruction. In an online course pre- and post-testing takes on additional meaning

Step-by-Step Course-Building Activity #19:
Applying Assessment Strategies

The following is an activity to apply assessment strategies and concepts to online courses.

1. Using the following methods/concepts of evaluation, develop an instrument or protocol for each of them that you can use in a course you teach:
   a. Self-evaluation
   b. Peer evaluation
   c. Authentic assessment
   d. Continuous evaluation
2. Field test the evaluations with a small group of students or a colleague.
3. Revise the evaluations based on your field test.

since it can assist in ensuring that instruction remains focused. These tests can also contribute data points for deciding what specific content needs to be retaught or reviewed by the class or individual students.

Use of Observational Data

This category may seem odd in the context of online learning. However, observing students online affords a rich opportunity to get to know students and assess what they are learning. The most outstanding feature is that there is a record of much of what occurs in class. Activities, assignments, and discussions can all be posted and saved. If students use chat rooms or IM these exchanges can be archived. In addition, voice conversations can be recorded and retained with permission from the participants.

The question of how to use this information to evaluate a student's performance remains. When teaching online we get to know a student's *voice* by reading Discussion Board postings and assignments. This allows us to assess, informally, where the student started in understanding the topic and what progress the student is making. In addition, these informal observations help alert us if students use other people's work or are floundering.

Coding methods. A formal way to evaluate a student's participation and work is to develop rubrics or systems of coding postings in Assignments or on Discussion Boards. Rubrics provide students with an understanding of the expectations for participation in class discussions and activities. They typically include guidelines specifying descriptors of performance for the following skills:

- completeness of thoughts
- understanding of the material
- incorporation of readings

- contribution to advancing the discussion
- timeliness of responses
- quality of writing

At each level of participation students are given direction, but there is enough leeway to permit them to interpret what it takes to earn points. See Figure 6.5 for a sample rubric.

Coding systems can be built so that students identify the type of communication they post. The categories to consider are (a) social interaction, (b) question about content, (c) observational comments, and (d) extensions of ideas. Providing categories helps students achieve clarity about their intentions.

Coding systems that have been developed and used for conducting research about online discourse (Love & Isles, 2006; K. Murphy et al., 2005; Newman, Webb & Cochrane, 1995) can also be used to evaluate the types and quality of students' online interaction and to test out various pedagogical concepts. This can be different from using coding systems in the online classroom to evaluate student work. However, these systems and the available research can help to inform how to guide course discussion and performance evaluation.

Informal observations. Observational data can contribute to student performance evaluation and increase the effectiveness of the course. At least twice during a course, we hold a voice conference using Skype. This occurs one-to-one and with small groups of students about a specific course topic. For example, in ECOMP 7104 *Technology in Education Thesis Project*, students are required to read a section of their classmates' thesis and share comments and questions about their classmates' work, orally. This type of conference allows us to get to know students better and vice versa. It is encouraging to hear students make comments like

 Oh, what was said about Susan's paper applies to mine. I'll fix it in mine.

Having a chance to speak with the faculty and my classmates reassures me that I'm on the right track.

Even the difficult group conferences in which conversation is strained tell us that we have work to do to build community among the students and to provide more support.

As with the *voice* in written work, the Skype conferences assist us in ferreting out possible inconsistencies between students' spoken and written communications and addressing them with a student. In an article about plagiarism, Rothman (2010) described a case in which a ghostwriter was given user information by a distance learner to do all types of assignments including tests and online discussion. One way in which we check on our own students is that we require a one-on-one, face-to-face interaction with them in every course. This makes it harder for a ghostwriter to successfully accomplish the assignments of one of our students. In addition, it builds a personal connection with the students so they may feel less inclined to be dishonest.

As instructors, we read all postings. It is often easy to see that some students are struggling with writing or other aspects of the course. We can and do use observation of both verbal and written student communication to offer assistance to these students. At Lesley University we can provide additional support from the online Writing Center. Information about the center is included in the syllabus, but sometimes students need a gentle nudge to make use of this free service. We assess this need through informal observation of student writing and voice conferences and use the same means to encourage use of the center when appropriate.

Other observations result in identifying outstanding students. We cheer them on to go beyond the standard coursework. This was the case with Barbara Green, a student in ECOMP 5007 *21st Century Teaching: Supporting All Learners on the Ability Spectrum*, whose writing skills are excellent. With encouragement she has had two articles published. She wrote,

Student Voice *It's rather surreal holding the magazine and looking at the article I submitted to you a year ago as a final project! Please continue to encourage your students to submit their articles.*

Observing students' contributions and then giving feedback can make a difference.

Weekly Reflection

Students can gain insight into their own progress and needs and think more deeply about a topic if they are guided toward that goal through reflections. Through student reflections instructors can assess whether the course is on track and how to proceed. The instructors of the Fulcrum Institute at Tufts University ask students to respond to the following questions in a journal or through postings on a weekly basis:

1. What is the most important thing you've learned from this week's session?
2. What surprised you?
3. What more would you like to know (or explore)?

These questions help highlight important themes of the week and supply substance for class discussions. The online environment lends itself well to reflective writing, since space can be set up for students to post reflections that are easily accessible by the instructor and others. In addition, students are not bound by a short period of time to write their thoughts. Taking time to contemplate what to share is a valuable activity and often helps students generate ideas that are clearly thought through.

Evaluation may be implemented in many different ways and has several purposes. One key feature is that it can be used to inform instruction and learning. Another is to build students' self-awareness and ownership of their learning progress and process.

Step-by-Step Course-Building Activity #20: Informal Assessment

The following is an activity designed to integrate informal assessment into your course.

1. Consider the two evaluation methods.
   a. Use of observation
   b. Weekly reflection
2. Consider the following:
   a. For what purpose(s) would you use each one?
   b. Explain your rationale.
3. Based on your students and the course content, develop guidelines to be placed in your syllabus and assignments for implementation of these two formative evaluation methods.

EVALUATING VARIOUS STUDENT ACTIVITIES AND PRODUCTS

In the online setting, just as in face-to-face learning, students are often required to complete assignments as part of their learning and evaluation process. Instructors may choose, as we do, to have students complete varied activities and products throughout the course rather than administer tests or quizzes periodically. Students know from the beginning that all coursework contributes to their grade. Along with grading students' assignments, it is vital that (a) there are clear guidelines or rubrics and (b) students receive feedback that will help deepen understanding of the content/skills as well as help to inform work on the next assignment. We discuss how to assess different types of assignments.

Multimedia

It is acceptable to have students submit assignments using a wide variety of media tools such as PowerPoint, podcasts, and videos. Moreover, instructors will want students to use varied media; it motivates them because students enjoy viewing and producing media. It provides a natural way for them to share and teach each other and makes teaching and learning more appealing.

Media assignments need to be evaluated on at least two dimensions: content and use of the medium. Some instructors may object to the latter. However, using media appropriately and well for communication has become an essential skill.

Whatever media students use, expectations about the quality of the product should be high and it is essential to provide guidelines. It is also important for the instructor to model the best possible use of media. This means aligning the medium with the objectives of the lesson. A rubric for podcast evaluation is shown in Figure 6.5.

Discussion

We have shared use of rubrics to help evaluate how well students are contributing to discussions (Figure 6.1 and Course-Building Activity #19). In addition, since we require a minimum number of substantive interactions during discussions about assignments, we use a table to track interactions as well as other grading related events. In Chapter 5, Figure 5.7, we present a table for tracking points earned for assignments, questions, and comments posted as well as responses to them. We keep the table in our course folder and use it as we read Discussion Board postings and assignments and after Skype conferences are completed.

George Blakeslee, a colleague at Lesley University, also uses a chart to track assignments. However, he shares the chart with all the students (without grades or points). In this way students can easily check to see if Blakeslee received an assignment and if they completed all the required tasks. This provides clarity about logistics, reduces student anxiety, and allows other communication between student and instructor to focus on substantive issues (personal communication, 2009).

Some instructors have students evaluate each others' Discussion Board postings (Hou, Chang, & Sung, 2007; McLuckie & Topping, 2004). Moodle and Blackboard have a built-in feature that makes it easy for students to rate their classmates' postings. We have not asked students to formally assess each others' postings, since we think it may create undue tension and competitiveness. We do ask students to make comments and suggestions.

However, we have found that in order to promote a lively and meaningful discussion it is critical to require participation and have the discussion be part of the grade, with the number of points for participation specified for each assignment. Students need to know that they will get credit for their role in discussions and that the interaction must be substantive. Along with the rubrics we give directions about class participation in our course guidelines, as seen in Figure 6.3.

Since discussing course content with classmates is a vital part of the students' learning environment, we work with students to create a comfortable learning community. We discuss how we use different techniques to nurture this in Chapter 5. By

Figure 6.3. Guidelines for Discussion Participation

A portion of the points earned for each assignment or discussion will be allotted to participation. Participation is defined as writing and posting substantive comments, critiques or questions relating to classmates' submitted assignments. Positive comments are encouraged, but the content of the comments or questions should contain thoughtful content-related observations. Your comments do not have to be lengthy, but they should be meaningful. Avoid just responding with statements such as *"Good job"* or *"I agree."* Instead, make statements such as *"I agree because . . ."* or *"I disagree because . . ."* or *"Your comments reminded me of . . ."* You should also ask questions for clarification or as a gentle challenge.

You will receive credit for the quality of your overall participation during the course, including responsiveness to nonrequired postings, Teachers' Room activities, and Skype conferences.

grading participation we let students know that interaction with classmates is vital. A colleague at a conference commented that his faculty do not have successful online discussions even though they give a grade for participation. In our conversation it became clear that the problem was giving only an overall grade rather than a grade for participation in each assignment/activity.

Case Study

We may ask a student to conduct a case study or decide what action to take based on a case study we offer. In both situations, there are no right or wrong answers to evaluate. When we assign either type of case study, we clearly indicate the components that should be included. In addition, students are expected to meet the general rubric found in Figure 6.4. The rubric is in the syllabus, since it applies to all assignments. This gives students an idea of the expectations for all assignments.

Group/Teamwork

As mentioned previously, we limit the amount of group work that we require to one or two assignments per course. The time and energy needed for collaboration can be a drain on learning and understanding course content. However, we do require some group or team activities, since the learning potential and thinking process that are necessary for collaboration are beneficial. Partner or teamwork allows students to use learning skills in their own way and to focus on portions of the assignment that may let them excel. For example, if a student has leadership skills he or she can take that role in a discussion or the development of a project. Or if a student is a good writer, he or she can offer to edit a written project. Alternatively if a student has strengths in media use, the student can offer to be the technician. There are many ways to allow students to use their strengths.

Figure 6.4. Assignment Rubric

A-	The student demonstrates all required competencies at expected graduate-level standards. Most of the products and performances are at an exemplary level and are submitted or demonstrated on time. Class participation is at an acceptable level.
B+	The student demonstrates required competencies at a satisfactory level. Most products and performances are submitted or demonstrated on time. Class participation is at an acceptable level.
B	The student demonstrates required competencies at a satisfactory level, but all expectations are not met. Most products and performances are submitted or demonstrated on time. Class participation is at an acceptable level.
B-	The student demonstrates required competencies at a marginally adequate level. The student is often late in submitting products or demonstrating competencies. Class participation is at an acceptable level.
C	The student demonstrates required competencies at a deficient level. The student is consistently late in submitting products or demonstrating competencies. Class participation is not at an acceptable level.

> **Step-by-Step Course-Building Activity #21: Evaluating Discussions**
>
> This is an activity to determine how to evaluate discussion as an element of an online course.
>
> 1. Decide how much emphasis you want to place on participation in discussion and what type of discussion you want students to have (Discussion Board, IM, voice, etc.).
> 2. Based on the samples in Figure 6.3 and Course-Building Activity #19, as well as others you might find, develop rubric/guidelines for discussions in your own course.
> 3. Share the rubric and your grading system with colleagues both online and not online and revise based on their feedback.
> 4. Use the system you devised with your students and revise again based on student feedback.

Since we teach graduate students, we usually have students work out how they will distribute the workload. However, we make sure some fraction of the assignment is reserved for clearly labeled individual work. By doing this we ensure that some portion of each person's contribution can be identified. This is also useful for grading.

Group work is not always problem free, regardless of the setting. Online, if there is a problem, students need to feel comfortable enough with the instructor to voice their concerns. Group projects are assigned midway through the course so students have had time to interact with and get to know us and their classmates. Every so often a student will email us to share his or her concern that a partner or group member is not participating fully. We counsel the student about how to handle the situation. Sometimes we intervene and check in with the student who has been reported to be problematic. If the student who has a problem does not respond to the satisfaction of the student who has raised the complaint (and we feel it is legitimate), we tell the latter to proceed with the project independently. We assess group projects as a whole but may give extra credit to portions that are written by individual students.

TECHNOLOGY CHOICES FOR EVALUATION

There are many online technology tools that can be used to evaluate student work. It is important to select these tools so that they match the purpose. Enthusiasm for technology can lead to using technology for its own sake. It is important to avoid this pitfall. The best case is when the tool transparently enhances learning. This means that the student spends little time learning how to use the tool and the tool is suited to the activity and content. The focus should be on the content of the course rather than the tools used. This may be a somewhat different issue for the instructor. Investigating which technology tool works the best and making it operational can take time.

We learn to use new tools and try them regularly. However, typically we try one or maybe two new tools per semester so that we do not become overwhelmed. Garrett (2006) also takes the approach of incorporating new technology gradually. In changing the course only slightly, if the new technology does not work as well as we would like, it affects only a few assignments. We evaluate how well the integration of a new technology works based on students' performance on the task and feedback on evaluations. After the course is completed we send out surveys asking students, anonymously, what they thought about the use of the new tool.

In discussing the use of technology tools for assessment we are referring to both traditional and less traditional ways to assess students' mastery of material. This includes automated Web-based evaluation tools; tools that are embedded in the LMS; as well as podcasts, voice communication (Skype), multimedia, and social-networking tools. The traditional method consists of using tests. The less traditional way includes student submission of projects using various media or participation in synchronous or asynchronous discussions.

Automated Assessment Tools

Tests and quizzes can be developed using a variety of online tools. Below we have listed a few current quiz sites that are available free or for a small fee. All of the following allow the instructor to have a free trial:

- QuizRevolution: This site provides tools for adding customized text, graphics, video, html, and feedback to your course. Quizzes can be embedded on a website, and you can also generate reports on scores. http://www.mystudiyo.com/
- Quia: This site has tools, templates, games, and quizzes created by others; individual storage space; and online grade books that can be customized. http://www.quia.com/web
- Quizstar: It enables the instructor to create, administer, and automatically grade quizzes online. It also allows the instructor to attach multimedia files, provides report tools, reuse, and share quizzes. http://quizstar.4teachers.org/
- Quizcenter: Use this site to create, administer, and grade quizzes online. It has password protection and quizzes can be edited or stored. http://school.discoveryeducation.com/quizcenter/quizcenter.html

Many other stand-alone Web-based testing sites are currently available and others will be developed. It is also worth noting that most LMSs offer built-in testing capabilities. Blackboard, for example, offers the instructor many test formats including either/or, essay, fill-in-the-blank, multiple-choice, jumbled sentences, matching, short answer and many more. Tests that have right and wrong answers can be graded automatically, allowing the scores to be placed in the grading center as soon as the test is completed. Other features include the possibility of randomizing questions to discourage students from sharing answers. If tests are part of an instructor's evaluation scheme there are many ways to take advantage of what the Internet and LMSs have to offer.

We must admit that we use tests infrequently, since most closed-book tests assess memorization. In addition, they do not lend themselves well to a constructivist approach. However, there are some conditions for which multiple-choice or fill-in-the-blank testing can be useful such as in getting a quick picture of whether students learned a particularly important piece of information required for continued development.

Other Tools

The online environment is well suited for using various technologies to support evaluation. Some of these technologies are Internet voice-based communication (Skype, Dimdim, Elluminate, etc.), podcasts, PowerPoint, Facebook, Twitter, and blogging. As new technologies develop, it is worthwhile to think about how they might be used and to experiment with them. Students who are taking online courses have basic technology skills. They are also generally comfortable using additional computer-related technologies. The instructor, of course, also needs to be comfortable with the technology. As we stated earlier, we recommend adding new technologies slowly, since the instructor needs to be more fluent with the technologies and to consider how they augment learning. Technology should not be used for its own sake; it needs to add substantially to instruction, an admonition we repeat often to ourselves.

Voice communication. We started using Skype in one course and then gradually expanded its use once we found that it added a valuable feature to our pedagogical tool kit. Skype (http://skype.org) is an easy-to-use free online voice conferencing tool. Initially we listed our Skype name on the syllabus and offered it as a way for students to communicate with us. We did this over a 3-semester period. Only one student responded.

Clearly, there had to be a better way to use this tool. An opportunity arose when we taught ECOMP 7104 *Technology in Education Thesis Project*. We began experimenting with requiring Skype by giving simple directions to students about installation and the requisite equipment. We decided to move some of the written comments about classmates' thesis development to small-group voice conferences in real-time using Skype.

Skype can be an excellent tool in gathering formative data. It gives students who have strong expressive language skills the opportunity to shine. During discussions it is possible to determine what misconceptions students have, their interests, and their overall commitment to the coursework. A rubric for conference participation can be developed and shared with students so that they know their conferencing responsibilities.

Voice conferences can also be conducted using good old-fashioned telephone technology. Haavind described how she uses individual telephone meetings with students to follow up on midstream self-evaluations about discussion participation, described earlier in this chapter. She reported that she is effusively supportive and asks if students have questions. Voice communication can be a way to connect with students and answer questions about evaluation issues. This can be particularly useful in formative evaluation.

Podcasts and vodcasts. According to Hew (2009), podcasts are primarily used by instructors to share information rather than for students to complete assignments. As instructors and students become more comfortable with this technology and their ability to communicate with it, we will see greater variety of use. Podcasts, auditory presentations that can be transmitted using the computer, and video podcasts, or vodcasts, are useful vehicles through which students may share their knowledge. Podcasts and vodcasts also allow students who have strong expressive language abilities to use them. If you ask students to share their vodcasts or podcasts with each other, auditory learners can also benefit.

Evaluating students' podcasts or vodcasts should be based primarily on the presentation of the content and completion of all components of the assignment. Some points or part of the grading should go to the skill with which students organize material and present it. It is important to model a good podcast presentation before you ask students to do one. In addition, guidelines or rubrics for developing a good podcast should be shared with students. Figure 6.5 shows a sample rubric we adapted from the RubiStar website (Rubistar.4teachers.org).

Presentation applications (PowerPoint, Prezi, etc.). Asking students to use a presentation application to share research or ideas is an alternative way for them to demonstrate their knowledge. We describe such an assignment using PowerPoint in Chapter 4 in Template 12. Students can be evaluated for these presentations almost in the same way that they are in a face-to-face classroom. However, there are some elements of this assignment that differ. The focus should be on the content of the PowerPoint file rather than on the student's presentation style. In addition, as Schafer (2006) indicates, the student can be asked to lead a discussion and be graded on facilitation skills. Students can also ask classmates to evaluate each other's participation in the discussion. Schafer models both PowerPoint presentations and discussion facilitation.

Web 2.0 tools (Facebook, Twitter, blogs, wiki, etc.). We discuss ways to use some of these Web 2.0 tools in other chapters in this book. Evaluating work that uses these tools is especially challenging because new Web 2.0 tools appear regularly and the *older* ones become less popular. The evaluation should not be dependent on the tool configuration but rather on how well the content is synthesized and analyzed when the tool is used. We recommend including the latest tools, since many students will already be familiar with them and appreciate being able to use an instrument with which they are already comfortable. To learn about the various tools mentioned and

Figure 6.5. Podcast Rubric

Category	4	3	2	1
Content	Covers topic in-depth with details and examples. Subject knowledge is excellent.	Includes essential knowledge about the topic. Subject knowledge appears to be good.	Includes essential information about the topic but there are 1–2 factual errors.	Content is minimal *or* there are several factual errors.
Presentation	Interesting, well rehearsed with smooth delivery that holds audience attention.	Relatively interesting, rehearsed with a fairly smooth delivery that usually holds audience attention.	Delivery not smooth, but able to hold audience attention most of the time.	Delivery not smooth and audience attention lost.
Sources	Source information collected for all graphics, facts, and quotes. All documented in correct works-cited format.	Source information collected for all graphics, facts, and quotes. Most documented in correct works-cited format.	Source information collected for graphics, facts, and quotes, but not documented in correct works-cited format.	Very little information was collected and documented in correct works-cited format.
Permissions	All permissions to use graphics "borrowed" from web pages or scanned from books have been requested, received, printed, and saved for future reference.	All permissions to use graphics "borrowed" from web pages or scanned from books have been requested and received.	Most permissions to use graphics "borrowed" from web pages or scanned from books have been requested and received.	Permissions were not requested for several graphics "borrowed" from web pages or scanned from books.
Aesthetics	Makes excellent use of font, color, graphics, sound, video effects, etc., to make the presentation high quality.	Makes good use of font, color, graphics, sound, video effects, etc., to make the presentation high quality.	Makes use of font, color, graphics, sound, video effects, etc., but occasionally these detract from the presentation content.	Use of font, color, graphics, sound, video effects, etc., but these often detract from the presentation content.
Mechanics	No misspellings or grammatical errors on captions or in speech.	One or two misspellings, mechanical errors, or both on captions or in speech.	Three misspellings, grammatical errors, or both on captions or in speech.	More than three errors in spelling or grammar on captions or in speech.
Workload (if group project)	The workload is divided and shared equally by all team members.	The workload is divided and shared fairly by all team members, though workloads may vary from person to person.	The workload was divided, but one person in the group is viewed as not doing his or her fair share of the work.	The workload was not divided *or* several people in the group are viewed as not doing their fair share of the work.

new ones as they appear, the instructor can do a Google search for sites and tutorials that explain how to use these social networks. The following are some of the most widely used Web 2.0 tools today:

- *Facebook.* In Facebook, class groups can be set up to discuss selected topics. LMSs such as Blackboard or Moodle have Discussion Boards for student conversation. However, as Haverback (2009) points out, one can expect "at least one member [in every class] to be on Facebook almost all the time because of its diverse and entertaining functionality" (p. 34). Facebook ensures rapid responses to questions and topics. This is also another good way to vary student assignments. Use of any social networking sites requires a review by the instructor to protect students' privacy.

- *Twitter.* According to Steve Dembo of Discovery Education in Silver Spring, Maryland, Twitter can be used "to conduct research or collaborate with classmates and their peers across the country" (quoted in Manzo, 2009). This is exactly what was done by Lisa Hogan, technology integrator in Topsham, Maine, who was a student in a Lesley course taught by Dan Lake. She found Twitter useful in learning the ideas of an innovative technology user. A description of how Lisa used Twitter is in Chapter 2, Figure 2.12. Although each communication is limited to 140 characters, Twitter can be used to direct students to articles about a topic being studied or to inspire them to do more research based on a tweet from an expert, classmate, or instructor.

- *Blogs.* Students can be asked to use a blog, that is, online journaling, as a way to exercise communication skills, share their thoughts and research, and have discussions with others. The literature (Kajder & Bull, 2003; Lamb & Johnson, 2006; Richardson, 2010) contains other ideas about how to have students use blogs. Blogs can be helpful in assessing students' abilities in many different areas. The key component of assessing learning through a student-created blog is to make sure that students are aware of how they are being evaluated. Whether choosing rubrics or a list of expectations, the focus should be on the content. A small fraction of the grade can include how well the blog is implemented.

- *Wiki.* Using a wiki is a great way to have students collaborate on developing a product or refining ideas. We have colleagues who ask their students to use a class wiki as a bulletin board. This does not take advantage of a wiki's capability for written material posted on it to be edited by anyone. In a class wiki, editing is limited to those enrolled in the course. Students can be asked to post their assignments on the wiki and then have classmates edit the work in order to improve it. It can also be used to help students who are working in teams to collaborate on the same document. João Freitas of Universidade Nova de Lisboa, Portugal, uses wikis in some of his hybrid classes and finds that students take pride in co-authorship of a class document (personal communication, 2010). On most wikis every edit is recorded with the name of the editor. Assessing this collaborative work can be tricky, since it is essential to encourage meaningful participation. Thus it may be useful to develop a system in which the edits may be counted and divided into categories such as grammar, elaboration, clarification, and content correction. Students might earn credit for each one of these categories. But, of course, the categories and expectations need to be clear.

With any of the Web 2.0 technologies it is vital to weigh the use of a tool with the time it may take students and the instructor to learn how to use it well and how appropriate it is to the learning task.

GRADING CRITERIA

There are many similarities between online and face-to-face grading. Participation is measured in both but instructors who grade in-class participation typically do not define what it means or use rubrics (Willard, 2010). In online courses it is easy to track class participation, since all Discussion Board participation is available and chats, voice conversations, and IMs can be recorded and saved.

Feedback on work is more important for students online, since there are no visual and few unplanned interpersonal cues about how well students are performing. Students need corrective feedback on each assignment because the instructor cannot walk around the room, patting students on the back saying, "Good job," or giving informal pointers for improvement.

Step-by-Step Course-Building Activity #22: Integrating Technology Tools

This activity provides a method for introducing and integrating technology tools, including those for student evaluation.

1. Review the section "Technology Choices for Evaluation."
2. Select one tool that you are familiar with and one that is new to you. Develop an evaluation activity using each of the tools you selected.
3. Create a rubric for the technology used for each of the selected tools and for the content. To avoid reinvention use RubiStar (http://rubistar.4teachers.org/) or another rubric-creating site. (Give credit to the rubric author.)
4. Field-test the evaluations with colleagues or students. Revise the evaluations based on the feedback.

Note: You may use this method to incorporate new technologies for evaluation in courses. You may want to use a new technology in courses and include it as a *gift* to students by offering all students full credit, since you are testing the appropriateness of the technology. After the course is completed, ask students for feedback. This will help you evaluate and refine your use of specific technology.

Typically there are more assignments to be graded online because assignments and activities make up the fabric of the course. There is no way for students to know they are on the right track unless they receive a grade or feedback. We do both of these; we also ask classmates to interact with each other for almost every assignment and activity. In this way students are receiving reactions to their work on a regular basis.

Another area to address is how to share grades and comments. Prior to obtaining Blackboard, we tried various schemes to maintain students' grades. We used a table or spreadsheet and periodically emailed each student his or her grade. We also tried emailing grades along with feedback on each assignment. Much to our relief when we started using Blackboard, we found the Grade Center. For each assignment we enter the name and potential numerical value. As students complete their assignment we submit their grade. The Grade Center holds the record of grades and the totals. A screen shot of a Blackboard Grade Center for one of our courses is shown in Figure 6.6.

When students log on to the Grade Center they are able to see only their own grades. In addition to numerical grades we send students comments and ask questions. We discussed the details of this in Chapter 5, including feedback templates and posting comments on the Discussion Board. For some assignments, we turn tracking on and edit or make comments directly on the student's work and send the work back to the student as an attachment.

The overarching goal in giving students grades and sending feedback is to assist them in understanding the content and how to improve their work.

Figure 6.6. Blackboard Grade Center

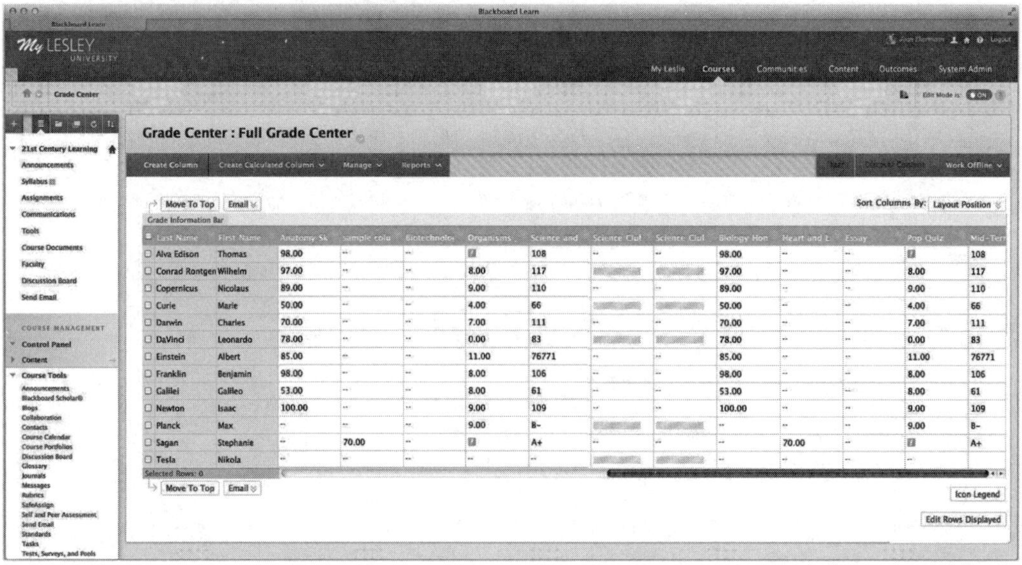

HIGH-STAKES TESTING

Currently many states in the United States require K–12 students to take tests at multiple grade levels to confirm that they have learned the prescribed content. This is considered high-stakes testing because graduation depends on it. This requirement may create a dilemma for instructors. It is well known that many instructors in face-to-face classrooms spend large portions of their instructional time teaching to the test. Thus all instructors must think about how they will support their students through this challenge. This support may involve teaching online students test-taking skills and certainly covering the content that the test addresses.

While high-stakes testing is currently enforced only in the K–12 setting there is a national movement to impose the same type of testing structure in the postsecondary environment. There are individuals who want to ensure that students who earn an undergraduate or graduate degree in a specific content area have a basic knowledge of the content. At whatever level, online instructors need to think about the impact that high-stakes testing can have on the courses they develop and on their students.

SUMMARY

In this chapter we have reviewed evaluation in all its various forms and uses. As we have also indicated, technology has made evaluation and tracking of progress online efficient and less difficult.

While evaluation is seen by some as an onerous and difficult task, it is an essential educational element. Students need feedback to know that they are learning. Evaluation needs to align with the content and the skills being taught and to match learning styles and the educational needs of students. It can direct the instructor to tailor activities, presentation of material, pace, and modes of delivery.

CHAPTER 7

Teaching Diverse Students Online

All student populations are becoming increasingly diverse and demands are being made on instructors to meet the needs of these learners. There is a great deal of information about teaching diverse learners in face-to-face settings. Although many of the same methods can be used online, face-to-face strategies may need to be adapted for online. In this chapter we discuss how to support a diverse student population online. The diversities include students with special needs, English language learners (ELL), gifted and talented (G&T) students, and students who are at-risk. In addition we describe the process of determining if a student, kindergarten through postsecondary, is eligible for special needs services and modifications and what those might be. We also include techniques to evaluate students with diverse learning needs. We share ideas about how to implement Universal Design for Learning (UDL), which can help all students by allowing them to use their learning strengths.

STUDENTS WITH SPECIAL NEEDS

Federal laws have been passed to protect and support students with special needs and individuals with disabilities. The laws relating to students are implemented locally and thus vary in how they are fulfilled. As a result it is necessary to check with each institution about the process of identifying and working with students with special needs. The process can be complicated and support for online students with special needs may be less than transparent. In this chapter, we describe ways to work with designated support staff, focusing on functional challenges and using appropriate online accommodations.

School Identification and IEP at K–12 Level

In the K–12 environment students are identified by an instructor, parent/guardian, or another educator in the setting. There is a state- and federally mandated process to follow once the student has been referred. The parent/guardian must be part of a team and give approval for an evaluation to take place. The student is evaluated and if identified as eligible for services, based on the evaluation, an **Individualized Education Plan (IEP)** is developed. The IEP contains goals and objectives resulting in a learning plan that usually includes accommodations. The IEP is confidential. However, professionals as well as the parent/guardian are entitled to see the IEP in order to understand how the learning environment is to be modified. Ideally, someone, usually a special education instructor, communicates with the classroom instructor about a student's eligibility for special services and the IEP. Together they work out appropriate modifications, some of which we share later in this chapter.

Student Self-Identification at Postsecondary Level

At the postsecondary level students need to self-identify. This is accomplished by contacting Disability Services at the institution of higher education and working with staff to verify eligibility for services either by presenting previous eligibility or through new testing. For students with physical disabilities, self-identification is fairly straightforward. Students with learning disabilities, ADHD, or emotional disabilities are often reluctant to become involved with special services. Many have had special education services for some time and are not eager to be singled out again. Some of them also feel that they want to make it on their own in their new adult setting. Regardless of what an individual higher education student decides to do, services should be available once eligibility is verified.

If a student chooses to receive services, it is the student's responsibility to inform each instructor. The student may then discuss his or her needs with the instructor or have the instructor work with disability services staff. If a student tells the instructor that modifications are needed, the instructor must check with the disability services office to verify eligibility.

Work with Designated Support Persons

Regardless of the level of the student, it is important to work with the office that provides support for the student and the designated support people. At the K–12 level, if a student has been identified as having special needs, staff should approach the instructor, face-to-face or online. If a student at the K–12 level seems to have a learning problem in an online course, it is a good idea to contact the special education department of the school or district that is responsible for the student. If the student has not been tested previously and shows signs of having a learning problem, it is important for the instructor to refer the student for an evaluation. If three or more of the indicators listed below are observed in the K–12 student, he or she might need to be referred; for postsecondary students, the instructor may suggest that the student seek assistance:

a. organizational problems
b. poor-quality written work as compared with peers
c. difficulty following directions
d. consistently late submission of work

    e. in voice interactions, difficulty expressing ideas or understanding other's ideas

    f. repetitive questions, that is, not processing or paying attention, unable to retain information, and related issues

At the postsecondary level the instructor does not refer students. At this level we are required to indicate the availability of services and the contact person. Figure 7.1 presents the standard information required by our university for every syllabus.

Institutions may organize their services differently. However, any institution of higher education receiving federal funds must offer support to individuals with disabilities.

We have worked with a few students who have physical disabilities and others with learning disabilities. In the former case, a student in our course was deaf. A university disability services staff member, with permission from the student, contacted us to make sure that all course material was accessible to the student. We also checked with the student to determine her needs. An online text-driven course is typically ideal for a student who is deaf. However, as noted previously, we always incorporate voice conferences in our course using Skype. Ultimately, an interpreter was hired to be with this student during our Skype conferences.

With another student, we noted that her writing skills were not strong and encouraged her to seek additional support in order to develop her writing. She told us that when she was in public school she was identified as having a learning disability, but

Figure 7.1. Disability Policy

Lesley University Policy Statement on Disabilities

Lesley University is committed to ensuring the full participation of all students in its programs. Accordingly, if a student has a documented disability and, as a result, needs some accommodation to complete course requirements, he or she should inform the instructor at the beginning of the course.

Americans with Disabilities Act

Students with documented special learning needs who may require accommodations for the course should speak with the appropriate disability person and the instructor within the first 2 weeks of class in order that appropriate and timely accommodations may be planned and necessary arrangements made.

    For students with learning disabilities and attention disorders, contact: Maureen Riley, Director, LD/ADD Academic Support Services, 23 Mellen Street, 5th floor

Phone: 617-349-8464

Fax: 617-349-8558

Email: mriley@lesley.edu

    For students with physical and psychiatric disabilities, contact: Laura Patey, Coordinator of Disability Services, 23 Mellen, 3rd floor

Voice: 617-349-8194

TTY: 617-349-8554

Fax: 617-349-8558

Email: lpatey@lesley.edu

that she had not contacted the university's disability services or the Writing Skills Center. She explained that she had successfully completed her other postsecondary degrees without support. This student worked hard and was able to complete the course, but she might have earned a higher grade had she received additional assistance or other accommodations for her special learning needs.

Technology Support for Accessibility

In addition to working with designated school personnel and the student, it is worthwhile to contact departments or individuals who provide technology support. Technology specialists may know about or have access to technologies that can assist online students who have a disability. If the technology specialists are not immediately aware of what is available they may be able to do research to find appropriate technology tools and also secure funds to purchase equipment. This works best as a collaborative process among all those involved but we mention contacting the instructional technology department so that this is not overlooked.

In some cases specialized software or hardware might need to be purchased for the student to provide access to the course material and to complete assignments. There are many free resources that can be found at the Apple special education site (http://www.apple.com/education/special-education/) or Microsoft's Windows accessibility site (http://www.microsoft.com/enable/default.aspx). But sometimes free tools are not sufficient, so it is useful to investigate all possible tools. There are many websites that provide information about the use of technology and students with special needs. Two of these are AbleData (http://www.abledata.com/) and the Center for Assistive Technology and Environmental Access (http://www.catea.gatech.edu/), which provide information about assistive technology.

Accessibility is also an issue that should be brought to the attention of those in charge of the institution's LMS. The presentation should be readable for those who have visual impairments. Most browsers allow the user to change the font size, but typically font color and backgrounds are controlled by an LMS administrator. The LMS should also be readable by text-to-speech screen readers. There are other features that need to be examined and monitored to ensure that the course is accessible to all students.

Websites that are used for class work also need to be accessible. A lot has been written about Web accessibility (Bray, Pugalee, Flowers & Algozzine, 2007; Brophy & Craven, 2007; Erickson, Trerise, VanLooy, & Bruyère, 2009; Freire, Russo, & Fortes, 2008; Kelly et al., 2009; Paulson, 2009). As the web has become a more central feature in our everyday lives, Web accessibility has become a more prominent issue. It is clearly unacceptable if students are unable to access a website that is the focus of an assignment. Some websites have a graphic indicating that they are **Bobby Approved** or complying with W3C accessibility recommendations. This means that the site meets certain basic accessibility features such as embedded text that describes each graphic representation. There are also accessibility tools that can provide assistance in evaluating a website's accessibility; the following are two examples:

    a. WAVE (Web Accessibility Versatile Evaluator),
       http://wave.webaim.org/index.jsp; and
    b. Site Valet: Quality, Accessibility, Standards Compliance,
       http://valet.htmlhelp.com/

We ask students in ECOMP 5007 *21st Century Teaching: Supporting All Learners on the Ability Spectrum* and ECOMP 6008 *World Wide Web as an Educational Resource* to determine how accessible their own school site is. About 90% of our students find that the sites fail the accessibility tests. Some of the problems are relatively minor and can be fixed, but the major barrier to doing this is developing administrator and webmaster awareness and then making Web accessibility a priority. Making accessibility a priority is often difficult to accomplish, given the myriad responsibilities associated with maintaining a website.

An assigned site needs to be accessible. A comparable situation in a face-to-face class would be to give the students a book in which students could read only some of the pages, while other books would be glued shut. The central concept is to determine what students' functional challenge is and if the lack of access to a website presents barriers to learning.

Functional Challenges

When trying to determine how to make accommodations for a student with special needs in an online course, the instructor may be told the category of disability the student has, such as visually impaired, learning disabled, or hearing impaired. This categorization might give the instructor a broad idea of what a student needs. However, it is more helpful to know what the student's functional challenges are, that is, what the student is and is not able to do in the online learning context. An IEP at the K–12 level should help establish both strengths and functional challenges. But whatever the student's level, one of the best ways to ascertain a student's abilities and functional challenges is to speak with the specialists who are familiar with the student and, most important, with the student directly. The instructor can then incorporate modifications that have worked well in the past and those that are acceptable to the student. Focusing on the course assignments and tasks and how the student might accomplish them successfully is the most direct way to accommodate a student's needs.

When we worked with students with special needs in a junior high school resource room at the beginning of every year, we interviewed students about their learning strengths and weaknesses. We found that our students were able to tell us as much as, and often more than, the testing results. The interview also served to build rapport and helped students take ownership of and have a commitment to their own learning.

A similar type of interview can be conducted using a voice conferencing system such as Skype. This is something we do with graduate students in our ECOMP 5007

21st Century Teaching: Supporting All Learners on the Ability Spectrum course to model the interviewing process.

The directions and questions, found in Figure 7.2, are posted before the conference so our students can determine how they learn best.

After we added this one-to-one interaction to our courses, we asked students whether they thought the discussion was effective. Thormann sent a survey after the course was completed and grades were submitted. Eighty-five percent of the 34 students responded. Students were generally positive. Of those who responded, 60% indicated that the one-to-one meetings were beneficial and 32% said that they

Figure 7.2. Individual Interview Assignment

Weeks 1 and 2: #4 Learning Strengths and Challenges

Purpose of Assignment: To think about your own learning strengths and challenges and to have a model for interacting with students.

Once you have acquired your Skype connection, you will sign up to "meet" with your instructor individually for 15 to 30 minutes. We will discuss your learning strengths and challenges, including the best way for you to learn concepts and skills in this course.

The discussion may serve as a model for you in working with your own students. Although you have records and reports from previous classes, it is often the case that students know a lot about their own learning process. Speaking with students is a good way for them to build awareness about their own learning styles and to assist them in defining their own learning goals. It also makes clear that they have a role to play in shaping their own learning. It also assists you as the instructor to provide appropriate teaching strategies.

The following are questions that I will ask you when we meet via Skype. Please also feel free to speak with me about other issues related to this course and your own learning process.

1. What subjects do you like the best? Do you know why?
2. How do you learn best?
3. What are your strongest and weakest learning modes (i.e., auditory, visual, hands-on)?
4. What can I, as your instructor, do to assist you to learn?

I will take notes during our meeting and send them to you to refer to and revise as you gain further insights into your own learning process.

I have posted times that I will be available for our individual discussions in the Teachers' Room. Please sign up for a time by replying to the posting titled "Individual Learning Discussion Schedule."

I look forward to meeting with each of you.

                                                                                            Joan

---

were somewhat helpful. We asked for comments about these one-to-one meetings; the following are two responses reflective of those students who found the meetings helpful:

 It was beneficial to 'meet' the professor via Skype. It made me feel more connected in the class and I felt more comfortable asking questions.

 It helped to realize that the professor was interested in the individual and unique needs of the students.

We used one-to-one meetings in courses with different subjects and the reaction to the meetings and the discussion topic varied. In one course the response was unanimously positive. In the other it was mixed. Based on this feedback from the survey we modified how we conducted these meetings.

Appropriate Accommodation Online

Support for developing accommodations for face-to-face students is fairly well established through K–12 special education departments and postsecondary disability services offices. But in the online environment this support may be less evident. Some departments and offices provide active support. Nevertheless, it is valuable for the instructor to have ideas about how to make accommodations for a student with special needs with or without assistance from staff at the responsible institution.

Assessment accommodations. It is important to allow students to complete their assignments and assessments in ways that complement their strengths and circumvent their functional challenges. This might mean that in doing an assignment or taking a test students are given more time or submit it in a different medium than prescribed. The latter may be extra effort for the instructor but the student's success is at stake.

If the student has a physical challenge it is necessary to determine the degree and type. If the student is visually impaired does this mean that the individual is blind or that small print is difficult to read? If a student has cerebral palsy is the individual able to use the keyboard or a voice recognition device? If a student has a learning disability it is vital to find out if the student is a visual, auditory, or kinesthetic learner. For a student with ADHD, autism, or emotional challenges, establishing what supports or modifications will help the student learn is essential. The strengths as well as the challenges should be understood so that appropriate supports can be made available.

Assistive technology (AT). There are numerous technological resources that can be put into place. We describe a few of them here. For students who are blind, text-to-speech software is invaluable. There is free software, but typically students are able to get assistance to purchase a more adaptable system such as JAWS (http://

www.freedomscientific.com/default.asp). If a student has some vision but needs text enlarged, there are free systems built into the computer operating systems offered by Apple, Microsoft, and other organizations. There are also commercial systems such as ZoomText (http://www.aisquared.com/) or WinZoom (http://getwinzoom.com/).

For individuals who do not have the manual dexterity to use the keyboard, there is speech-to-text software that will produce words on the screen as a person speaks. DragonNaturallySpeaking (http://www.nuance.com/naturallyspeaking/) is one of the better-known products. There are also adaptive keyboards such as Intellikeys, offered by Intellitools (http://www.intellitools.com/). Or, instead of submitting a written assignment, a student might complete the work by producing a voice document using free software such as Audacity (http://audacity.sourceforge.net).

A student with a learning disability, ADHD, or an emotional challenge may find using some of these technology tools more compatible with their learning modality than the traditional approach of writing a paper or taking a written test would be. The instructor's primary concern is to know that a student has mastered the necessary content and gained skills in the process. Thus students should be given the opportunity to complete their assignments and assessments in nontraditional ways. Whether or not students have a documented special need, all individuals should be supported and encouraged to complete assignments in a way that best meets their learning style. This idea leads to the concept of Universal Design for Learning (UDL).

Step-by-Step Course-Building Activity #23:
Assistive Technology Services and Devices

This activity is designed to determine the services and assistive technology (AT) devices that are available for students with special needs.

1. Contact the special education department or disability services office of your educational institution and find out what services they provide for students with special needs online, how the services are offered, and what an instructor's role is in the process. Get copies of all documents pertaining to the services provided and instructor responsibilities.
2. Find out what type of technology support is provided for online students with special needs and the process used. Technology Services may have to be contacted to find out what is available. Consider a student you either have or anticipate working with and develop a list of technology supports you could provide for that student.
3. Learn something about assistive technology (AT) by engaging with the technology and the special education or disabilities services personnel. In addition, check out the Apple and Microsoft disability websites.
4. Make a list of technology supports that you might use now and in the future and match them with all the functional challenges you can think of.

UNIVERSAL DESIGN FOR LEARNING (UDL)

Universal Design for Learning (UDL) was first developed and promoted in the educational context by Center for Applied Special Technology (CAST) (http://cast.org). UDL was derived from architectural universal design (UD), which employs inclusive features such as curb cuts designed to assist people in wheelchairs. But curb cuts are also useful to others, including parents with baby strollers, the elderly, cyclists, or those with wheeled suitcases or shopping carts. Edyburn (2010) points out that although UDL has its roots in architectural design, UD should be viewed differently from UDL. UD is relatively static, while UDL is a dynamic process. Edyburn writes that with UDL "much more attention must be devoted to the complex interactions between learning objectives, learner characteristics, performance support strategies, technology, and outcome" (p. 36).

Rose and Meyer (2002) of CAST describe research about how individuals learn and have developed UDL principles based on this research. CAST disseminates these principles to guide instructors and maintains that using instructional methods that address the needs of students with disabilities benefits all students. Edyburn (2010) concurs that conceptually this makes sense, but also suggests that research that directly addresses the overall benefits of UDL needs to be conducted. In many cases CAST recommends using technology to enhance learning experiences for all students. Making UDL accommodations for diverse learning styles has implications for teaching online.

Incorporating UDL practices into online courses from the beginning is advisable. This allows the instructor to be ready for almost any learner with special needs as well as to expand learning opportunities for all students. Students can discover their learning style by using tools such as VARK, a guide to learning styles (Visual, Auditory, Read/Write, Kinesthetic, http://www.vark-learn.com/english/index.asp). In addition, as indicated above, the instructor can interview students to help them think about how they learn best. Students can then use tools and methods available to enhance their learning and output. A course may also be retrofitted to incorporate UDL principles. As with all our suggestions, we recommend that when adding new elements or experimenting with something unfamiliar, it is best to integrate the new material slowly. We did just that with UDL. Figure 7.3 presents an announcement posted some years ago for our students as we started to retrofit ECOMP 5007 *21st Century Teaching: Supporting All Learners on the Ability Spectrum* with UDL.

Interestingly, one student in the course proceeded to submit almost all her assignments in an alternative format. Shortly after this announcement was posted this student wrote,

> **Student Voice** *I decided since we now can present our case study in different formats (thanks, UDL) I created a photo story about my school.*

This student is a technology coach and saw the UDL alternative as an opportunity to experiment with new software that she was asked to evaluate for her schools.

Although she did not have a disability, she seized the opportunity, since she admitted that she was not fond of writing.

Another student, who works as a librarian and technology specialist, embraced UDL. We asked her why. She responded,

Student Voice *I decided to do a video for a couple of reasons. One is that I believe that it's important for students to be excited about a project. This excitement will help propel the learning process and will be evident in the final product. Creating a slideshow and video is more fun for me than writing a traditional paper. I can be creative and use my own artistic license to portray my interpretation of the subject. . . . Secondly, I knew that I wanted to incorporate some video clips from the video that I was assigned to watch. I know from experience a slide show/video format can make for an authentic presentation experience, or as you said bring it to life. When I am in an audience, I always appreciate this type of presentation. Plus, it usually stays with me a little longer than just text.*

We learned a lot about having students submit assignments in alternative formats. Although we indicated that all assignment components needed to be addressed, the first student did not always do this. We are now more specific about what alternative assignments need to contain and spell out the components for both standard and nonstandard assignments. In addition, we found that it was more difficult for us to evaluate assignments that were submitted orally. We are accustomed to reading written assignments.

Being more specific about the content has helped but it will still take us time to adjust to digesting and commenting on material we have to listen to rather than read. For example, it is not possible to embed a feedback comment quickly in the oral media environment. We learned about our own learning styles and are expanding

---

Figure 7.3. UDL Options

Dear 5007ers,

In an effort to incorporate Universal Design for Learning (UDL) principles in our course, I invite you to use alternative presentation formats and tools when submitting your assignments. (We will focus more on UDL later in this course but this message is an effort to implement some UDL before we study it.) Instead of submitting a standard written report, you may submit a PowerPoint slideshow with voiceover, an audio file, video, graphic displays, a website, or other means of completing your assignment.

You may use any tool to which you have access (and know how to use). In addition, the ability to view or read your submission must be free and available to everyone in the class.

If you choose an alternate approach to complete your assignment *all* components of each assignment must be addressed. You may want to select a different approach based on your preferred learning style or for the fun of it. If you have any questions about this, please pose them in the Teachers' Room or email me.

Joan

---

our methods of giving feedback, including using auditory feedback with tools such as Audacity and Skype conferencing.

The general guidelines for UDL in face-to-face instruction can be used online with modifications. Barbara Gibson and other colleagues at Lesley University have described engaging all students by (a) getting, (b) focusing, and (c) maintaining students' attention.

Some of the ways to get students' attention is by using storytelling or asking them to describe their own experiences to introduce a topic. We do this in a number of assignments (see Chapter 2, Figure 2.4, and Chapter 3, Figure 3.3). Using humor to get students' attention can be helpful. However, in the online environment this can sometimes backfire because the humorist cannot see the visual or hear the auditory reaction and vice versa. To help our students understand that we are teasing, we use emoticons after a joke (-: or include words in parentheses: (grin), (ha, ha). We advise that sarcasm *never* be used, since it is more often hurtful than helpful. Another way to get attention is to begin an assignment with a question or problem that needs to be addressed. Also, when launching an assignment or activity, the instructor should convey genuine enthusiasm to serve as an inspiration.

To help students stay focused, illustrations, including pictures, graphics, or diagrams, are useful. Students can also be encouraged to develop their own images as memory aids. A librarian/technology specialist in one of our classes mentioned this. **Graphic organizers** may be used to help students visualize concepts and ideas as well as keep track of the steps necessary to complete an activity. If appropriate to the activity or assignment, the instructor can provide exemplars or demonstrations. Hands-on activities that actively engage students work well for most students. We use these, knowing that learning by doing helps solidify understanding (see Chapter 3, Figure 3.9, and Chapter 4, Figures 4.1 and 4.7).

Maintaining interest throughout an assignment, activity, or even the semester is vital. Having students converse with each other about the content keeps them involved. In some of the assignments students can work in small groups with guidelines about the structure and expectation of group work. As noted previously, we require involvement in most assignments. We keep students accountable with rubrics and also include discussion participation in the grading structure. To ensure that discussions hold the students' interest, we use open-ended questions, promote critical thinking, and have students moderate discussions. In discussions the instructor can keep the conversation pertinent by modeling interaction and coaching students about how they might respond to their classmates. One student emailed us at the end of our course, writing

Student Voice *One more thing, kudos to you for participating in the Discussion Board. No teacher has ever done that before. They have always provided great personal feedback on assignments through email, but not on the Discussion Board. This definitely added a new and improved dimension.*

The preceding suggestions are all good practices to capture, focus, and maintain students' attention. These and additional actions for implementing UDL were shared by Barbara Gibson and James Keefe at a workshop funded by a Teachers for a Competitive Tomorrow U.S. Department of Education grant. The workshop materials were adapted from work done by CAST and the Access Center at Colorado State University. We have added the context of online to these UDL ideas.

Respect for Diversity

To implement UDL online, a climate in which diversity is respected needs to be created. This can be accomplished during introductions and throughout the course by the instructor consciously asking about and showing interest in students as individuals. Encouraging students to share ideas that reflect their unique qualities also creates acceptance and appreciation of individual differences.

Evaluation for All Students

We have written about students' completing assignments in alternative or nontraditional ways. This allows them to exercise different communication skills to share what they have learned. It is particularly important for individuals with special needs to have this opportunity and it also enhances every student's communication repertoire. Students can do oral presentations using podcasts or **Jing**, complete projects individually or in groups, assemble e-portfolios, write journals, offer video and share a performance. We consider assignments to be the core of our evaluation process, so by varying the means for assignment completion, we broaden the way in which students can be evaluated.

Adaptive Devices

To facilitate students' access to and fulfillment of assignments it is beneficial to make available an array of assistive or adaptive devices. For individuals who are eligible for services, obtaining devices may be achieved through a special education department or disability services office. Assistive technology (AT) may include adaptive keyboards, screen magnifiers, screen readers, alternative input devices, among other items. Some of these devices or software, such as text-to-speech screen readers or screen magnification, can be offered to all students free or at minimal cost. The key issue is that students are able to access and complete all online assignments. Thus if a video is part of an assignment, captioning is essential for those who have a hearing impairment or for those who learn best by reading text. In addition, documents and textbooks should be available in digital format for text-reading devices. All written material we present is available digitally so that students can access it. We sometimes recommend textbooks, but they are not required. If we do feel the need for a text we find one that is available on the university **ebrary** or **NetLibrary**. For those who have an eligible **print disability** there are regulations to consult from the National Instructional Materials Accessibility Standard (NIMAS) and associated organizations.

Auditory Input

In addition to voice conferences to address an auditory learning style, we have started to present many of our directions orally and in print. We use free recording software such as Audacity (http://audacity.sourceforge.net) and offer the directions for both auditory and visual learners. We post the audio files along with the text. It does take extra time but we often catch typos, missing words, and confusing directions when we read aloud. Hearing the instructor's voice and inflection contributes to students' understanding of the assignment and helps to build a relationship with the instructor.

Group Work

Another technique in using UDL in an online setting is to provide opportunities for partner work, study groups, and cooperative learning. Group work can allow students to use their strongest or preferred learning mode. We want to ensure that students are able to perform to their potential and so we use some partnering or group work in our courses. A challenge in evaluation of these activities is determining the level of contribution of each person in a group exercise. We address this by asking for students to "cc" us on some of their communications, and also by having each student do some part of the assignment independently. We also encourage peer mentors because students learn a great deal from teaching each other. Working with others addresses the issue of students feeling isolated in the online learning process.

Clear Expectations

All students benefit from understanding what they are expected to do in a course as well as how they will be evaluated. In our courses each assignment begins with a purpose, so that students know what we hope they will gain from completing it. We have general rubrics and guidelines, as well as required components, for each assignment.

Segmented Assignments

As appropriate, we give frequent assignments that are brief, that is, rarely more than 1 week in duration. Assignments are related to each other, but short assignments enable students to focus on one issue at a time. They eventually put it all together. As one student in ECOMP 5007 *21st Century Teaching: Supporting All Learners on the Ability Spectrum* wrote in her impressions about the course,

It gave me an opportunity to rethink and add appreciably to my perceptions about inclusion and students with . . . learning challenges. . . . What I particularly liked was the fact that several of the assignments provided me with opportunities for meaningful discussions with the special education teachers in my school and with others, both within and outside of my district, a positive experience.

Assignments are broken down into component parts. We number the parts and place them sequentially. If students complete one element at a time, they find assignments less formidable. It works for us when we are faced with a large task such as writing this book. (-: An additional and related concept is to divide large or long-term projects into smaller chunks.

This complements another online teaching guideline. That is, students should be given portions of a large assignment to prevent their waiting until the last minute to complete it. In our ECOMP 7104 *Technology in Education Thesis Project*, which involves writing a very long document, we have students submit a weekly assignment. This results in many students making comments like these:

This has really been a very stress-free way to write our papers.

I must say that you have made this very painless and easy to work on. Working on each chunk at a time and then blending it all together was a wonderful way to finish. I had worked so hard and so much on my thesis that until I broke it apart, I was unable to see where things might change.

There is a skill to segmenting assignments. For us it is part of a tool kit that we have honed over the years. For those who need assistance we suggest you look at Lodewyk, Winne, and Jamieson-Noel (2009); Mager (1962); and Siegel and Siegel (1975).

Specific Feedback

Doing large projects a segment at a time with clear and specific feedback on each segment lets students know that they are being supported and gives them direction about how to improve. This is good for all students but especially useful for students with special needs. They need to know what they are doing well as well as the mistakes they are making. In some courses we post public feedback indicating what is positive about an assignment. When other students read the comments, they learn some good skills.

We also encourage students to ask questions. This relieves students' anxieties and helps us in our role as mentor/coach to assist and clarify. We suggest that students ask some of their questions in the Teachers' Room forum but we also make it clear that they can email us or reach us on Skype.

Time as an Accommodation

In online courses instructors are urged to let students know what the assignments are in advance. This helps all students schedule their work. If students see that some of the assignments will take a long time they can plan accordingly. This is also a way for students to get the *big picture* and anticipate what they need to do. We post all assignments for those who need to have all the assignments available. But we post each assignment in a separate folder so that those who do not want to look ahead or who would be overwhelmed are able to focus on 1 week at a time.

Due dates are essential in helping students know how to pace themselves. We allow time extensions for students who contact us and ask for them. We make it clear that we prefer that students meet the due date. However, our goal is to have students learn successfully, so it is better to give time extensions to students rather than have them turn in inferior work.

Plan Ahead for Accommodations for Students with Special Needs

Many issues need to be addressed in order to provide appropriate accommodations for online students with special needs. We have discussed them above. The accommodations are similar to those that are made in face-to-face classrooms, but online, most need to be instituted in advance. For example, providing oral as well as written directions is different in a face-to-face classroom. In the face-to-face classroom an instructor can pick up written material that has been distributed, and read it if necessary. That flexibility is harder to achieve in an online environment.

UDL affirms the concept that all students are able to benefit by having accommodations available to match their learning style. Other groups of learners who also benefit from modifications in teaching strategies are English language learners (ELL), gifted and talented students, and at-risk students. We present strategies for online courses that can help these students succeed.

Step-by-Step Course-Building Activity #24: Incorporating UDL

This activity helps in the development of a plan to *incorporate UDL ideas* in online courses so as to support students with diverse needs.

1. Consider some of the UDL ideas presented here.
2. Make a list of the UDL ideas that you already use in your teaching and compare them with the ideas in this chapter. Develop plans to use them in your online course.
3. Select at least two UDL concepts that are new to you to use in a future course. Develop a plan to incorporate them in your online course.
4. Share your ideas with colleagues who work with students with diverse needs, both special education professionals and nonspecialists. Revise your plans based on their feedback.

ELL (ENGLISH LANGUAGE LEARNERS)
OR ESOL (ENGLISH FOR SPEAKERS OF A SECOND LANGUAGE)

The online environment supports learning by individuals in distant places. By definition this means that more students from diverse backgrounds, language groups, and cultures are taking online courses. Even if we focus only on learners who attend educational institutions in the United States, many students are from other cultures and may also be ELL students. As stated by Smith, Teemant, and Pinnegar (2004), a key to being successful as a student in the United States is the ability to understand the patterns in the English-speaking culture. Learning is social and language is a social tool (Smith et al., 2004).

When we first started teaching online we had ELL students from other cultures enroll in our courses. We recall a young woman from Italy and a man from Korea. We did not have previous experience or expertise in teaching ELL students and ended up being successful with the Italian student but woefully unsuccessful with the Korean student. Although the Italian student's English was not perfectly grammatical, she was able to do the assignments and understood what was expected. We did not penalize her for her lack of English language skills but focused on the ideas she shared. We also spoke with her a few times to clarify some misconceptions. In addition, the Italian student was conversant with a Western style of constructivist and developmental teaching that we use in our courses.

We struggled immensely to help the Korean student succeed but in the end unfortunately failed. We followed the same tactic of ignoring his lack of English language skills with the Korean student as with the Italian student. However, he did not understand what he needed to do to complete the assignments. We emailed back and forth giving him specific feedback as to where he had a problem and how he could improve his work. In the end he and we were unable to communicate well enough to help him succeed. For one of his assignments he copied the posting of a classmate who wrote a case study and simply changed the Western names to Korean names. We explained to him that what he did was plagiarism and that we did not accept plagiarized work. But even this communication did not seem to be well understood. In the end we had to fail this ELL student, which did not please us, and surely did not please the student.

We learned from these experiences. Adding an assignment that requires vocal contact opens up channels of communication. This turned out to be valuable for all students. We contacted the university to suggest that online students be required to pass the **Test of English as a Foreign Language** (**TOEFL**) to ensure some basic level of English language competence. With the Korean student we guessed that one of the problems was that our teaching/learning system may have been out of synch with his. The solution we arrived at, as we have mentioned before, is to be explicit about the teaching method we are using. We think this is a start but attention needs to be paid to both the language and cultural challenge, which will only increase as more teaching and learning go online.

There are specific techniques that are recommended by educators who specialize in working with ELL students. We adapt some of them to the online environment. Helping ELL students to be comfortable with the use of the language helps students in their acculturation and learning. By using varied assessment and learning tools ELLs may become more at ease with English. Also, by viewing classmates' assignments that use English as well as graphics helps deepen the ELL students' language and content understanding.

Some in the ELL field (Abedi, 2006; Spinelli, 2008; Xu & Drame, 2008) recommend using sociocultural assessments with ELL students to accommodate for their differences. Sociocultural educational roots can be found in Vygotsky's writings (1986). The sociocultural approach "emphasizes the interdependence of social and individual processes in the co-construction of knowledge" (John-Steiner & Mahn, n.d.). The primary focus is to assess students according to their cultural background, for example, asking students to reflect on an aspect of the topic that is being taught based on their home country experience. The instructor needs to understand the impact of culture and first language on the way an ELL student (or any student) understands the world, and take this into consideration when teaching and evaluating the student.

In teaching ELL students it is important to use content the bilingual student can identify with and finds relevant. Useful assignments and assessments are based on "improving rather than merely auditing student performances (Wiggins, 1998)" (Smith et al., 2004, p. 40). Instructors need to be able to judge the quality of student performances on authentic tasks. Smith et al. also indicate that in the assessment process it is useful to ask questions that are "central to learning content, language, and general cognitive skills. Assessment should focus more on what is to be learned than on the assessment. . . . Assessment item structure is important, going from simple to complex, concrete to abstract, familiar to unfamiliar and situated to general" (p. 45).

It is also valuable to have students set goals against which measurement can occur. This can empower ELLs to take hold of their own learning process. Developing exemplars for students to compare their work against guides them to improve the quality of their work.

The instructor should also be sensitive about how well the student has integrated the language, culture, and content. With this in mind the instructor should separate language learning from content learning in the evaluation process by making accommodations in grading. To evaluate ELL students, Smith et al. (2004) also suggest that the instructor "gather samples of evidence from assisted, unassisted, individual, and group performances in familiar and unfamiliar contexts on several occasions"(p. 44). This process helps the instructor to assess in which context the student performs best and under what circumstances the student may need extra practice or support. This echoes UDL and the approach of building a community of learners to help support the ELL learner in the midst of first-language learners (New Zealand Ministry of Education, n.d.). Building a community of learners is discussed in Chapter 5.

Whenever possible, instructors can use pictures, vodcasts, diagrams, and non-verbal prompts. Students can also use those alternative means to complete their assignments. Assignments and assessment that can be read by text-to-speech systems can support the ELL student in understanding the evaluation. These students can use speech-to-text software to dictate their thoughts and edit their ideas. There are also language translation programs that might be productively used.

Relationships with the instructor and classmates are essential ingredients in a sociocultural assessment model. The instructor's role can be more supportive by providing encouragement and specific feedback so that students understand how they can improve and reach their goals (Smith et al., 2004). Another strategy is to help ELLs understand when and how to ask for assistance. We make a special effort to reach out to students, by asking them if they need assistance from the beginning of the course. We also, at times, suggest that they seek the support of the writing center and classmates.

Prabhu (2009) reports on a number of software companies that offer programs to help ELL students increase their skills in reading and math. Some of the software provides directions or instruction in the student's native language. While use of these programs appears to be helpful to comprehension, taking high-stakes tests can still be a major stumbling block for ELLs whether face-to-face or online. Prabhu (2009) also writes, "The American Federation of Teachers (AFT) has urged the NAEP [National Assessment of Educational Progress—a national exam] to alter the way it tests ELLs so that educators will get more accurate data to inform their instruction and close the achievement gap" (p. 9).

As with UDL, the ideas presented here are appropriate for all students. However, for the ELL and the student with special needs the difference between success and failure almost always revolves around the instructor's awareness of the student's needs and providing accommodations.

GIFTED AND TALENTED

Gifted and talented students are enrolling in online courses because they provide them with the opportunity to study subjects that their school does not offer (either advanced or a specialized curriculum), to be able to move more quickly through course content and to fit into their schedules (Siegle, 2004). The successful K–12 online gifted and talented learner is typically self-motivated and driven to learn.

A study was conducted by Nicholas and Ng (2009) about gifted students who participated in a 6-month online follow-up to a summer science experience. The researchers found that one of the reasons some of the students had limited success was that they lacked motivation because they were not evaluated for online participation. Further, the authors suggest, using a constructivist approach (discussed in Chapter 2) and having students create a public artifact to be seen and critiqued by an audience larger than the teacher provides a greater incentive for students. The authors also claim that since adolescent students use social networking tools on a regular basis, these tools should be incorporated into learning projects.

In our courses we always find students who are advanced or expert. Since we teach at the university level we do not label these individuals as gifted. However, we do differentiate how we engage with these students. We find these students in a variety of ways. In some courses we ask students to complete a **SurveyMonkey** questionnaire to help us get to know them and also to find out what they know about the topics we are teaching. This helps us to modify course content. Also, we read students' postings, especially their introductions, carefully and observe what they share and how they express themselves.

Once we determine that some of the students in the course have advanced knowledge or skills, we offer or require these students to complete alternative assignments. At first we send out a message to all the advanced students and then we negotiate with each of them. For example, in ECOMP 6008 *The World Wide Web as an Educational Resource* students are required to create and publish an educational website. Through the introduction and survey, we find that a portion of our students are already accomplished website developers. In some cases they are even webmasters for their school system. Once we determine their level of expertise we provide them with a list of alternative assignments, one of which is open-ended. We work with these experienced students individually to develop an assignment similar to the scope of the original one. Every alternate assignment has its own grading criteria. The purpose of differentiating assignments is to help students grow and gain new skills and knowledge based on their ability and expertise. We are especially interested in motivating and *pushing* all students, including gifted students, to make significant gains.

AT-RISK STUDENTS

It seems reasonable that online courses would be beneficial for students who are having difficulty in a traditional school setting, that is, students who are considered to be *at-risk*. The term at-risk has many roots and does not refer only to the ability to master academic knowledge. Those students who are at risk may be so for a variety of reasons, such as behavioral problems, poverty, or phobias (Durden, 2009). Rushton (2002) described a virtual school program that was instituted for at-risk students in San Antonio, Texas. PLATO's Web Learning Network curriculum delivered online was used as the instructional intervention. After analyzing one semester of student participation in the virtual school program, Rushton indicates that for at-risk students face-to-face contact is needed to supplement the online learning. Parent or guardian involvement increased success. Schomburg and Rippeth (2009) reported that having students participate in online courses in computer labs with adult support resolved the problem of a high failure rate that at-risk students experienced when taking online courses at home. The Schomburg and Rippeth (2009) research indicates that "when asked to make comments or suggestions for the lab, the two most common responses from students were that they liked working at their own pace and that their success was due to the help they received from the adults (e.g., the virtual lab aide, a state testing tutor, the guidance counselor, and the in-school suspension monitor) in the school" (p. 35). What is important with at-risk students is that they need a great deal of support, whether learning online or face-to-face.

From these two reports and others (Durden, 2009; Watson & Gemin, 2008) it is clear that virtual learning can help students who are at risk. This means not only helping them by providing time management skills, tutoring, and encouragement but also guiding them in test-taking and assessment. Many of the techniques suggested in this chapter can also be used with students who are at risk.

SUMMARY

All learning environments, face-to-face and online, are welcoming greater numbers of diverse students. In the online setting accommodations for these diverse learners need to be applied thoughtfully. Many face-to-face techniques that are currently in use must be modified for the online setting. Most important, instructors and administrators need to be mindful of the presence of diversity in online education in order to ensure the success of all their students.

CHAPTER 8

Dealing with Dilemmas

We write about teaching online from a positive perspective. But as with every human endeavor, there are challenges. In our book we explore the difficulties we have experienced, such as resistance to online learning; instructor, student, and administrative readiness; and access. Ethical issues and instructor preparation have also not been easy to contend with. We have struggled with many of these and found most to be resolvable. Challenges, new and old, will continue to intrude on our teaching and development of high-quality courses. We persist in searching for answers through our own practice, through feedback from students and colleagues, and by adopting ideas that others offer. In this chapter we look at dilemmas and challenges as an explicit focus.

RESISTANCE TO ONLINE LEARNING

There has been a fair amount of skepticism over the years about online learning, expressed by all stakeholders—educators, students, parents, and the community. Oettinger and Marks (1968) present a two-page chart listing those who have input into what happens in schools. As pointed out by these authors, it is difficult to introduce and sustain change in the educational system, since so many constituents, including legislators, businesspeople, the school committee, teachers' union, and religious organizations, have a voice. Although Oettinger and Marks were generally referring to K–12 schools, a similar set of constraints exists in higher education.

Some parents, particularly those who are not **digital natives**, have difficulty understanding how their child could learn in an online course. This is not the way they learned. They have many questions. How will students be supervised? Who will make sure that students are keeping up with their work? Don't students spend enough time on the computer already? Is it unhealthy for students to do more work on the computer? Will students be isolated?

Educators have similar concerns. They wonder: How will instructors learn to teach online? Who will develop the courses? What type of support will instructors and students need/receive? Can all content areas be taught online? How will the amount of time spent teaching online be compensated? Will it take more time than face-to-face teaching? Who owns online courses?

Students may be reluctant to take courses online because they wonder if the course will be equivalent in value to their face-to-face courses. Will it be hard to learn online?

Can they get help when they need it? How will they be able to prove it is their own work? How can they use what they find on the Web?

Administrators are concerned about issues such as teacher training, support, access, and finances. Who will pay for what—for example, students' computers? How does the institution establish and maintain online learning operations? What is the best way to mediate differences in opinion and attitude among constituents about online learning?

All these questions and concerns are valid. Many need to be resolved by the stakeholders themselves, working together. Since rapid growth of online learning continues to be reported and predicted (Flynn, 2010; Murray, 2006; Van Dusen, 2009), such decisions need urgent attention. One hopeful sign is that instructors, who ten years ago told us that it was impossible to teach their courses online, are now embracing this format, some with enthusiasm and others with resignation. Regardless of their attitude toward online teaching, many instructors are now recognizing that they must and can teach online and their students can and do learn.

SKILLS READINESS

In order for students and instructors to excel, they need to be prepared to learn and teach online. There are numerous online learning-readiness-survey sites, open to any student, and are offered by colleges, universities, and school districts that provide online learning. At the university level, Marygrove College and Lesley University have readiness surveys, and at the K–12 level, Anaheim Union High School and the Internet Academy, located in the state of Washington, have them. It is instructive to examine some of these sites to get a sense of what is expected. The sites explore issues from technology capabilities to learning styles to motivation. There are also teacher standards online. The first two listed below are for K–12, the third is for higher education:

- iNACOL (International Association for K–12 Online Learning), http://www.inacol.org/research/nationalstandards/NACOL Standards Quality Online Teaching.pdf
- NEA (National Education Association), http://www.nea.org/assets/docs/onlineteachguide.pdf
- Principles of Effective Online Teaching: Best Practices in Distance Education, Faculty Focus Special Report, Magna Publications, 2010. http://www.eou.edu/bb/workshops/10 Principles of Effective Online Teaching.pdf

In higher education, many books have been written about teaching online (Conceiçáo, 2007; Meyers, 2002; Palloff & Pratt, 1999; Rovai, Ponton, & Baker, 2008), and there are countless articles with recommendations about how to teach online (Armstrong, 2007; Barczyk, Buckenmeyer, & Feldman, 2010; Desai, Hart, & Richards, 2008; Li & Irby, 2008; Menchaca & Bekele, 2008; Ryan, Carlton, & Ali, 2004). The consensus is that if participants are not prepared, the online venture is likely to fail. At all levels, students and instructors must be aware of the skills and attitudes that are needed and make sure that those are in place before starting an online course.

Instructors need the same skills that students require. In addition, instructors must be able to teach (Menchaca & Bekele, 2008) and be knowledgeable in their area of expertise—no different from face-to-face teaching—and have the flexibility to work in an online format. Working in an online format means being able to meet the online teaching standards/recommendations. Given the rapid rate at which online learning is growing, it is imperative that instructors and students get ready sooner rather than later.

ACCESS AND AVAILABILITY

Barriers to access and availability can be translated into lack of resources such as funding to support infrastructure and personnel. We discuss access for special needs, ESL, gifted, and at-risk students in Chapter 7. However, there are important access issues for those who are not in these categories. Two examples include access to school support services and to the technology itself.

School Support Services

Students' success in online courses may depend on school services support. At the Henry Hudson Regional School District in New Jersey, Caruso (2008) explains, the district requires a recommendation from a teacher and a counselor to enroll in a course. In addition, all students must spend one period a day in a computer lab

---

Step-by-Step Course-Building Activity #25: Student Readiness Skills

This activity helps clarify student readiness skills.

1. Review two online readiness surveys.
2. Write student expectations to place in the course guidelines or syllabus that are based on some of the readiness surveys you reviewed.
3. Determine what school services are available to online students in a school you work in or know.
4. Write a description of the services students can use to place in course guidelines, or syllabus, with a rationale.

doing coursework with facilitators. Durden (2009) maintains that having on-site guidance counselors to aid students is preferable to using counselors employed by virtual schools. Our opinion is, whatever the configuration, both students and instructors need to know how to access support.

Students can also benefit from peer experiences such as belonging to a club or team. Enrichment lectures, arts events and other activities can enhance student learning. Institutions offering online education should consider ancillary activities that enable socializing with peers and create affiliation with the institution.

Technology for All Students

To participate in online learning all students must have appropriate technology. Although Li and Irby (2008) discuss the advantages of online learning for those who were formerly denied access to higher education due to financial constraints, it is still the case that students or their schools need funding to pay for courses, purchase and maintain equipment, and have high-speed access (Jones, 2008; Stuart, 2008). It now is insufficient to have access to the Internet only in a public place such as a school or library. Public places often have blocked sites to protect users from hackers and other intrusions.

The challenge is to find ways to make the Internet broadly available to students and instructors. Some efforts have been made by organizations that distribute older computers to schools or Nicholas Negroponte's One Laptop per Child (OLPC) initiative, originally focused solely on the developing world (http://en.wikipedia.org/wiki/One_Laptop_per_Child), is now available in the United States. Such programs are helpful but not adequate for all those who need access in developed nations.

STUDENT INTEGRITY ISSUES

Plagiarism and cheating are problems that plague all educational institutions. They are considered particularly problematic in the online format. We present ways to avoid or prevent plagiarism, such as using software tools, shaping assignments, and configuring test protocols. We also share ideas about how to detect and address plagiarism if it does occur.

Plagiarism-Prevention Techniques

Early in our online teaching, we determined that a fraction of our students plagiarized. We discovered this by comparing the language used in conversations on the Discussion Board postings and language used in formal posted assignments. We simply took questionable phrases of about 10 to 14 words and Googled them. When we did this, we often found that whole paragraphs of text had been copied from the web. Once we established that a student had copied material we started an email conversation with the student about the copied text. We emailed so that we had a written record of the exchange. We also *locked down* the assignments so that the student was not able to remove the offending work. We were and are very careful in our initial communications to give the student the benefit of the doubt and do not use the term plagiarism. However, if the student denies the inappropriate copying and we have definitive proof, our language about the behavior becomes stricter. Figure 8.1 presents the last email that we sent to a student who plagiarized on two assignments.

Although there may be only a few plagiarism cases, they are unpleasant and take a lot of time. It is better to adopt techniques to prevent plagiarism such as spelling out the university's academic-integrity rules in the course guidelines.

Since the early days when we used Google to check for plagiarism, we have added measures that seem to eliminate plagiarism, at least as far as we can tell. One of these measures relates to the type of assignments students do for our courses, specifically, assignments that create the need for unique responses and focus on synthesis, analysis, and evaluation. For longer tasks, we build in checkpoints as a deterrent. When we ask students to read articles and write reports we often ask them to find their own articles. The reports must include information and resources using APA format. Although students are introduced to APA early in the program, to solidify their understanding of this style, the first academic assignment asks students to review and implement APA rules. Figure 8.2 shows an APA assignment that we require in almost every course.

By having students write this paper about APA, we are making sure that they actively engage with the resources we provide. We have a feedback template that emphasizes proper citations and that is designed to avoid plagiarism and give credit to others.

It is fortunate if the host university has a subscription to Turnitin (turnitin.com), another tool to thwart plagiarism. Turnitin is an online plagiarizing defense product. We turn this tool around: Instead of submitting work to check for plagiarism, we require students to post their own work on Turnitin to make sure they are not copying

Figure 8.1. Final Email to a Student Who Plagiarized

Dear Bettie,

I have consulted with the Technology in Education Division Director regarding the paper you submitted for your last assignment. I know that one section of the paper is not your writing. Other portions of this paper may be yours. As a result of your action and lack of respect for others' work you will not receive credit for this assignment. An incident such as this in another course will have dire consequences.

If you use other authors' work without giving appropriate credit again in another class, you will face official scrutiny based on the university's academic integrity policy. Copying someone else's work without giving credit is considered plagiarism and in the academic community it has serious consequences. As stated in the syllabus, the policy is found at http://www.lesley.edu/policies/catalog/integrity.html. You should reread this very carefully before enrolling in other courses.

I have cc'd this message to various Lesley administrators so that they will be fully aware of what has occurred and will notify any future instructors of yours.

You have done some reasonable work for this course and I am sad that I had to take the action your paper forced me to take.

Joan

Figure 8.2. APA Assignment

Week 1: Assignment #2 APA

Individual Project

Purpose of Assignment: To learn and review elements of appropriate APA use and citation of material from other sources.

1. Select one of the following sites (a or b). At minimum read the sections indicated.
   a. American Psychological Association (APA) format posted by Purdue University (http://owl.english.purdue.edu/handouts/research/r_apa.html). Use the menu at the left side of the screen and read at least the following sections:

   - *General Format*
   - *In-Text Citations: The Basics*
   - *In-Text Citations: Author/Authors*
   - *Reference List: Basic Rules*
   - *Reference List: Author/Authors*
   - *Reference List: Electronic Sources*

   b. "The Basics of APA Style," on APA's official website (http://www.apastyle.org/learn/tutorials/index.aspx). Be sure to read/listen to Slides 9–21, which include information about use of language and references. Also, read some of the links on APA's web page "Frequently Asked Questions About APA Style," especially those addressing electronic citations (http://www.apastyle.org/learn/faqs/index.aspx).

2. Write a brief paper using appropriate APA format. Include the following:
   a. Indicate whether you have used the Purdue or APA site.
   b. A brief summary of how and when in-text citations are used.
   c. A rationale for why APA might be helpful for readers and writers and in what context it is helpful.
   d. A description of how various Web resources should be cited.

Additional information is available in American Psychological Association ([APA] 2010) (*Publication Manual of the American Psychological Association* [6th ed.]) and works listed in course readings for this week.

Due Date: This assignment is due on the date indicated in the syllabus, assignment chart, and Discussion Board, not before or after.

Readings

APA. (2010). Frequently asked questions about APA style. Retrieved from http://www.apastyle.org/learn/faqs/index.aspx

Barowy, W. (2005). APA format in three steps, by example. Retrieved from http://www.lesley.edu/faculty/wbarowy/apa/

Mages, W. K. (2009). APA exposed. Retrieved from http://gseacademic.harvard.edu/~instruct/articulate/apa_mod/APA_Intro/player.html

Purdue University. (2010). OWL Purdue online writing lab. Retrieved from http://owl.english.purdue.edu/handouts/research/r_apa.html

Figure 8.3. Turnitin

I have set up a Turnitin website for you to post your assignments. This will help you make sure that you have not used other authors' words inappropriately. Turnitin will alert you if you have quoted others' works in excess and you will be able to fix that before submitting the assignment. You need to post assignments to Turnitin *before* submitting them to the course Discussion Board.

inappropriately, before they submit. Figure 8.3 shows the directions and reasons for using Turnitin that we share with students in most courses.

We check Turnitin to make sure that students are using it and to see what the results are. We are able to see all submissions, while students are able to see only their own. If students do not use Turnitin, we send out a message pressing them to use it. Once it is used, students seem to appreciate the opportunity to correct and improve their citation skills. Students also realize that we have this tool available to us, which we believe diminishes the temptation to copy others' work.

There are additional procedures that we use to help avoid plagiarism:

- having voice conversation to discuss what a student has submitted and letting the student know that this will happen periodically
- having exchanges about assignments on the Discussion Board
- shaping and personalizing assignments so that copying is not a wise option for students

Shaping Assignments to Avoid Plagiarism

Strom and Strom (2007) have a 9-item list of ways to shape assignments that can help to minimize plagiarism and cheating for middle and high school students in face-to-face classes. Most of their ideas can also be applied to all levels of online courses. We have used many of these ideas and find that they generally work. We have selected some of Strom and Strom's items that we think are most salient in preventing plagiarism online. Following each item, we provide an example of how we apply these principles in order to discourage student dishonesty in our online assignments:

1. The purpose of every project should be clear; identify anticipated benefits; and invite dialogue regarding methods, resources, and the types of products that are acceptable for submission. (Strom & Strom, 2007, p. 112)

Example: The purpose and benefits of every assignment are indicated at the top of each assignment (Chapter 4, Figures 4.2, 4.3, and 4.4) and on the Assignment Page (Chapter 2, Figure 2.7). The method of submitting products is expanded by the UDL approach discussed in Chapter 7.

4. Emphasize higher-order thinking and creative behavior. Instead of reporting only knowledge, student participation should involve practice with higher-level abilities

identified in *A Revision of Bloom's Taxonomy: An Overview* (Krathwohl, 2002). (Strom & Strom, 2007, p. 112)

Example: Students are asked to compare and contrast, analyze, and synthesize as well as create knowledge. Almost all our assignments do not have right or wrong answers. We have students read, experience, conduct interviews, or gather information to come up with solutions or ideas of their own (see Chapter 4, Figures 4.4, 4.5, and 4.7).

6. Encourage varied types of information gathering. Submissions might include a hard copy of located web data accompanied by the same information summarized and interpreted in a student's own words, results drawn from polls or interviews, and descriptions of steps in an experiment (Strom & Strom, 2007, p. 113).

Example: We not only encourage but require students to use varied resources in doing their assignments (see Chapter 4, Figures 4.2, 4.4, and 4.6).

8. Allow students to reflect, revise, and improve their final product. Having access to suggestions from classmates who have read their work and being expected to revise their product supports perseverance and teaches students how to accept constructive criticism (Strom & Strom, 2007, p. 113).

Example: For some major projects students are required to revise and improve their work. They have both instructor and classmate feedback (see Chapter 4, Figure 4.5, and Chapter 6, Figure 6.2).

9. Consider the use of oral critique. This method allows students to make their views known verbally, permits classmates to practice offering helpful criticism, enables teachers to call for clarification when points are unclear, and eliminates the use of technology tools for deception (Strom & Strom, 2007, p. 113).

Example: As illustrated by Skype conferences, we use oral interactions and critiques at least once during a course (see Chapter 2, Figure 2.4).

Talab (2000) has additional suggestions such as requiring specific components, asking students to use multimedia, and requiring that they cite all sources used, which includes graphics, pictures, video clips, and so on. As can be seen from the examples, we use many techniques suggested by Strom and Strom (2007) in our assignments. In an online course, there are more frequent assignments that substitute for in class face-to-face time. Assignments need to be varied. They should each contain elements of plagiarism prevention. There is no foolproof method of dealing with plagiarism. However, by making students aware of the impact of dishonesty and of school policies, it is possible to decrease plagiarism or even eradicate it.

Preventing Cheating on Tests

If testing is needed to assess student progress, there are procedures that can minimize cheating, similar to those in face-to-face education. A proctor can be hired to monitor an online or paper-and-pencil test at a specified location. If tests are multiple choice, students can be tested on individual subsets of the items. As a result, students in the same cohort will be taking different tests on the same subject. If the same items are used, they should be randomized. Tests need to be timed unless a student is eligible for untimed testing through special education services.

Cheating on tests is one of the more difficult issues to resolve online. As a result and in part because of our constructivist teaching philosophy, we do not use tests. In some content areas testing is necessary and so some of the suggested interventions above may be useful.

Student Work Done by Others

Colleagues ask how we know that students are doing their own work. To some extent this problem also exists in face-to-face classrooms. Other people can write papers for students. However, there are some safeguards that we have already mentioned, including voice conferences, emails, and Discussion Board postings. By requiring multiple ways of interacting, we detect when there are wide differences in communication styles and content knowledge. Still, it is very difficult to prove that someone else is doing the work. Ultimately we believe that a student does not want to cheat, since he or she is the one who suffers.

PROFESSIONAL ISSUES FACING INSTRUCTORS

The instructor confronts a variety of challenges when moving from traditional face-to-face teaching to an online format, challenges ranging from applying school rules to observing copyright laws.

Application of School Rules When Online

It is important to uphold school standards and regulations when teaching online, but it is not always so easy to figure out how to do that. For example, how can we make sure that students attend class? We adapt the attendance rule by giving students assignments that we estimate will take the same amount of time as a 3-hour class plus about 6 to 9 hours of homework time. We also have a due date for every assignment. Other institutions may have different rules about how to handle online attendance.

Appropriate behavior is another aspect that needs attention. We have had to deal with inappropriate behavior only a few times. In one case, the student used

---

Step-by-Step Course-Building Activity #26: Preventing Plagiarism

This activity focuses on developing *methods to prevent plagiarism.*

1. Make a list of the ways you might be able to prevent cheating and plagiarism.
2. Make a list of tools that are available for you and your students to use to enhance student integrity, such as plagiarism detection software, or a school policy.
3. Use the two lists created in steps 1 and 2 to develop a plan delineating what steps you will take to prevent cheating and plagiarism.
4. Include guidelines for student integrity in your syllabus or course guidelines.

---

a swearword in a posting on the Discussion Board. We struggled with whether we should remove the posting and tell the student why or ask the student to remove it. We felt that we needed to act quickly, so that the class would not be disrupted. In the end, we decided to ask the student to remove it and explained why we wanted it removed. Luckily, the student understood, was apologetic, removed the posting, and did not use offensive language again.

In another incident, the student decided to do *her own* assignment rather than the one that was given. We pointed out to the student that she had not done the required work. She responded by telling us that no one was going to tell her what to do. We then consulted with the program director. As it turned out, this student had a history of problem behavior. We attempted to work with the student by explaining the course rules, but she continually responded in a combative fashion. We were lucky—this student decided to drop the course.

As is evident, it takes some creative thinking to figure out how to apply school rules and standards to the online classroom. The best solution is to avert problems by being explicit about expectations. When daunting infractions arise, it is good to discuss them with colleagues. We find that either they have dealt with similar situations before or together we decide on the best course of action.

Providing Aid to Students in Need

We wrote about procedures and ideas for assisting students with diverse needs in Chapter 7. A challenge arises if an institution does not have policies or support that an instructor believes would be sufficient to help each student. Instructors can try to provide as much support as possible on their own and with the help of colleagues. It is also advisable to contact the direct supervisor and other appropriate staff at the institution, describe the student's issues, and request advice. Assistance may not be immediately available, but the instructor raises awareness and contributes to ensuring support for future students. As pointed out by various authors (Caruso, 2008; Durden, 2009), and by us earlier, institutions also have a learning curve as they start offering online courses.

Copyright and Online Resources

As with face-to-face courses, instructors need to be aware of how to use printed material while following copyright laws. It is especially important for instructors to serve as models for students and use materials correctly. We have adopted the policy of getting most of our materials from online sources.

Lesley University subscribes to multiple online databases. As a result, we and our students have access to a broad array of resources, including scholarly articles, newspapers, journals, magazines online, ebooks and streamed video. We assign specific readings and require our students to do research using Lesley's database resources. Doing such research opens up a wide world of information to our students. By using the Lesley online library resources, we stay within copyright laws, since the tuition helps to pay for all library resources. It would be easier for our students if we just posted the articles for them. However, copyright laws indicate that we can distribute articles only once. To stay within the law we provide the citation and, where we can, the database in which we located the article.

If an institution does not have wide-ranging online resources, more work is required to find appropriate material. The advantage of using online databases is that they include works that have been vetted by an editorial board or peer reviewers. Since anyone can publish on the web, the reader needs to filter information to determine if the content is accurate. Google Scholar provides access to some published work, but links sometimes lead only to abstracts. To get a full text document, it is often necessary to have a subscription to the publication or pay a fee for reprints. We have used Google Scholar and found the perfect article only to realize that we do not have a username and password to a proprietary site. This can be very frustrating. We then go to our databases and search but we rarely meet with success in these cases. We have to be satisfied with what we have or order a reprint.

For many courses it is possible to find good resources on the Web without having access to databases. In either case it is important to honor copyright laws and make sure that materials are vetted or give students tools to evaluate the efficacy of unscreened sites.

Changing Role of Instructor

Throughout this book we have discussed how the online teaching role is different from face-to-face. Some challenges for instructors who move from face-to-face to online teaching include transforming courses to an online format, getting to know students at a distance, time management when there is 24-hour access, building collegiality with other instructors who may not be in the office across the hall, and finding satisfaction in teaching in a new way. We describe our experiences and how an instructor who is new to online might handle these issues to help ease the transition. However, each person will need to find his or her own way.

Transforming courses. We found transforming courses to an online format to be exciting and demanding. It stretched our brains and forced us to think differently. When we started teaching online there was little guidance. We were fortunate that we had taught face-to-face for quite a while, knew our audience (K–12 teachers), and were knowledgeable about the content we were planning to teach. We would recommend that anyone contemplating building an online course have this background.

Our face-to-face teaching experience led us unconsciously to adopt a constructivist mode for online teaching. We borrowed a colleague's syllabus to see what she was doing, wrote our own syllabus, and figured out how we would manage the course. Much of what we did initially was trial, error, and instinct. When literature started to appear, it confirmed what we were already doing. We also adopted ideas from others. For example, Palloff and Pratt (1999) suggest that students are required only to participate in group assignments a few times per semester because of the amount of time required. When we read the book we were not requiring more than two group assignments but were thinking of increasing the number to boost student interaction. We took Palloff and Pratt's suggestion to heart and require no more than two group assignments.

The part of moving courses online that we enjoy the most is thinking up ways for students to learn the same or similar content without being in class. It keeps us fresh and makes courses that we teach more interesting to us.

Getting to know students. In a face-to-face course, we are able to get to know students by proximity. We like to think about time spent with online students as *quality time*. In a face-to-face classroom, we can definitely see the students, but we often have no idea if they are paying attention or what they think about what is going on. Since we require online students to post assignments weekly and interact with each other and us in a substantive way, we know when and how well students are paying attention. We also have some idea about what they are thinking. Students cannot sit in the back of the classroom daydreaming. Or at least if they want to, they do it on their own time (smile).

Participation and due dates are essentials of the course. When students miss deadlines because of intruding problems or responsibilities, students let us know what is going on in their lives. Recently one of our students was involved in a court case that resulted in her missing a couple of assignments. When the student returned we worked with her so that she could make up the work. We would like to think that because of our support and understanding during this confusing time, she worked harder when she was able to refocus on coursework. Typically, in a face-to-face course students just skip class, because they might be embarrassed to share this type of information.

The Coffee Shop and the Teachers' Room forums in our LMS also help us to know students better. As we describe, the Introduction assignment (see Chapter 3, Figure 3.4) creates a personal connection from the start of the course. These interactions continue throughout the course and everyone continues to get to know each other as the semester proceeds. This is in part due to our voice conversations and also the *voice* that we *hear* through students' formal assignments and informal interactions on the Discussion Board. Overall, we feel that we know students in a different way in online courses. In a face-to-face classroom, we get to know a small number of students well. Online, we know all our students reasonably well, since we hear each person's *voice* repeatedly.

Time management. Time management and the number of hours that it takes to teach an online course can, at first, be overwhelming. Some instructors would like to mimic a face-to-face schedule that consists of 3 hours on a specific day of the week and established office hours. This does not work well for online students. Since students are emailing and posting to the Discussion Board at all times of day and night throughout the week, the instructor needs to be responsive and responsible almost as it is happening.

We have learned a few lessons about controlling the time we spend and how we manage our time. We know that we will need to spend about a week or two prior to the course, transferring our course content from the previous semester, revising the syllabus and assignments, and adding new readings. We spend time thinking about the changes that we want to make in the course. The time spent up front is worthwhile, since well-prepared materials will save time while the course is running. If we have made mistakes in the syllabus, assignments, or any of the material, there is always a student who will notice it. If there are too many errors, students lose confidence.

To make our revisions more efficient we do not edit on the LMS, since the embedded word processor is not as robust as our regular one. We keep all our course materials in document files. We edit the files, then copy and paste or attach the revised course materials into the LMS course site. This document file is a record of the entire course, which we keep on our computer as a backup. Some of our colleagues have reported to us that they set up their entire course before class started and it disappeared a few days later. We groaned for them. We would also groan for ourselves, but at least we always have a backup. Another advantage of using our word processor is that it contains grammar, spell-check, and other writing supports that help us. (Those embedded in LMSs are often cumbersome.) Using our regular word processor helps ensure that we have as few writing errors as possible.

Assignments are due on Monday or Tuesday so that students are able to work on them during the weekend, since most of our students have full-time weekday jobs. This also allows us to spend weekday time reading assignments and sending feedback. Due dates for assignments are different for K–12 students and undergraduates whose main *job* is attending school.

We have described how we facilitate the course and build community in Chapter 5. Some of the interactions serve a dual purpose, the one we mention above, and using time wisely. For example, we use group messages, postings in the Teachers' Room, and Announcements when we reply to a student's question. If one student has a question we surmise that others have the same question. In the template we use to send feedback directly to individual students there is a section that contains specific comments and question about students' work. As we have said before, we save time by posting these personalized statements on the Discussion Board for the entire class to respond to.

Student moderators save instructor time by acting as facilitators for part of the course. As Thormann's research indicates, student moderation also enhances learning. Still another technique is to have student team leaders handle organizational tasks such as convening groups and scheduling Skype conferences. Saving time can also be as simple as encouraging students to help each other by responding to classmates' questions in the Teachers' Room or privately. All this aids in building community and shifting to a student-centered approach and saves us time.

Raines (2011) lists ten ways to be a more efficient instructor. We have mentioned many on her list. Raines's main theme is to set up systems and activities that anticipate student questions such as a *to-do list* for students. In addition, she suggests that the instructor set up a weekly schedule for him- or herself to do specific course activities such as *Monday and Tuesday for reading and grading assignments.* By using a series of techniques and patterns we are able to teach courses of high quality and respond to student needs but not be totally swamped.

Intellectual property. The question of who owns a course that was developed by an instructor while working at an institution has not been definitively determined. According to Kranch (2009), instructors may claim that a course is similar to a book or video they produced while working for an institution. Books and videos are considered the property of the instructor.

Institutions, on the other hand, may believe that by contributing resources for the development of an online course, they are entitled to ownership of the course. Kranch suggests dual ownership in his statement

> Granting intellectual property rights of distance education materials to the sponsoring institution best preserves the institution's investment of staff, resources, and name. Including in this ownership the provision that authoring faculty retain the perpetual right of use, augmentation, and remuneration best preserves the faculty member's investment of creativity. (p. 355)

A concern about academic freedom if institutions hold the copyright for online courses is implied by Talab (2007). She cites some ways in which faculty can negotiate with institutions in order to maintain intellectual property rights to online courses such as using collective bargaining, developing institutional policies, and avoiding individual contracts. Many institutions do not have such policies. However, as online learning proliferates, this issue may become part of every teaching contract. Institutions and instructors or the legal system must resolve these ownership challenges.

Collegiality with other instructors. We find that collegiality is similar in online and face-to-face teaching for maintaining currency of our content. In face-to-face education, we gain insights into our subject matter with colleagues by having discussions, attending conferences in our content area, and talking in the corridors. There is a slight difference with online teaching. There are fewer, if any, corridor chats. And it takes a little extra effort to make connections with people who are not in the same physical space but it is worth it when we do.

Finding satisfaction in teaching. We do miss the eye contact, smiles, and thoughtful faces of our students. But we do not miss the travel, *schlepping* materials to class, worrying about the comfort and workability of the physical space, and other annoying aspects of face-to-face teaching. Our main satisfaction comes from being able to *see* our students learn. We experience this from reading their postings, assignments, positive comments they write to us, and course evaluations that we receive.

Teaching canned courses. Some institutions hire instructors to teach courses with all the content prepared by outside course developers. This is often done to make sure that specific course content is addressed or to relieve instructors of having to develop a course. In assigning instructors to teach a canned course it is important that they are knowledgeable in the content area, agree with the teaching philosophy used, and are comfortable with the rules of interaction that the institution requires. Some instructors may find using courses that are prepared by others limiting if they are not allowed to bring their own material into the course or if they cannot alter the syllabus (Kramarae, 2007).

A study of university faculty members conducted by Proctor (2007) found that faculty members were averse to using canned courses because preset content offended them. They felt like facilitators as opposed to instructional guides, and it interfered with their creativity.

Faculty may also be concerned about academic freedom. And there is the issue of wanting to use an individual instructor's strengths in knowledge and teaching style. If courses are proscribed, instructors' expertise and enthusiasm for teaching their specialty may be lost. Many adjunct faculty members bring rich experiences to their teaching. An example is Ran Hock, who teaches a number of courses relating to use of the Internet. His writing about the Internet includes four books and numerous articles. When he teaches ECOMP 6008 *The World Wide Web as an Educational Resource*, Hock draws on his in-depth knowledge of search engines. When a course is co-constructed by those from other institutions who are expert in the subject, faculty members are able to share unique skills and knowledge with students.

Since we have always developed our own courses, it would be difficult for us to teach a canned course, one that we could not modify. In addition, having the flexibility to revise the course during and after each semester helps to keep the course relevant to students' interests and needs. It also keeps the course fresh for the instructor who constantly brings in new materials and tries new ways to engage students.

Decisions about professional issues of online teaching influence how well we perform our work. We have come to terms with many of them, including transforming our courses, time management, getting to know students, collegiality, and

> **Step-by-Step Course-Building Activity #27: Professional Issues**
>
> This exercise assists in understanding and preparing to deal with *professional issues relating to teaching online.*
>
> 1. Make a list of the professional issues that you think will affect you in your online teaching.
> 2. Ask a colleague or colleagues to make a list also.
> 3. Compare your lists and discuss how you hope to handle these challenges.
> 4. Read at least 3 articles relating to the professional issue on your list.
> 5. Write down your plans and exchange lists with your colleague.
> 6. Set a time (6 or 9 months) to meet again to examine your lists to see how and if you resolved the challenges and to discuss any new ones.

satisfaction with teaching. Others, such as intellectual property and teaching canned courses, are still in question. Time and more experience will clarify how these issues are resolved.

EDUCATOR PREPARATION MODELS

State departments of education have been accrediting K–12 teachers for years. State agencies have begun to spell out standards for online teachers. In 2006 Georgia instituted the Online Teaching Endorsement (http://www.gapsc.com/Rules/Current/EducatorPreparation/505-3-.85.pdf). Deubel (2008) wrote that four states now have specific endorsements for online teachers. In 2010 the Massachusetts Board of Elementary and Secondary Education discussed the promulgation of "regulations necessary to implement innovation schools, including regulations pertaining to a new 'virtual public school' online learning option." (http://www.doe.mass.edu/boe/docs/0410/item6.html).

Higher education instructors are not licensed individually but accreditation is addressed by having the institution reviewed by an outside organization such as the National Council for Accreditation of Teacher Education (NCATE), and the state department of higher education. These and other accrediting agencies are now including evaluation of distance education programs.

As online teaching and learning opportunities expand, oversight organizations understand that instructors need to use different skills and methods to be successful and qualified. In the future accreditation may become a prerequisite for teaching online.

Higher Education Online Programs

Many universities offer certification and master's degree programs to assist instructors in gaining experience and learning how to teach online. Most of the programs are offered in an online format. Figure 8.4 shows a list of some of these university programs.

Figure 8.4. Higher Education Online Programs

Type of Program	University Name
Master of Education in e-Learning Technology and Design	Jones International University
Teaching Online Certificate Program	Lesley University
Graduate Certificate in Online Teaching and Learning and Masters of Arts in Teaching with an Online Teaching Emphasis for K–12 Teachers	New Mexico State University
e-Learning and Online Teaching Certificate	Stout University of Wisconsin
Certificate in Online Teaching and Learning	University of Florida
Illinois Online Network The Master Online Teacher certificate	University of Illinois
Certificate in Foundations of Distance Education and Joint Certificate: e-Learning and Instructional Design	University of Maryland
Teaching Online Certificate	University of San Diego Extension
Distance Education Certificate Program	University of Wisconsin–Madison

Enrolling in an online course or program is a good way to understand online teaching, fill in knowledge gaps, and learn different techniques. By taking courses online, it is possible to get a sense of what enrolled students experience and it is good to note whether instructors implement the ideas they espouse. Becoming familiar with how different faculty members organize their courses and materials, as well as the types of assignments, technology, and assessments they use is also helpful. These are all experiences that can help build a personal instructional tool kit.

Online Teaching Assistant or Internship

In the Lesley University Technology in Education program it has been our practice to have new instructors work with an experienced instructor as a teaching assistant (TA) before teaching on his or her own, whether face-to-face or online. We screen potential instructors and select those who have both knowledge of the content and teaching experience. In both formats the TA works with us while we teach so that he or she does not have to reinvent the assigned course, to maintain consistency across course content and so that both we and the potential instructor can see if there is a match between his or her capabilities and the Technology in Education program needs.

Figure 8.5. Preparing Students for a TA

Dear Thesis Writers,

We are lucky to have Richard Hill join us as my co-instructor this semester. He is well versed in the use of technology in the educational setting as well as conducting research. In the future Richard (he prefers to be called Rich) will be teaching ECOMP 7104 for Lesley and for this reason he will work with us this semester to become familiar with this course and also help shape your thesis writing.

As co-instructors Rich and I will be ccing each other when we communicate with you so that we will all be *on the same page* or I guess the expression should be *on the same screen*.

Joan

We recently had a new instructor work with us as an online TA. Shown in Figure 8.5 is an example of how we introduced our TA since we asked him to take on a portion of the teaching role under our guidance.

In this online model the experienced instructor and TA work closely together so that the TA learns some of the online teaching principles that we follow. Institutional online teaching practices vary widely, so potential instructors, whether knowledgeable about online or not, need to do a teaching assistantship. We also have instructors who are not experienced online teachers take a course in online teaching offered by Lesley.

Another hands-on model for learning how to teach online is by doing an internship. Prabhu (2009) writes "Six University of Central Florida (UCF) education majors are in the middle of a seven-week internship where they are working hand-in-hand with FLVS teachers." This "first-of-its-kind internship program" online (Prabhu, 2009) is followed by 7 weeks in a traditional classroom.

In-School or University Programs

Schools and universities also provide their own programs to support instructors who need to teach online. Institutions offer face-to-face and online courses as well as peer mentoring for the development and implementation of courses. De Simone (2006) writes that "it is important to institute a training program for initial preparation and ongoing support that is sensitive to the needs of the teacher and the learning goals." She also indicates that focusing solely on how to handle the technology is insufficient and lists the need for support that includes most of the topics we address in this book.

However training is offered, it is important to make available ongoing support for instructors so that they can continue to grow and share what they have learned. It can be difficult for institutions to do this because of time and funding constraints, but the payoff is high in terms of keeping instructors enthusiastic and skilled.

Step-by-Step Course-Building Activity #28:
Appropriate Professional Development

This activity helps in the evaluation and selection of the most appropriate professional development option.

1. In addition to reading this book, make a list of options that are available to you for professional development relating to the content area you teach and to teaching online.
2. Gather information about what each professional development opportunity offers.
3. Compare and contrast these opportunities.
4. Make a list of the strengths and weaknesses you bring to online teaching.
5. Based on your lists, select one of the professional development opportunities to participate in that will strengthen your teaching capacity.
6. Continue to do this activity at least once a year!

STUDENT RETENTION

Much has been written about student retention in online courses (Allen, 2006; Gaide, 2004; Hannum, Irvin, Lei, & Farmer, 2008; Nichols, 2010). Concern about retention is one barrier to using online learning at some universities because of the effect on enrollment and matriculation (Allen & Seaman, 2007). Research and expert opinion stress that there is a need for learner-centered principles, clear student expectations, strong support services, and targeted interventions when necessary.

At Lesley we have a low drop-out rate. This may be due to the small size of online classes that allow instructors and students to form personal relationships, use a constructivist student-centered teaching philosophy, and provide support services. These services include a 24/7 help line for technical problems with the LMS, an online writing support center, and an advising system. In addition, we are teaching self-selected adult learners who are enrolled in a degree program. The students are highly motivated and for the most part are pleased to take control of their own learning. Without some of these conditions, the retention rate could potentially decrease. However, institutions and instructors need to be clear so that students understand what is expected, and supportive so that students can complete their courses and programs.

SUMMARY

There are many challenges to tackle when teaching online. The first hurdle is getting stakeholders to agree that it is a viable option for them. Next is making sure that instructors and students are prepared and have access to the appropriate technology. Once online learning is under way, structuring learning so that students are prevented from plagiarizing needs to be attended to. Students also require sufficient support so that they are able and motivated to complete their courses.

Instructors are faced with their own dilemmas such as how to apply school rules and copyright laws. They must deal with changes required to become instructors in an online environment. Seemingly obvious issues such as time management, building collegiality, and finding satisfaction need to be addressed so that they do not get in the way of effective instruction in a new teaching format. In addition, facing professional issues such as dealing with intellectual property or being required to teach a canned course may arise. Locating professional development to support teaching in general and online teaching specifically can be another challenge. All these issues are surmountable but do take time, commitment, and cooperation from all those involved in online education.

CHAPTER 9

Looking to, and at, the Future; and Conclusions

We agree with Chris Dede, Timothy E. Wirth Professor in Learning Technologies at the Harvard Graduate School of Education, who responded to our questions about online learning by saying,

> Online learning is better than face-to-face teaching for some types of students: Learners who are shy and will not participate in face-to-face discussion, students who think slowly but deeply and benefit from time to respond, learners for whom English is a second language, etc. Online learning also breaks the limits of classroom discussion: limited time face-to-face only one person can speak at a time. And students who develop skills in learning online will enter the workplace well equipped to work collaboratively across distance and to participate in online training. (Email correspondence, November, 2010)

We also believe that online learning will transform the way everyone learns so that online education holds new promise for all students in the future.

Every day in the media there are reports about changes in technology that are possible, desirable, easy, or difficult to achieve or inevitable. Scores of bulletins and newsletters arrive by email and are posted on the web daily, hinting at or announcing new developments and opportunities: the cloud, the increasing power and variety of mobile devices, a plethora of social networking opportunities. Concomitantly come the articles about the risks and questions that these new prospects engender. Publications such as *EdWeek*, *SmartBrief on Ed Tech*, *ASCD SmartBrief*, the *Washington Post Technology Daily Report*, and *Campus Technology* report regularly about the assets and potential liabilities of online developments.

From all of these reports, it is possible to discern the trends (LeBaron, 1994). The details, however, are more difficult to envision. We do know that technology will get smaller and more portable, and each instrument will have greater functionality.

This evolution of technology, social attitudes, and budgetary considerations are having an impact on online teaching and learning. The modern debate about education has been on the front page since the National Commission on Excellence in Education published *A Nation at Risk: The Imperative for Educational Reform* (1983). Since that time technology has become a major player in the educational field. We have seen certain themes emerge. These include providing adequate and equal technology access, ensuring that a majority of teachers are using technology for teaching and learning, and offering sufficient instructional and maintenance support. These elements are necessary for the successful use of technology in schools and have been the source of much debate. As we have indicated, these are issues in online learning as well.

It is almost inconceivable today that students, from elementary to graduate school, can study without access to online educational resources and instruction. Judah Schwartz, faculty member at Tufts University and principal investigator at the Fulcrum Institute, told us,

> I believe online learning will play an increasing role at secondary level as school systems confront the increasing costs of providing staff in relatively narrow areas of the curriculum (advanced physics and other sciences, foreign languages, etc.). At elementary levels I think the impact of technology is likely to be felt, indeed is already being felt, in the move many school systems are making toward online curricular materials—particularly open-source curricular materials. Higher education will, in my view, rely more and more heavily on online instruction. (Email correspondence, November 24, 2011)

It is also predictable that online education will replace a significant portion of in-school building education and will be an element of every individual's learning experience. Given the growth in online learning in K–12 and higher education, there is a need for policies to be developed around funding, teaching credentials, and quality assurance. Several states—Michigan, New Mexico, and Alabama—require an online course for graduation (Hicks, 2011). Some high schools are also making the same decision.

In a 2005 keynote speech, our colleague Alan November said, "Within 5 years from today, all of your high school students will take at least one course online in order to graduate." Although this has not occurred yet, we are on our way to this reality.

For higher education, a Sloan Consortium survey reported that "more than one in four college and university students now take at least one course online" (Allen & Seaman, 2010). Another prediction is that

> by 2015, 25 million post-secondary students in the United States will be taking classes online. And as that happens, the number of students who take classes exclusively on physical campuses will plummet, from 14.4 million in 2010 to just 4.1 million five years later, according to a new forecast. (Nagel, Online learning set, para. 1, 2010)

This final chapter explores emerging developments that will affect online teaching and learning, such as the evolution of technology, gaming, home schooling, the impact of online learning, tools, globalization, and **m-learning**. We also address the need for educator preparation in the light of these changes.

GAMING AS LEARNING

While it has long been accepted that play is the work of kindergarteners, typically this attitude has not held for older students. Based on our experience computer games were not highly regarded early in their appearance on the educational scene. The same was true for use of computer simulations, which are now seen as useful learning experiences.

In the 1960s, organizations such as the Educational Development Corporation (EDC) developed simulations for student use based on original historical documents so that students learned to think and work like historians. Simulations that re-created Caesar's march on Rome and traced the triangular trade in rum, cotton, and slaves were two memorable examples of this development. Students used original source documents to construct a historical account, created maps, and challenged each others' conclusions. At that time, the Xerox machine was the latest technology. Teachers made copies of student work so the class members could look at each other's products simultaneously. In this way, they learned how to write for different audiences (Gray, 1997). In 1964 the overhead and opaque projectors were new tools in schools. Teachers made transparencies of student work so all eyes could focus on one paper and students could learn grammar and composition together. Now the **interactive whiteboard** and interactive teaching technologies serve these purposes. Today's video games are almost in a different universe but both the 1960s simulations and today's games represent stages in this evolution.

Today, digital storytelling, video games, and cell phones are being tapped to make U.S. history lessons more engaging for middle and high school students. The Corporation for Public Broadcasting (CPB) and EDC are developing these approaches. EDC's Bill Tally, senior researcher and designer at the Center for Children and Technology (CCT), wrote, "We've found these games and tools can really engage kids' imaginations, help them look at evidence, and get them thinking about events in the past and their significance today" (Tally, History games tell the story, para. 6, 2009).

The MITRE Corporation developed "virtual reality," used to train firefighters and jet plane pilots. VR mitigates the many risks and high costs associated with teaching professionals in the field. Both examples were prototypes for gaming as learning. On the Harvard Graduate School of Education site, Dede's work is described as

> assessing Augmented Reality Simulation Games that use mobile computers to teach students mathematics and literacy skills. In games such as 'Environmental Detectives' and 'Mad City Murder,' students confront complex multi-dimensional problems that demand higher-order thinking skills confronting environmental and public health issues. (Grants support Chris, n.d., para. 2)

Most of these learning games can now be played on the web and therefore can be an attractive element of teaching and learning. Games capture the imagination of younger people, both teachers and students. Games have not only gained a place in face-to-face classrooms but will also play a larger role in online learning. We demonstrate this in Chapter 4 by describing game-like activities such as simulations, role-playing, and class newspaper publishing. With today's ubiquitous technology, gaming can be universally accessed and can serve students at all levels well if games, whether used synchronously or asynchronously, are well designed. Students are focused on solving the same problem as individuals, pairs, or teams. De Freitas and Griffiths (2007) report that research is being conducted to determine the efficacy of using online gaming for learning and training purposes. These authors believe that the use of gaming provides motivation and can also help build collaboration skills for learners (De Freitas & Griffiths, 2007). Although Deubel (2006) shares some reservations about online gaming, she adds that benefits to the list above include potential for "customized learning, promotion of generalizable long-term memory skills, planning and problem solving and improving mental agility" along with many others. Deubel lists more than a dozen educational games. Making all this easier and more affordable is the growing acceptance of mobile phones (see below) as learning tools to expand learning through gaming as well.

The future looks bright for life and learning online. Companies like Legacy Interactive are developing environments, such as a virtual hospital, to engage students in potential medical careers. Their website proclaims,

> Whether you're looking for fun games to play or need the perfect training product for your workforce, you've come to the right place. Each of our two synergistic divisions— Legacy Games and Legacy U—informs the other, resulting in world-class products that exploit the latest trends in mobility, social networking, gaming and learning. (http://www.legacyinteractive.com)

Second Life, IMVU, and Kaneva represent other versions of gaming as they combine with virtual worlds to provide new opportunities for teaching and learning.

HOME SCHOOLING (K–12)

Home schooling has been available *forever* (think of Socrates teaching Plato). In our experience in Massachusetts in the mid-1980s, the local school district superintendent had to approve separate applications for each student in any resident family that wanted the child home schooled. In a town of approximately 30,000 people, there were perhaps four requests in 6 years. Those were challenging days for a home-schooling parent—no Internet to supply materials and networks, no easily contacted community.

In recent years the line between home schooling and taking online classes while enrolled in school has blurred. We have found parents requesting that their child stay at home for part of the program and at school for the rest. This is a 21st century offshoot of the off-campus experiences of the 1970s, when high school students were allowed to leave the building for specific educational and personal opportunities. That practice was not universally successful. Home schooling undoubtedly will continue to grow, especially given the online learning possibilities we have described in this book.

Regardless of the reason parents choose this path, they find home schooling easier to manage now because of available technology. Social networking and open educational resources (OER) offer unending opportunities. There were 1.5 million home-schooled students in the United States in 2007, according to the U.S. Department of Education's National Center for Education Statistics (NCES), as reported in December 2008. And home schooling will continue to grow.

Companies such as eTAP and Global Student Network support online home schooling by offering whole curriculums and specialized online instruction such as writing courses (http://time4writing.com), even guitar lessons (http://www.riffinteractive.com/). Lips and Feinberg (2008) write about the growth in home schooling and mention the option of low-cost online support for curriculum and tutorials for students. In Ohio, the Graham Local Schools are reaching out to home-schooling families by establishing the Graham Digital Academy, which now enrolls home schoolers (Demski, 2010).

IMPACT OF ONLINE LEARNING ON FORMAL SCHOOLING

More schools will accept and encourage students to take online courses, even require them. They will develop and offer more courses for subjects that are typically under-enrolled, such as high-level science or math and some foreign languages, or when the needed expertise is not available. This is a viable solution for children who are homebound or for families that travel. The accessibility of otherwise unavailable courses offers a solution to a major problem in schools: keeping advanced students motivated and supporting students who need reinforcement as they learn. This approach also supports military families, expatriates, athletes, and performers.

Several states, among them Florida, Georgia, Michigan, Virginia, Illinois, and Maryland, have virtual high schools funded by their legislatures. Massachusetts approved a virtual "Innovation School" under new legislation (http://www.k12.com/mava/).

There is now an industry that supports virtual schooling because online learning is good for students who are at risk, students who have learning disabilities, students who are gifted and talented, or students who want to learn a topic or subject not available in school.

This solution is also promoted by the federal government. In the National Education Technology Plan released in April 2010, we read that

> with online learning, learners can gain access to resources regardless of time of day, geography, or ability; receive personalized instruction from educators and experts anywhere in the world; and learn at their own pace and in ways tailored to their own styles and interests. Moreover, it enables our education system to leverage the talents and expertise of our best educators by making their knowledge and skills available to many more learners. (U.S. Department of Education, p. 69)

Resources will continue to open up. Hafner (2010) describes the state of the open educational resources movement and how higher education faculty members are developing courses and making once private courses available online, with integrated video. This movement started when MIT (Massachusetts Institute of Technology) put its course materials online but now includes other universities like Yale and Carnegie-Mellon as well as iTunes U (http://www.apple.com/education/itunes-u/). The slogan of iTunes U is "Learn anything, anytime, anywhere."

Increasingly, higher education institutions are placing their library holdings online by digitizing content for easy access by both scholars and students and to protect valuable archives. The K–12 educational system is following the lead of higher education, while meeting its constituents' age-appropriate needs. The K–12 enterprise is moving to e-texts to save money, avert the damage to students' backs caused by overloaded backpacks, and provide access to up-to-date materials. Online learning can solve a nature-based challenge. According to McCown (2010,

> A new pilot project at the Mississinawa Valley school system in Ohio is testing the idea of replacing snow days, or 'calamity days' as Ohioans call them, with "e-days": days when students do their lessons online instead of in the classroom. (McCown, As snow days rack up, para 2)

Increasingly, studies are conducted and position papers written on various aspects of K–12 teaching online. Archambault and Crippen (2009) examine experiences of K–12 teachers who reported on their background, reasons for choosing to teach online, and their concerns. Huett, Moller, Foshay, and Coleman (2008) make a plea for a careful examination of instructional design for K–12 online learning. The authors urge educators to think differently and focus on new ways to engage students. Rice (2009) conducted a study asking experienced distance education stakeholders what their recommendations were for K–12 distance education in the next 5 years. In order of importance, their priorities were the following:

1. Evaluation of course design and delivery
2. Best practice
3. Accountability
4. Access
5. Online learning/learners
6. Professional development
7. Accreditation/standards
8. Funding
9. Technology

The University of Massachusetts at Amherst, suffering from cuts in staffing and increases in students, decided to offer more online courses, as reported in the *Boston Globe* (Jan, 2010). One student commented that being in a lecture hall felt exactly like being online. He could see the board and the teacher. On the other hand, a faculty member said he can reach many more students online than in a lecture hall that is limited to 230 seats.

For both K–12 and higher education, the evidence is clear that online education will become more prevalent. It is even possible to teach physical education online (Grayson, 2010). There are interactive online flashcards to teach facts about health, game rules and other topics; lesson plans for P.E. teacher use; video demonstrations; and more.

DIVERSITY AND GLOBALIZATION

As our society evolves, we can expect to have a more diverse student body and community, whether of students living in the United States or of those studying online from other countries. Diversity brings attendant advantages, such as cross-fertilization of ideas and multiple perspectives. It also engenders divides: digital natives versus **digital immigrants**, English as the national language versus retaining other native languages, and teaching in a variety of languages or making translation programs available.

Another important element is differing expectations about schooling that diverse groups bring. The challenge is to make sure that the proper tools are available to different students. Technology and learning online provide the opportunity to enable accommodations. These include language translation and immediate access to up-to-the-minute information through search engines and online journals. ASCD is now publishing an international version of its *InfoBrief*. And there are instruments available now such as Skype, Cisco's Telepresence, and Elluminate that allow many people from across the world to meet in real-time.

MOBILE PHONES AND M-LEARNING

Related to globalization of online learning is the use of mobile and smart phones, or m-learning. We predict that m-learning will become an integral part of the online learning experience. The reason for this belief is that even in remote and economically deprived areas of the world cell phone use is ubiquitous. In India the *Hindustani Times* reported,

> By October 2006, there were 130 million mobile phones in India, with six million new phones being purchased every month. With the arrival of third-generation telephony and growing sales in rural areas, Indian mobile phone users are going to exceed the 300 million mark by 2011. (as cited in Tenhunen, 2008, p. 515)

Hesse (2007) writes about mobile phone use in Africa and the expectation that it will expand tremendously. It is a short jump from easy access to mobile phone technology to learning online. Tufts University Medical School and Christian Medical School in India have partnered in using m-learning to reach remote locations in India (Vyas, Albright, Walker, Zachariah, & Lee, 2010). Paul Resta (2010), a faculty member at the University of Texas in Austin, shares his insight into the use of mobile phones worldwide for learning.

Since a large portion of the world's population has access to mobile phones, and smart phones are becoming more widely available to greater numbers of people, m-learning will serve to educate greater numbers of students. Leichman (2010) writes about Michal Yerushalmy, who in her travels in India "saw that students were more likely to have cell phones than computers, and that even in schools equipped with PCs, Internet service was sometimes spotty." Yerushalmy worked with others to develop Math4Mobile,

> [an application] that can be installed on most cell phones, enabling these devices to perform mathematical functions from elementary school geometry to high school calculus. It has proved to be a hit with teachers in several countries, particularly in South America and South Africa. This new approach is also being piloted in Israeli-Arab schools under the auspices of the Al-Kasemi Academic College of Education. (Leichman, Interacting aroung math, para. 1, 2010)

Yerushalmy has also established a website with a colleague in India to use mobiles to enable a distance mentoring system for school teachers to support teaching of math and science in remote and rural communities (http://mobilegurukul.org/index/aboutus).

Ubiquitous mobile phone access is not the only reason that we foresee m-learning's increased popularity; the new generation of students already use their mobile phones constantly and are comfortable with this technology. As we understand it, they would not dream of studying, doing research, writing, or, in fact, living, without their smart devices.

PREPARING FOR TEACHING ONLINE

Educator preparation programs that lead to certification or licensure need to ensure that educators understand how to teach and learn online by experiencing high-quality online education themselves. While this is an easy statement to make, changing educator preparation is complex. There are constraints posed by private and public institutions, federal and local regulations, funding, history, institutional independence, and other factors. The International Association for K–12 Online Learning (iNACOL) provides standards, promising practices, and policy advisories. The National Commission on Teaching and America's Future (NCTAF) explores the conditions necessary to prepare educators well for the 21st century. Teaching with technology to enable learning has been slow to take hold in institutions of higher education, but they are now becoming models of online teaching and learning, as mentioned in Chapter 8.

It is helpful that several national organizations have spoken about online K-through-16 teaching and learning. The Council for Higher Education Accreditation (CHEA), an organization that coordinates accreditation activity in the United States, is fully aware of the challenges and implications of online education and has, since 2001, explored how to assess online higher education teaching and learning. The National Education Association (NEA) has a guide for K–12 educators interested in online teaching and learning.

SUMMARY

Nagel (2010) indicates that, by practically every measure, "electronic learning is experiencing unprecedented growth and will continue to do so for the foreseeable future" (The future of e-learning, para. 1). He cites a 2010 report by the research firm Ambient Insight "showing that electronic learning, by dollar volume, reached $27.1 billion in 2009 and predicting this figure will nearly double that by 2014, with academic institutions leading the way."(para. 1). However, it will take planning and agreement among the various stakeholders, including K–12, higher education, and educator preparation programs, along with support from high-level governmental agencies, to move the online initiative along. Many states have already started this process. In the interval, all of us need to explore and experience online learning and teaching for ourselves, our children, and our communities.

Glossary

ADHD (Attention deficit hyperactivity disorder): a disorder characterized by inattentiveness, inconsistencies, hyperactivity, impulsivity, or a combination of these behaviors. This designation describes individuals who display levels of the preceding, which are not reflective of the normal range of behavior for a child's age and development.

Artificial intelligence (AI): the theory and design of systems of computer software and hardware that simulate intelligent human behavior.

Assistive technology (AT): any item, piece of equipment or product that is used to increase, maintain, or improve the functional capabilities of individuals with disabilities. This legal definition was first set forth by the Individuals with Disabilities Education Improvement Act (IDEA) of 2004.

Asynchronous: not in real-time. In the context of the online classroom, it means that students and the teacher are online at different times.

Behaviorism: as it pertains to education, a philosophical orientation to teaching that focuses only on the objectively observable aspects of learning.

Blended (or Hybrid) learning: a combination of face-to-face and online instruction.

"Bobby Approved": a certification indicating that a website is accessible to individuals with disabilities. "Complying with W3C" also indicates accessibility.

Constructivist approach: an instructional approach in which learners build knowledge for themselves, each learner individually developing meaning as he or she engages in the learning process.

Digital immigrant: someone who grew up without computer technology and adopted it later.

Digital native: a person who from childhood has lived with and used computers and the Internet.

ebrary/NetLibrary: digital services to library patrons that provide online distribution of information.

English language learner (ELL): term used to describe individuals for whom English is not the first language learned and who do not speak English proficiently. Other terms are: Students with limited English proficiency (LEP), Second language learners (SLL) and English as a second language (ESL)

Emoticon: a text expression usually constituted from punctuation symbols, representing a writer's mood, for example, ":-)", ":-(", and ":-D". They are often used to alert a reader to the tone of a statement, and can improve understanding of the text.

Evaluation: a process of collecting data to demonstrate effectiveness of an intervention and to provide a measure of performance.

Gifted and talented (G & T): designation for students who are defined as having high ability and who are capable of outstanding performance.

Graphic organizer: an image that helps arrange information and ideas for understanding, remembering, or writing about. Mind maps and concept maps are other terms that are used to describe these tools.

Guided practice: an instructional method in which the instructor provides students with ways to grasp and develop concepts or skills while monitoring each student's progress.

Individualized Education Plan (IEP): a written plan for a student identified as eligible for special education services. It is developed by an educational team including parents and specifies the student's academic and sometimes social goals and objectives as well as the methods to attain them.

Interactive whiteboard (IWB): a teaching and learning tool, sometimes referred to as an Interactive Teaching Tool (ITT), that consists of a large whiteboard display surface connected to a computer and projector. A projector displays the computer's desktop onto the board's surface. Users can control the computer using a pen, finger, stylus, or other pointing or writing device on the board's surface.

Jing: an application that allows a person to take a picture or short video of what is displayed on a computer screen and share it instantly through email, IM, Twitter or blog.

Jigsaw method: a cooperative learning technique in which students become an "expert" on some aspect of a unit of study. After investigating that area, the "experts" exchange information and learn from each other.

Learning style: approaches or ways that people prefer to learn, for example, visually, verbally, or aurally. Knowing one's learning style helps one develop strategies to compensate for weaknesses and capitalize on strengths.

M-learning: learning with mobile technologies such as handheld computers, MP3 players, netbooks and smart phones.

Moodle: a learning management system (LMS), that educators use to create and teach courses online.

Netiquette: a set of social conventions that help to facilitate and make online interaction courteous and respectful.

Open source: describing materials and applications available on the Internet that can be accessed without cost and modified by tech-savvy users.

Podcast: a series of digital media files (either audio or video) that are released episodically and downloaded via a syndication-based Web feed.

Print disability: an inability to read print effectively because of a visual, physical, perceptual, developmental, or cognitive disability.

Provisioning: having teaching and learning resources ready to use at the start of an instructional experience.

RSS (Really Simple Syndication): a family of web feed formats used to publish frequently updated works, such as newscasts, in a standard format.

Rubric: a set of categories and criteria for assessing individual student assignments, including levels of potential achievement for each criterion.

SMS (Short Message Service): a service allowing the exchange of short text messages between mobile device users.

Social networking: building and reflecting relationships among people who have the same interests and/or participate in the same activities on the Web.

Storyboard: a visual way to display information in a sequential or hyperlinked sequence such as a progression of illustrations. This method is frequently used to plan a video, animation or website.

SurveyMonkey: online software that enables a user to create his or her own Web-based questionnaires.

Synchronous: meaning *in real-time*; students and the instructor are interacting online at the same time.

Threaded discussion: an online discussion by email, online messageboard, or internet forum in which messages are organized, either topically or chronologically, and displayed visually in hierarchical form.

TOEFL (Test of English as a Foreign Language): a common requirement for university and college admissions as well as an English proficiency test for students whose first language is other than English.

Virtual world: an online community, usually a computer-based simulated environment, in which users relate to each other to develop ideas or computer objects and complete tasks. In education virtual worlds are intended as experiences in which participants can learn and experiment safely.

Vodcast: the short form of "video podcast" which is online delivery of video content.

Web accessibility: a designation for websites that are usable by individuals with disabilities.

Webquest: an inquiry-based online activity in which students solve a problem or meet a challenge by reading, analysing, and synthesizing Web-based information.

Wiki: a term used to describe a website set up for a group of users who can work together to modify and edit the content of the website.

Course Guidelines for ECOMP 7104
Technology in Education Thesis Project

Dear 7104 Students,

I am looking forward to being *in class* with you this semester. The course has been designed to help you synthesize and expand your knowledge about issues relating to use of technology in the schools. It is also a course about knowledge production for the larger academic community and your role in this process.

Please read the following information and the syllabus carefully. Refer to this document and the syllabus when you have questions about reading requirements, APA format, grading, due dates, group assignments, or posting assignments on Blackboard. You may want to print the whole syllabus or key portions, such as the Assignment Chart, Guidelines for Online Discussion and Participation, and Assignment Rubrics.

If you have any questions please feel free to contact me.

Joan

Exemplars

To get an idea of what other students have done for their thesis projects, including length, format, topics, and writing, please look under the Course Documents link and click on Thesis Exemplars. Although these theses, written by Lesley EdS graduates, are research studies, by reviewing them you will get a sense of what your thesis might look like. As you know, we changed thesis format to meet your needs.

Components: Components of a thesis vary but generally it contains some standard elements in a set order. You may, however, vary the elements, add or delete sections, and change the order as appropriate to your topic. Below is a suggested outline for thesis components and order:

Title Page

1. Abstract
2. Introduction
3. Literature Review
4. Plan

     a. Setting
     b. Contextual justification: Problem or Purpose
     c. Project Plan (goals, objectives, resources, time frame, etc.)
5. Implications
     a. Challenges
     b. Risks
     c. Benefits
6. Conclusion
7. Reference List
8. Appendixes (optional)

Posting Assignments

All assignments should be available to all participants and must be submitted to the class Discussion Board in the appropriate forum. You are asked to post work in a public place so that we will all be able to learn from and support each other and discuss issues that are raised. Sharing your work and giving and receiving feedback from colleagues are practices that members of a scholarly community do on a regular basis.

Question About Course Materials

If you have questions about course content or administrative issues, post questions in the Teachers' Room forum under the Discussion Board button. Please read the questions or comments in this forum regularly. Respond to your classmates' questions, pose your own, and read the responses from your classmates and from your faculty member.

When you notice that there are new and unread messages in the Teachers' Room forum it is important to read them, since they may contain crucial information about your assignments and the course content from a classmate or faculty member.

Format for Posting Assignments

All assignments must indicate the title of the assignment in the subject line and be posted on the Discussion Board in the appropriate forum.

To make it easier for your classmates to access your assignments (decreasing the number of clicks and difficulty opening files), please write the assignments with your word processor and then copy and paste the assignment in the text box in the appropriate Discussion Board forum. For formatting purposes, please attach the document also.

Blackboard will not accept symbols in the file name, such as "#" or "&." It is best to use only the underscore or period symbols as part of the file name, since Blackboard will accept these.

All assignments submitted as attached files *must* have a file name that includes an abbreviation of the assignment name and *the student's name or initials*. Examples: litrev_joan.doc or litrev_jt.doc. Repeated failure to follow file-naming guidelines will result in points being deducted from your grade.

Due Dates

All assignments must be posted no later than the day the assignment is due, unless otherwise indicated. *The due date is indicated in a table within the syllabus, in the first file in the assignments area, and on the Discussion Board.*

All assignments are due no later than 12:00 midnight (your local time) on the day indicated on the assignment chart. If you are unable to post on the due date, you must contact the faculty member prior to the due date and receive permission for an alternative posting date. After 2 days, if you do not contact the faculty member and the assignment is not posted, points will be deducted.

For some assignments, you are required to comment or ask questions about classmate's posting. However, please feel free to read, ask questions, or comment on any posting. This is your classroom. Anytime you have a question or comment, please contribute to the appropriate forum, the Teachers' Room, or the Coffee Shop.

Grading

Students will receive credit based on grading criteria indicated in the Assignment Rubrics and the Online Discussion and Participation Guidelines. To receive full credit assignments must address all components of the assignment.

You will be graded on the quality of the written material, including grammar and content, the appropriateness of the material presented, and your ability to analyze and process content.

Faculty will give general feedback on the technical aspects (grammar, punctuation, usage, APA, etc.). However, you are responsible for remedying technical aspects of your writing. If you need assistance, I strongly recommend that you contact the Center for Academic Achievement (www.lesley.edu/academic_centers/caa/online_tutoring.html).

Your assignments need to directly address *all* portions of the assignment as outlined in the assignments. In addition, your projects should reflect originality, complexity, and applicability to your topic. The length of the submitted projects should be such that its content provides complete coverage of the assignments and all of its components.

Each assignment should be a synthesis of your thinking and research, including the following:

1. What you have read, observed, experienced, and information gathered.
2. How you interpret what you have read, observed, experienced, and information gathered.
3. What you understand based upon what you have read, observed, experienced, and information gathered.

Assignment Rubrics

Grade	Rubric
A	The student demonstrates all required competencies at an exemplary level at the times specified by the instructor. Products and performances are worthy of dissemination beyond the confines of the class. Class participation is at an exemplary level.
A-	The student demonstrates all required competencies at expected graduate-level standards. Most of the products, performances, or both are at an exemplary level and are submitted on time. Class participation is at an acceptable level.
B+	The student demonstrates required competencies at a satisfactory level. Most products and performances are submitted on time. Class participation is at an acceptable level.
B	The student demonstrates required competencies at a satisfactory level, but all expectations are not met. Most products and performances are submitted on time. Class participation is at an acceptable level.
B-	The student demonstrates required competencies at a marginally adequate level. The student is often late in submitting products or demonstrating competencies. Class participation is at an acceptable level.
C	The student demonstrates required competencies at a deficient level. The student is consistently late in submitting products or demonstrating competencies. Class participation is not at an acceptable level.

Posting to Blackboard

To help guide you in understanding *classroom* participation in our online environment please review the Guidelines for Class Discussion and Online Participation. In addition, please be sure to read Posting Due Dates and Format for Posting Assignments.

Guidelines for Class Discussion and Online Participation

Level of Participation	Comments and Responses
Excellent	Integrate views Deepen dialogue Build on ideas of other postings Go beyond information given Stimulate additional thought about the topic Feedback is constructive, specific, and supportive Well written Accurate, original, and relevant
Above Average	Contains most of the above qualities and makes a significant contribution.
Average	Contains some of the above qualities and contributes some to the conversation.
Minimal	Contains a few of the above qualities and may add a social and collegial presence.
Unacceptable	Contains none of the above.

The class discussion and online participation guidelines are drawn from various sources, including the following:

Haavind, S. (2004) Teacher as online facilitator. In I. Zimmerman, & A. Koufman-Fredrick (Eds.), *Mission possible: Reaching all learners with technology*. Boston: MASCD.

Pelz, B. (2004) (My) three principles of effective online pedagogy. *Journal of Asynchronous Learning Networks, 30*(8). Retrieved from http://www.sloan-c.org/publications/jaln/v8n3/v8n3_pelz.asp

Wiggins, G., & McTighe, J. (1998). *Understanding by design*. Alexandria, VA: Association for Supervision and Curriculum Development.

Group Assignments and Discussions

A portion of the points earned for each assignment or discussion will be allotted to participation. *Participation* is defined as writing and posting substantive comments, critiques, or questions relating to classmates' submitted assignment. Positive comments are encouraged, but the content of the comments or questions should contain thoughtful content-related interactions. Your comments do not have to be lengthy, but they should be meaningful. Avoid just responding with statements such as "Good job" or "I agree." Instead, make statements such as "I agree because . . ." or "I disagree because . . ." or "Your comments reminded me of . . ." You should also ask questions for clarification or as a gentle challenge.

You will also receive credit for the quality of your overall participation during the course, including responsiveness to nonrequired postings, Teachers' Room activities, and Skype conferences.

Skype Discussions

At least twice during the course you will be asked to participate in a Skype conference with a faculty member or with a faculty member and a group of classmates. If you don't already have Skype, in preparation for the conferences you will need to set up and test Skype to make sure it works. You will need the following:

1. a high-speed connection (cable or DSL) for the computer
2. Skype software (downloaded from http://skype.org/)
3. a microphone and speakers.

Use of Skype is free (for Skype-to-Skype clients), although there are services and products you can buy.

If you do not have high-speed access at home, you can check to see if your school or library will allow the use of Skype or get together with a classmate or friend who has high-speed access. If neither of these are possible, we can use SkypeOut and VOIP (Voice over Internet Protocol) which allows your faculty members to contact you at no cost and include you in a group voice conference.

The ideal, of course, is to get Skype so you can experience using it. In the past students who are newly introduced to this have become Skypeaholics . . . a money-saving affliction at worst. For example, one student wrote the following: "I wanted to thank you for using SKYPE. My daughter and her two sons (ages 12 and 7) left for Japan yesterday morning. They will be away for at least 6 months. I'm delighted to be able to use SKYPE with them while they are away."

Reading and Research Requirements

As part of this course, you are required to develop your own reading list based on the project and topic you decide will serve as your thesis. You are expected and required to use the Lesley Library databases to find appropriate publications as well as using other resources such as libraries, websites, and interviews. There are also some required readings in the course and a bibliography that you will find helpful.

Lesley Library Databases

Lesley provides extensive online databases that may be found by clicking on the mylibrary tab within myLesley.

Lesley's Library provides a tutorial on using the library at http://mail.lesley.edu:81/searchpath/. You may want to use this as a review to prepare you for your library research.

The Education Research Guide is at http://lesley.edu/mylesley/supportcontent/library/general_content/education_research_guide.htm

E-Books

There are links for e-books on the mylibrary page on myLesley. Lesley's ebook database, Ebrary, has been expanded from just 3,000 academic books in education to 38,000 academic books in all areas of study. You can set up your own *bookshelf*. In addition, you can highlight passages, take notes, and bookmark particular pages to return to at anytime.

APA Format

You should use APA format when citing sources and submitting your assignments. The primary concern is that you use other people's work appropriately. Hopefully, throughout your program you have paid close attention as to how APA citations are used. If not, this is the time to do it! For specific examples of appropriate use, please examine the following article by Mary Seegers, a Lesley University graduate:

Seegers, M. (2001). Special technology possibilities for students with special needs. *Learning and Leading with Technology, 29*(3), 32–39.

A description of the APA style and format can be found at the following locations:

APA (2009). *Publication manual of the American Psychological Association* (6th edition). Washington, DC.
APA (2010). *Frequently asked questions about APA style*. Retrieved from http://www. apastyle.org/learn/faqs/index.aspx
Mages, W. K. (2009). *APA exposed*. Retrieved from http://gseacademic.harvard. edu/~instruct/articulate/apa_mod/APA_Intro/player.html
Purdue University (2010). *OWL Purdue online writing lab*. Retrieved from http://owl. english.purdue.edu/handouts/research/r_apa.html

Line Spacing

Although APA requires double spacing and a title page, for this course please use single spacing and do not use a title page. However, be sure to remember to put your name and a title on your paper in a header or footer or at the top of the paper. It is easier to read single-spaced assignments on screen and in print, and I don't need a title page if it is in the header or on the first page. For these reasons, I ask you to change these APA format requirements for this course only. Thanks.

Persistent URL

You will note that for some of the readings found on the Lesley databases I have indicated Persistent URLs as a convenience for students. The use of Persistent URLs is a service provided for students enrolled in the Lesley program. You must be logged into myLesley for Persistent URLs to function. The inclusion of Persistent URLs in a reference list or bibliography does not conform to the sanctioned APA format. When you cite sources in your APA reference list do *not* use Persistent URLs.

Academic Integrity

All Lesley students are responsible for understanding and using all components of the academic integrity policy, which are found at http://www.lesley.edu/policies/ catalog/content_acad_policies/acad_integrity_5_09.pdf.

Writing Skills

As a student enrolled in a degree-granting program at Lesley, if you want or need to improve your writing, one-on-one online writing support is available. You can email drafts of your papers to Lesley's online writing center. Writing advisors will review your work and provide you with feedback to

1. Make suggestions for improving organization, clarity, and cohesiveness.
2. Identify errors in punctuation, usage, and mechanics (including citation formats) and provide advice on correcting them.

3. Answer any questions relating to research techniques and idea development.

The service provided by the Center for Academic Achievement is available for the entire duration of your enrollment at Lesley University. Writing advisors will respond to a submission in 48 hours. Guidelines for this service are posted under the Course Documents button titled Center for Academic Achievement. For more details on this service, please visit www.lesley.edu/academic_centers/caa/online_tutoring.html.

Email Addresses

Your email address on Blackboard, which is our *classroom* for this course, is listed as a Lesley email address and will be the address we use to communicate with each other over the course of the semester.

All graduate students have automatically been issued a Lesley University email address as part of the course enrollment process. This email address will be the primary address Lesley will use to communicate with you.

You are able to access your email directly through the Internet(https://mymail.lesley.edu) or through myLesley. To access email through myLesley (http://my.lesley.edu/):

1. Locate the "Check Your Lesley Email" link on the "Welcome" page.
2. Click on "Check Lesley Email Now"
3. Enter your Lesley user name and password when prompted.

If you would like, you will be able to forward this email to another of your email accounts through myLesley or directly through Lesley Online Information System (LOIS). However, if you do this, please remember to update the forwarding address if your other email address changes. From myLesley (http://my.lesley.edu/):

1. Locate the "myLesley Support and System Updates" area and within that the "Update Your Email Address" section.
2. Click on the link to "forward your Lesley email to another account."
3. Enter your Lesley username and password.
4. Enter the email address to which you wish to forward the message.
To access this feature from LOIS directly (http://www.lesley.edu/lois)
1. Click on the "log in" tab.
2. Enter your Lesley username and password.
3. Under the Personal Profile heading select "Forward Lesley Email to Another Address."
4. Enter the email address to which you wish to forward the message.

Socialization

Please use the Coffee Shop forum for sharing personal information, including your photos, exciting events in your life, comments about sports, your hobbies, and your family.

References

Abedi, J. (2006). Psychometric issues in the ELL assessment and special education eligibility. *Teachers College Record, 108*(11), 2282–2303.

Allen, I. E., & Seaman, J. (2007). *Online nation: Five years of growth in online learning.* Retrieved from http://www.sloan-c.org/publications/survey/pdf/online_nation.pdf

Allen, I. E., & Seaman, J. (2010). *Learning on demand: Online education in the United States, 2009.* Retrieved from http://sloanconsortium.org/publications/survey/pdf/learningon-demand.pdf

Allen, T. H. (2006). Is the rush to provide on-line instruction setting our students up for failure? *Communication Education, 55*(1), 122–126.

Alonso, A., Manrique, D., & Vines, J. M. (2009). A moderate constructivist e-learning instructional model evaluated on computer specialists. *Computers and Education, 53*(1), 57–66.

Archambault, L., & Crippen, K. (2009). K–12 distance educators at work: Who's teaching online across the United States. *Journal of Research on Technology in Education, 41*(4), 363–391.

Armstrong, S. (2007). Virtual learning 2.0: Professional development is a whole new ballgame for educators who teach online. *Technology and Learning, 28*(4), 26–30.

Baran, E., & Correia, A. P. (2009). Student-led facilitation strategies in online discussions. *Distance Education, 30*(3), 339–361.

Barczyk, C., Buckenmeyer, J., & Feldman, L. (2010). Mentoring professors: A model for developing quality online instructors and courses in higher education. *International Journal on ELearning, 9*(1), 7–26.

Beldarrain, Y. (2006). Distance education trends: Integrating new technologies to foster student interaction and collaboration. *Distance Education, 27*(2), 139–153.

Blau, I., & Caspi, I. (2009). What type of collaboration helps? Psychological ownership, perceived learning and outcome quality of collaboration using Google Docs. In Y. Eshet-Alkalai, A. Caspi, S. Eden, N. Geri, & Y. Yair (Eds.), *Proceedings of the Chais conference on instructional technologies research 2009: Learning in the technological era* (pp. 48–55). Raanana, Israel: The Open University of Israel.

Bray, M., Pugalee, D., Flowers, C., & Algozzine, B. (2007). Accessibility of middle schools' web sites for students with disabilities. *The Clearing House: A Journal of Educational Strategies, Issues and Ideas, 80*(4), 169–176.

Brenner, S. (2007). Distance education in the public high school. *Distance Learning, 4*(4). 29–34.

Brophy, P., & Craven, J. (2007). Web accessibility. *Library Trends, 55*(4), 950–972.

Caruso, C. (2008). Bringing online learning to life. *Educational Leadership, 65*(8), 70–72.

Cavanaugh, C., & Blomeyer, B., eds. (2007). *What works in k-12 online learning.* Eugene, OR: International Society for Technology in Education.

Cavanaugh, T., & Cavanaugh, C. (2008). Interactive maps for community in online learning. *Computers in the Schools, 26*(3–4), 235–242.

Chalker, C. S., & Stelsel, K. (2009). A fresh approach to alternative education: Using malls to reach at-risk youth. *Kappa Delta Pi Record, 45*(2), 74–78.

Chang, S. H., & Smith, R. A. (2008). Effectiveness of personal interaction in a learner-centered paradigm distance education class based on student satisfaction. *Journal of Research on Technology in Education, 40*(4), 407–427.

Chapman, C., Ramondt, L., & Smiley, G. (2005). Strong community, deep learning: Exploring the link. *Innovations in Education and Teaching International, 42*(3), 217–230.

Chen, N., Ko, H., Kinshuk, & Lin, T. (2005). A model for synchronous learning using the Internet. *Innovations in Education and Teaching International, 42*(2), 181–195.

Chou, C. (2003). Interactivity and interactive functions in Web-based learning systems: A technical framework for designers. *British Journal of Educational Technology, 34*(3), 265–279.

Claybaugh, K. (2005). Colorado Springs District creates digital school in local mall for "disenfranchised" students. *THE Journal (Technological Horizons in Education), 32*(7), 32–35.

Coffey, H. (2009). *Zone of proximal development.* University of North Carolina at Chapel Hill. Retrieved from http://www.learnnc.org/lp/pages/5075.

Cole, J., & Foster, H. (2008). *Using Moodle: Teaching with the popular open source course management system.* Sebastopol, CA: O'Reilly Media.

Conceição, S. C. (Ed.). (2007). *Teaching strategies in the online environment.* San Francisco: Jossey-Bass.

Cowan, K. (2009). Learning across distance. *The Education Digest, 74*(9), 4–9.

Croxton, J. S., Van Rensselaer, B. A., Dutton, D. L., & Ellis, J. W. (1989). Mediating effect of prestige on occupational stereotypes. *Psychological Reports, 64*(3), 723–732.

Customers question tech industry's takeover spree. (2010, July 8). *eSchool News.* Retrieved from http://www.eschoolnews.com/2010/07/08/customers-question-tech-industrys-takeover-spree/

Dawson, S. (2006). A study of the relationship between student communication interaction and sense of community. *The Internet and Higher Education, 9*(3), 153–162.

De Freitas, S., & Griffiths, M. (2007). Online gaming as an educational tool in learning and training. *British Journal of Educational Technology, 38*(3), 535–537.

De Simone, C. (2006). Preparing our teachers for distance education. *College Teaching, 54*(1), 183–184.

Dede, C. (2004). Planning for "Neomillennial" learning styles: Implications for investments in technology and faculty. Harvard Graduate School of Education. Retrieved from http://citeseerx.ist.psu.edu/viewdoc/download?doi=10.1.1.119.9896&rep=rep1&type=pdf

Demski, J. (2010). Winning back homeschoolers. *THE Journal (Technological Horizons in Education), 37*(1), 20–21.

Desai, M., Hart, J., & Richards, T. (2008). E-learning: Paradigm shift in education. *Education, 129*(2), 327–334.

Deubel, P. (2006). Games on. *THE Journal (Technological Horizons in Education), 33*(6), 30–41.

Deubel, P. (2008, January 10). K–12 Online teaching endorsements: Are they needed? *T.H.E. Journal.* Retrieved from http://thejournal.com/articles/2008/01/10/k12-online-teaching-endorsements-are-they-needed.aspx

Dillon, S. (2010, February 12). Wi-Fi turns rowdy bus into rolling study hall. *New York Times.* Retrieved from http://www.nytimes.com/2010/02/12/education/12bus.html

Dion, K., Berscheid, E., & Walster, E. (1972). What is beautiful is good. *Journal of Personality and Social Psychology, 24*(3), 285–290.

Doe, C. (2007). A look at . . . secondary-level software and webware. *MultiMedia and Internet@Schools, 14*(2), 21–25.

Donovan, M. S., Bransford, J. D., & Pellegrino, J. W. (Eds.) (1999). *How people learn: Bridging research and practice.* Washington, DC: National Academy Press.

Driscoll, K. (2007). Collaboration in today's classroom: New web tools change the game. *MultiMedia and Internet@Schools, 14*(3), 9–12.

Durden, S. R. (2009). School guidance counselors: Are they distance education's biggest ally? *Distance Learning, 6*(3), 47–52.

Eagly, A. H., Ashmore, R. D., Makhijani, M. G., & Longo, L. C. (1991). What is beautiful is good, but . . . : A meta-analytic review of research on the physical attractiveness stereotype. *Psychological Bulletin, 110*(1), 109–128.

Edelstein, S., & Edwards, J. (2002). If you build it, they will come: building learning communities through threaded discussions. *Online Journal of Distance Learning Administration, 5*(1). Retrieved from http://www.westga.edu/~distance/ojdla/spring51/edelstein51.html

Edyburn, D. L. (2010). Would you recognize universal design for learning if you saw it? Ten propositions for new directions for the second decade of UDL. *Learning Disability Quarterly, 33*(1), 33–41.

Erickson, W., Trerise, S., VanLooy, S. L. C., & Bruyère, S. (2009). Web accessibility policies and practices at American community colleges. *Community College Journal of Research and Practice, 33*(5), 405–416.

Flynn, W. J. (2010). Five trends that are changing the educational landscape. *The Catalyst, 39*(1), 29–40.

Freire, A. P., Russo, C. M., & Fortes, R. P. M. (2008). The perception of accessibility in web development by academy, industry and government: a survey of the Brazilian scenario. *New Review of Hypermedia and Multimedia, 14*(2), 149–175.

Fulcrum Institute for Education in Science. (2007). *ED211: Some of what matters about matter* [Course materials]. Tufts University and TERC (Technical Education Research Centers, Inc.), Medford, MA.

Gaide, S. (2004). Community College Identifies Student Expectations as Key Element in Online Retention. *Distance Education Report, 8*(15), 4–6.

Garrett, N. (2006). New technologies help build learning communities. *Distance Education Report, 10*(13), 1–6, 2–3, 6.

Garrison, C., & Ehringhaus, M. (2009). Formative and summative assessments in the classroom. Retrieved from http://www.nmsa.org/Publications/WebExclusive/Assessment/tabid/1120/Default.aspx

Grants support Chris Dede's research in emerging technologies. (n.d.) Retrieved from the Harvard Graduate School of Education website: http://www.gse.harvard.edu/academics/masters/tie/faculty/dede.html

Gray, J. (1997). Jim Moffett: 1929–1996: An appreciation. *The Quarterly, 19*(1), 33–34.

Grayson, J. (2010). Virtual P. E.? No sweat! *T.H.E. Journal, 37*(1), 28–31.

Groen, J., Tworek, J., & Soos-Gonczol, M. (2008). The effective use of synchronous classes within an online graduate program: building upon an interdependent system. *International Journal on ELearning, 7*(2), 245–264.

Hafner, K. (2010, April 16). An open mind. *The New York Times*, p. 16L.

Hannum, W. H., Irvin, M. J., Lei, P. W., & Farmer, T. W. (2008). Effectiveness of using learner-centered principles on student retention in distance education courses in rural schools. *Distance Education, 29*(3), 211–229.

Hatfield, E., & Sprecher, S. (1986). *Mirror, mirror . . . : The importance of looks in everyday life.* Albany: State University of New York Press.

Havard, B., Du, J., & Olinzock, A. (2005). Deep learning: The knowledge, methods, and cognition process in instructor-led online discussion. *The Quarterly Review of Distance Education, 6*(2), 125–135.

Haverback, H. R. (2009). Facebook: Uncharted territory in a reading education classroom. *Reading Today, 27*(2), 34.

Hendrikz, O., Prins, G., Viljoen, J-M., & Du Preez, C. (2009). *The use of mobile phones in enhancing academic performance in distance education: An African perspective.* Retrieved from http://www.ou.nl/Docs/Campagnes/ICDE2009/Papers/Final_paper_069hendrikz.pdf

Henze, M. (2009). Demystifying "constructivism": Teasing unnecessary baggage from useful pedagogy. *Christian Education Journal, 6*(1), 87–112.

Herrington, J., Reeves, T., & Oliver, R. (2006). Authentic tasks online: A synergy among learner, task, and technology. *Distance Education, 27*(2), 233–248.

Hesse, B. J. (2007). A continent embraces the cell phone. *Current History, 106*(700), 208–212.

Hew, K. F. (2009). Use of audio podcast in K–12 and higher education: A review of research topics and methodologies. *Educational Technology Research and Development, 57*(3), 333–357.

Hicks, M. (2011, February 8). E-learning requirement could hurt Idaho students without Internet. Associated Press.

Horton-Salway, M., Montague, J., Wiggins, S., & Seymour-Smith, S. (2008). Mapping the components of the telephone conference: an analysis of tutorial talk at a distance learning institution. *Discourse Studies, 10*(6), 737–758.

Hou, H., Chang, K., & Sung, Y. (2007). An analysis of peer assessment online discussions within a course that uses project-based learning. Interactive Learning Environments, 15(3), 237–251.

Houck, C. (2004). Practical ways to make workplace distance learning accessible. *Learning Circuits*. Retrieved from the American Society of Trainer and Developers website: http://www.astd.org/LC/2004/0804_houck.htm

Hudson, B., Hudson, A., & Steel, J. (2006). Orchestrating interdependence in an international online learning community. *British Journal of Educational Technology, 37*(5), 733–748.

Hudson, H. T. (2009). How to teach with wikis. *Instructor, 119*(2), 66–67.

Huett, J., Moller, L., Foshay, W. R., & Coleman, C. (2008). The evolution of distance education: implications for instructional design on the potential of the web. *Tech-Trends: Linking Research and Practice to Improve Learning, 52*(5), 63–67. doi: 10.1007/s11528-008-0199-9

Hughes, M., Ventura, S., & Dando, M. (2007). Assessing social presence in online discussion groups: a replication study. *Innovations in Education and Teaching International, 44*(1), 17–29.

iNACOL (International Association for K–12 Online Learning). (2010). *Fast facts about online learning*. Retrieved from http://www.inacol.org/press/docs/nacol_fast_facts.pdf

Islam, Y. M., & Doyle, K. O. (2008). Distance education via SMS Technology in rural Bangladesh. *American Behavioral Scientist, 52*(1), 87–96.

Jan, T. (2010, December 19). A course correction. *Boston Globe*. Retrieved from http://www.boston.com/news/education/higher/articles/2010/12/19/overbooked_classes_strain_umass_faculty_students/

Jewell, V. (2005). Continuing the classroom community: Suggestions for using online discussion boards. *The English Journal, 94*(4), 83–87.

John-Steiner, V., & Mahn, H. (n.d.). Sociocultural approaches to learning and development: A Vygotskian framework. Retrieved from http://webpages.charter.net/schmolze1/vygotsky/johnsteiner.html

Jones, J. G. (2008). Issues and concerns of directors of postsecondary distance learning programs regarding online methods and technologies. *American Journal of Distance Education, 22*(1), 46–56.

Kajder, S., & Bull, G. (2003). Scaffolding for struggling students: reading and writing with blogs. *Learning and Leading with Technology, 31*(2), 32–35.

Kelly, B., Sloan, D., Brown, S., Seale, J., Lauke, P., Ball, S., & Smith, S. (2009). Accessibility 2.0: Next steps for web accessibility. *Journal of Access Services, 6*(1&2), 265–294.

Kelly, R. (2005, December). Project-based learning: A natural fit with distance education. *Online Classroom*, p. 2, 7.

King, A. (1993). From sage on the stage to guide on the side. *College Teaching, 41*(1), 30–36.

Kolb, L. (2007). *No need for "clickers" when you have a cell phone!* Retrieved from http://www.cellphonesinlearning.com/2007/12/no-need-for-clickers-when-you-have-cell.html

Kramarae, C. (2007). Gender matters in online learning. In M. G. Moore (Ed.), *Handbook of distance education* (2nd ed., pp. 169–180). Mahwah, NJ: Lawrence Erlbaum.

Kranch, D. A. (2009). Who owns online course intellectual property? *Quarterly Review of Distance Education, 9*(4), 349–356.

Lamb, A., & Johnson, L. (2006). Blogs and blogging, Part II. *School Library Media Activities Monthly, 22*(9), 40–44.

LeBaron, J. (1994). A quasi-plausible scenario: Colleen's challenges, circa 2001. Retrieved from http://www.ikzadvisors.com/wp-content/uploads/2010/02/Colleen-Boxton.pdf

Lee, M., McLoughlin, C., & Chan, A. (2008). Talk the talk: Learner-generated podcasts as catalysts for knowledge creation. *British Journal of Educational Technology, 39*(3), 501–521.

Legg, T. J., Adelman, D., Mueller, D., & Levitt, C. (2009). Constructivist strategies in online distance education in nursing. *Journal of Nursing Education, 48*(2), 64–70.

Leichman, A. (2010, November 30). Math goes mobile. *Israel 21c Innovation News Service.* Retrieved from http://israel21c.org/201011308542/culture/math-goes-mobile

Li, C., & Irby, B. (2008). An overview of online education: Attractiveness, benefits, challenges, concerns and recommendations. *College Student Journal, 42*(2), 449–458.

Librero, F., Ramos, J. A., Ranga, A. I., Triñona, J., & Lambert, D. (2007). Uses of the cell phone for education in the Philippines and Mongolia. *Distance Education, 28*(2), 231–245.

Lips, D., & Feinberg, E. (2008). *Homeschooling: A growing option in American education.* Retrieved from the Heritage Foundation website: http://www.heritage.org/Research/Reports/2008/04/Homeschooling-A-Growing-Option-in-American-Education

Lodewyk, K. R., Winne, P. H., & Jamieson-Noel, D. L. (2009). Implications of task structure on self-regulated learning and achievement. *Educational Psychology 29*(1), 1–25. doi: 10.1080/01443410802447023

Love, K., & Isles, M. (2006). "Welcome to the online discussion group": Towards a diagnostic framework for teachers. *Australian Journal of Language and Literacy, 29*(3), 210–225.

Mager, R. (1962). *Preparing instructional objectives.* Belmont, CA: Fearon.

Manzo, K. K. (2009). Twitter lessons in 140 characters or less. *Education Week, 29*(8), 1–14.

Maushak, N. J., & Ou, C. (2007). Using synchronous communication to facilitate graduate students' online collaboration. *The Quarterly Review of Distance Education, 8*(2), 161–169.

McCown, D. (2010, December 28). As snow days rack up, discussion turns to e-days. *Tricity News.* Retrieved from http://www2.tricities.com/news/2010/dec/28/snow-days-rack-discussion-turns-e-days-ar-739373

McInnerney, J. M., & Roberts, T. S. (2004). Online learning: Social interaction and the creation of a sense of community. *Educational Technology and Society, 7*(3), 73–81.

McLuckie, J., & Topping, K. J. (2004). Transferable skills for online peer learning. *Assessment and Evaluation in Higher Education, 29*(5), 563–584.

McPherson, V. (2009). Practical applications of Web 2.0: Bring your community together. *Knowledge Quest, 37*(4), 62–63.

Menchaca, M., & Bekele, T. (2008). Learner and instructor identified success factors in distance education. *Distance Education, 29*(3), 231–252.

Merrill, M. D., & Gilbert, C. G. (2008). Effective peer interaction in a problem-centered instructional strategy. *Distance Education, 29*(2), 199–207.

Meyers, K. (2002). *Quality in distance education: Focus on online learning: ASHE-ERIC higher education report.* Hoboken, NJ: Wiley.

Miller, C., Veletsianos, G., & Doering, A. (2008). Curriculum at forty below: A phenomenological inquiry of an educator/explorer's experience with adventure learning in the Arctic. *Distance Education, 29*(3), 253–268.

Miller, K. (2008). Teaching science methods online: Myths about inquiry-based online learning. *Science Educator, 17*(2), 80–87.

Mims, C. (2003). Authentic learning: A practical introduction and guide for implementation. *Meridian: A Middle School Computer Technologies Journal, 6*(1). Retrieved from http://www.ncsu.edu/meridian/win2003/authentic_learning/

Mueller, J. (2006). Authentic assessment toolbox. Retrieved from http://jonathan.mueller.faculty.noctrl.edu/toolbox/

Murphy, E., & Rodriguez-Manzanares, M. A. (2009). Sage without a stage: Expanding the object of teaching in a Web-based, high-school classroom. *International Review of Research in Open and Distance Learning, 10*(3), 1–19.

Murphy, K., Mahoney, S. E., Chen, C-Y., Mendoza-Diaz, N., & Yang, X. (2005). A Constructivist model of mentoring, coaching, and facilitating online discussions. *Distance Education, 26*(3), 341–366.

Murray, C. (2006, November 7). Study: Virtual-school enrollment explodes. *eSchool News.* Retrieved from http://www.eschoolnews.com/2006/11/07/study-virtual-school-enrollment-explodes/

Nagel, D. (2010, March 3). The future of e-learning is more growth. *T.H.E. Journal.* Retrieved from http://thejournal.com/articles/2010/03/03/the-future-of-e-learning-is-more-growth.aspx

Nagel, D. (2011, January 26). Online learning set for explosive growth as traditional classrooms decline. *Campus Technology.* Retrieved from http://campustechnology.com/articles/2011/01/26/online-learning-set-for-explosive-growth-as-traditional-classrooms-decline.aspx

The National Commission on Excellence in Education (1983). A Nation at risk: The imperative for educational reform. Retrieved from http://teachertenure.procon.org/sourcefiles/a-nation-at-risk-tenure-april-1983.pdf

New Zealand Ministry of Education. (n.d.). *Holistic development—Kotahitanga.* Retrieved from http://www.educate.ece.govt.nz/learning/curriculumAndLearning/Assessmentforlearning/KeiTuaotePae/Book2/HolisticDevelopment.aspx

Newman, D. R., Webb, B., & Cochrane, C. (1995). A content analysis method to measure critical thinking in face-to-face and computer supported group learning. *Computing and Technology: An Electronic Journal for the 21st Century, 3*(2), 56–77.

Nicholas, H., & Ng, W. (2009). Engaging secondary school students in extended and open learning supported by online technologies. *Journal of Research on Technology in Education, 41*(3), 305–328.

Nichols, M. (2010). Student perceptions of support services and the influence of targeted interventions on retention in distance education. *Distance Education, 31*(1), 93–113.

Oettinger, A., & Marks, S. (1968). *Run computer run: The mythology of educational innovation.* Cambridge, MA: Harvard University Press.

Oishi, L. (2007). Working together: Google apps goes to school. *Technology & Learning, 27*(9), 46, 48.

O'Sullivan, D. (2003). Online project based learning in innovation management. *Education and Training, 45*(2/3), 110–118.

Palloff, R., & Pratt, K. (1999). *Building learning communities in cyberspace.* San Francisco: Jossey-Bass.

Palloff, R. M., & Pratt, K. (2001). *Lessons from the cyberspace classroom: The realities of online teaching.* San Francisco: Jossey-Bass.

Paulson, L. D. (2009). W3C adopts web-accessibility specifications. *Computer, 42*(2), 25–26.

Payne, C. R., & Reinhart, C. J. (2008). Can we talk? Course management software and the construction of knowledge. *On the Horizon, 16*(1), 34–43.

Prabhu, M. (2009). New programs help English-language learners. *eSchool News, 13*(1), 9. Retrieved from http://www.eschoolnews.com/2009/12/11/new-programs-help-english-language-learners/

Prabhu, M. (2010). Technology gives kids constant media access. *eSchoolNews*. Retrieved from http://www.eschoolnews.com/2010/01/22/technology-gives-kids-constant-media-access/

Proctor, D. W. (2007). The canned courses controversy: Faculty perceptions of courses created by others. *Distance Education Report, 11*(10), 4–7.

Ragan, L. (2007). *Best practices in online teaching—during teaching—assess messages in online discussions*. Retrieved from the Connexions website: http://cnx.org/content/m15035/1.1/

Raines, D. A. (2011, January 24). Be efficient, not busy: Time management strategies for online teaching. *Faculty Focus*. Retrieved from http://www.facultyfocus.com/articles/online-education/be-efficient-not-busy-time-management-strategies-for-online-teaching/?c=FF&t=F110124

Resta, P. (2010). *Transformation: Redefining public education for the 21st century*. Retrieved from http://www.education.nh.gov/innovations/documents/redefining-development-script.pdf

Rice, K. (2009). Priorities in K–12 distance education: A Delphi study examining multiple perspectives on policy, practice, and research. *Journal of Educational Technology and Society, 12*(3), 163–177.

Richardson, W. (2010). *Blogs, wikis, podcasts, and other powerful web tools for classrooms*. Thousand Oaks, CA: Corwin Press.

Rose, D. H., & Meyer, A. (2002). *Teaching every student in the digital age: Universal design for learning*. Alexandra, VA: ASCD.

Rothman, J. (2010, November 23). The Shadow Scholar. *Boston Globe*. Retrieved from http://www.boston.com/bostonglobe/ideas/brainiac/2010/11/the_shadow_scho.html

Rotstein, A. H., & Associated Press. (2005, August 19). iBooks replace textbooks at Arizona high school. *The Seattle Times*. Retrieved from http://seattletimes.nwsource.com/html/nationworld/2002445320_nobooks19.html

Rourke, L., & Anderson, T. (2002). Using peer teams to lead online discussions. *Journal of Interactive Media in Education, 1*(1), 1–21.

Rovai, A. P., Ponton, M., & Baker, J. (2008). *Distance learning in higher education: A programmatic approach to planning, design, instruction, evaluation, and accreditation*. New York: Teachers College Press.

Rushton, H. (2002). Fine-tuning an online high school to benefit at-risk students. *T.H.E. Journal, 30*(4), 33–38.

Ryan, M., Carlton, K., & Ali, N. (2004). Reflections on the role of faculty in distance learning and changing pedagogies. *Nursing Education Perspectives, 25*(2), 73–80.

Saphier, J., Haley-Speca, M. A., & Gower, R. R. (2008). *Skillful teacher: Building your teaching skills*. Acton, MA: Research for Better Teaching.

Schafer, P. (2006, June). Online presentations encourage critical thinking, peer interaction. *Online Cl@ssroom*, 2–8.

Schomburg, G., & Rippeth, M. (2009). Rethinking virtual school. *Principal Leadership, 10*(4), 32–37.

Secker, J. (2008). Case study 5: Libraries and Facebook. University of London Centre for Distance Education: LASSIE: Libraries and Social Software in Education. Retrieved from http://clt.lse.ac.uk/Projects/Case_Study_Five_report.pdf

Shea, P., Sau Li, C., & Pickett, A. (2006). A study of teaching presence and student sense of learning community in fully online and Web-enhanced college courses. *The Internet and Higher Education, 9*(3), 175–190.

Siegel, E., & Siegel, R. (1975). Ten guidelines for writing instructional sequences. *Journal of Learning Disabilities, 8*(4), 203–209.

Siegle, D. (2005). Six uses of the Internet to develop students' gifts and talents. *Gifted Child Today, 28*(2), 30–36.

Skinner, B. F. (1963). Operant behavior. *American Psychologist, 18*(8), 503–515.

Smith, M. E., Teemant, A., & Pinnegar, S. (2004). Principles and practices of sociocultural assessment: Foundations for effective strategies for linguistically diverse classrooms. *Multicultural Perspectives, 6*(2), 38–46.

Spinelli, C. G. (2008). Addressing the issue of cultural and linguistic diversity and assessment: Informal evaluation measures for English language learners. *Reading and Writing Quarterly, 24*(1), 101–118.

Strom, P. S., & Strom, R. D. (2007). Cheating in middle school and high school. *The Educational Forum, 71*(2), 104–116.

Stuart, R. (2008). Adapting to the era of information. *Diverse Issues in Higher Education, 25*(21), 13–15.

Talab, R. S. (2000). Copyright, plagiarism, and Internet-based research projects: Three "golden rules." *TechTrends: Linking Research and Practice to Improve Learning, 44*(4), 7–10.

Talab, R. S. (2007). Faculty distance courseware ownership and the "Wal-Mart" approach to higher education. *TechTrends: Linking Research and Practice to Improve Learning, 51*(4), 9–12.

Tally, B. (2009). History games tell the story. Education Development Center, Inc. Retrieved from http://www.edc.org/newsroom/articles/history_games_tell_story

Tenhunen, S. (2008). Mobile technology in the village: ICTs, culture, and social logistics in India. *Journal of the Royal Anthropological Institute, 14*(3), 515–534. doi:10.1111/j.1467-9655.2008.00515.x

Thormann, J. (2008, March). Student moderators in online courses. *Online Classroom*, pp. 1, 7.

Tinker, R., & Haavind, S. (1996). Netcourses and netseminars: Current practice and new designs. *Journal of Science Education and Technology, 5*(3), 217–223.

Treacy, B. (2007). What's different about teaching online? How are virtual teachers changing teaching? *Kentucky Virtual High School Newsletter, 1*(2). Retrieved from http://edtechleaders.org/documents/teachingonline.doc

U.S. Department of Education, National Center for Educational Statistics. (2008, December). *1.5 Million Homeschooled Children in the United States in 2007* (Report no. NCES 2009030). Retrieved from http://nces.ed.gov/pubs2009/2009030.pdf

U.S. Department of Education. (2010, November). *National Education Technology Plan 2010.* (Contract No. ED-04-CO-0040, Task Order 0002). Retrieved from http://www.ed.gov/sites/default/files/netp2010.pdf

Van Dusen, C. (2009, November 1). eSN Special Report: Beyond virtual schools. *eSchool News*. Retrieved from http://www.eschoolnews.com/2009/11/01/esn-special-report-beyond-virtual-schools/

Verges, J. (2011, January 31) Roosevelt takes a leap into online gym class. *Argus Leader*. Retrieved from http://pqasb.pqarchiver.com/argusleader/access/2253247871.html?FMT=ABS&date=Jan+31%2C+2011

Vyas, R., Albright, S., Walker, D., Zachariah, A., & Lee, M. Y. (2010). Clinical training at remote sites using mobile technology: An India-USA partnership. *Distance Education, 31*(2), 211–227.

Vygotsky, L. (1986). *Thought and language*. Cambridge, MA: Massachusetts Institute of Technology Press.

Watson, J., & Gemin, B. (2008). NACOL: Promising practices in online learning: Using online learning for at-risk students and credit recovery. Retrieved from http://www.inacol.org/research/promisingpractices/NACOL_CreditRecovery_PromisingPractices.pdf

Wighting, M. J., Liu, J., & Rovai, A. P. (2008). Distinguishing sense of community and motivation characteristics between online and traditional college students. *Quarterly Review of Distance Education, 9*(3), 285–298.

Willard, C. (2010, February 22). Reconsidering grading students on class participation. *Faculty Focus*. Retrieved from http://www.facultyfocus.com/articles/teaching-and-learning/reconsidering-grading-students-on-class-participation/?c=FF&t=F100222-FF

Xu, Y., & Drame, E. (2008). Culturally appropriate context: Unlocking the potential of response to intervention for English language learners. *Early Childhood Education Journal, 35*(4), 305–311.

Index

Note: Page numbers followed by f indicate figures. *Italicized* page numbers indicate glossary definitions.

About the Authors

Joan Thormann, Ph.D., is a professor in the division of Technology in Education at Lesley University. Since 1996, she has been developing and teaching courses online. She has supported other faculty members in designing and implementing online courses and been a staunch advocate of the online-teaching format. Her recent research has focused on examining online-teaching strategies such as using synchronous conferencing and student moderating to build learning communities and engender greater student ownership of the learning process. Prior to working at Lesley, Dr. Thormann taught in K–12 public and private schools, worked for an educational software company, and was at the Massachusetts Department of Education, where she developed, implemented, and directed projects relating to technology for students with special needs. Professor Thormann has served on many advisory boards and presented at over 100 conferences nationally and internationally. She edits a column on technology and special needs for *Learning and Leading with Technology*. In addition to numerous published articles, she has co-authored books about technology and education, including *Learning Disabled Students and Computers: A Teacher's Guide Book, Microcomputers in Special Education: An Introduction to Instructional Applications,* and *Literacy in a Science Context.* In 2010, she received a Massachusetts Computer Using Educator's Pathfinder award for demonstrated leadership in the ability to find effective pathways for planning, integrating, and facilitating aspects of technology in education.

Isa Kaftal Zimmerman, Ed.D., is currently the principal of IKZ Advisors, an educational consulting firm serving educators and stakeholders in the Science, Technology, Engineering, and Mathematics (STEM) fields. She has been a superintendent of schools, a high school principal and assistant principal, a junior-high-school teacher, and both division director of the Technology in Education Program and associate professor at Lesley University. As a principal and superintendent, she pioneered technology in schools for instruction and productivity in Massachusetts and started the Massachusetts Association of School Superintendents Technology Task Force. She was also chair of the Massachusetts Commissioner of the Department of Elementary and Secondary Education's Educational Technology Advisory Council (ETAC) for two terms. She was Senior Fellow at the University of Massachusetts Donahue Institute and the University of Massachusetts President's Office until the spring of 2009. In this capacity she planned and organized the STEM annual Summit from 2006 to 2008, created and monitored the attendant website, led the development of a state STEM plan outline, and networked stakeholders. She also oversaw the Commonwealth Information Technology Initiative (CITI) K–12 program.

She was appointed to the Governor's STEM Advisory Council in January 2010 and to its Operation Board in January 2011. She is the co-editor and contributor to two books published by the Massachusetts affiliate of ASCD (*Beyond Technology: Learning With The Wired Curriculum* and *Teaching: A Career, A Profession*) and has a chapter in *Technology In Its Place: Successful Technology Infusion in Schools*. She continues to write about leadership, technology, and STEM in both published journals and online.